*About the Aut*

**Jill Black**, a working mother herself, is a
with her husband and two young children. Her previous books
include *A Practical Approach To Family Law* and *Divorce: The Things
You Thought You'd Never Need to Know*.

## Babies!
**A Parent's Guide to**
**Surviving (and Enjoying!) Baby's First Year**
*Christopher Green*

## The First Five Minutes
**You May Never Get a Second Chance to**
**Make a First Impression**
*Norman King*

## Intangible Evidence
**Exploring the Paranormal World**
**and Developing Your Psychic Skills**
*Bernard Gittelson*

## Loveshock
**How to Recover**
**From a Broken Heart and Love Again**
*Stephen Gullo Ph.D. and Connie Church*

## The Tao of Health, Sex and Longevity
**A Modern, Practical Approach to**
**the Ancient Way**
*Daniel Reid*

## The Working Mother's Survival Guide
*Jill Black*

# SELF-HELP FROM SIMON & SCHUSTER

# THE
# WORKING MOTHER'S
# SURVIVAL GUIDE

## Jill Black

S I M O N   &   S C H U S T E R

LONDON • SYDNEY • NEW YORK • TOKYO • TORONTO

First published in Great Britain by
Simon & Schuster Ltd in 1989

Copyright © Jill Black, 1989

**Simon & Schuster Ltd**
**West Garden Place**
**Kendal Street**
**London W2 2AQ**

Simon & Schuster of Australia Pty Ltd
Sydney

British Library Cataloguing-in-Publication Data available
ISBN 0–671–65501–9

Typeset in Baskerville by Selectmove Ltd, London
Printed and bound in Great Britain by
Richard Clay Ltd, Bungay, Suffolk

# Contents

England and Wales have a different legal system from Scotland and Northern Ireland. The advice in this book is based on the laws of England and Wales, although many of the points made apply equally in all parts of Great Britain.

# Introduction

Some months ago, I shared the lift in the court building with another barrister whom I had not seen for some time.

'What are you doing with yourself these days?' he enquired.

'I'm writing a book,' I replied.

'What's this one about?' he asked.

'How to survive as a working mother,' I said.

'Well that won't take you long,' he said. 'Just tell them to hire a nanny – that's all there is to it, isn't it?'

And off he went, immaculate in every detail, brain uncluttered by domestic trivia, no pangs of guilt at pursuing his career at the expense of his children's happiness and not even the smallest smear of breakfast cereal on his suit.

If you too look at life through rose-tinted spectacles, this book is not for you. It is for the rest of us, struggling to fill every unforgiving minute with 70 seconds' worth of distance run.

The idea of a survival handbook for working mothers came to me in 1982 soon after I had had my first child, Charlotte. There was so much I needed to know. It was not just that I needed factual details about maternity rights and childcare facilities. I also needed to know whether other mothers felt as mixed up as I did about leaving my new baby to go back to work, whether other mothers fell asleep exhausted in front of the TV at the end of each working day, whether I was the only one who had ever served up frozen beefburgers every day for a week.

By the time Andrew was born in 1986, I had learnt such a lot. I had used a childminder for 18 months, I had tried a nursery for 6 months and I had managed to engage and keep a nanny. I had found out how to live with guilt and fatigue, how to cram the week's shopping into one half-hour swoop on the local supermarket and how to create an illusion of domestic order by stuffing the worst of the mess into a cupboard, polishing the taps and sticking a vase of fresh garden flowers in a prominent position in the hall. Once more it occurred to me, why not pass the information on?

This time, I was foolish enough to propose my idea to a publisher. How I thought I would have time to write a book, practise full time as a barrister and be a wife and mother I cannot imagine – by the time I reflected upon the practicalities, I had already signed the contract.

So many other working mothers have helped with this book by talking about their own experiences and passing on tips. I am grateful to all of them. Various people have read the drafts of some of the chapters. I would like to thank them for their invaluable comments and, in particular, to thank the National Childminding Association for their kind permission to publish certain of their forms. I am also indebted to my agent, herself a working mother, for all her understanding and encouragement, and to my publishers who have waited patiently and with astonishing forbearance for the manuscript. As for my family and Helen, our nanny, thanks are not really sufficient – without them, there would not be a book at all.

Except for Charlotte, all children are male in this book. I apologise to any female children who may feel put out by this. I do not intend to imply that they are any less important – it is simply a question of convenience.

# 1

# To work or not to work?

T o work or not to work?
 This is a question you are likely to ask yourself over and over again throughout your tour of duty as a working mother. This chapter is therefore not only for would-be working mothers agonising over the initial decision but also for seasoned campaigners pondering retirement.

Although the chapter has a practical bias, do not be misled into thinking that practical considerations are the only ones that matter. It is every bit as important to consider the emotional side of life as a working mother. You might be lucky enough to secure a first-class nanny, to have oodles of help at home from your husband, an understanding boss and an adaptable child, but you will still be a failure as a working mother if you cannot cope with your own feelings. Chapter 2 deals with the sort of emotional problems that beset most of us from time to time. Read it before you make up your mind.

## What do you think?

This is what really matters because you are the one who is going to have to live with the decision. Be wary of your own emotions and try not to let them interfere with your deliberations, particularly during pregnancy and the early days of motherhood. However rational you are normally, your emotions can play tricks on you during this initial period, robbing you of the capacity to make a sensible choice about what to have for supper let alone about whether to go back to work or not. Keep your options open for as long as you possibly can because this weepy, sentimental phase *will* pass eventually, although having a baby does change your priorities permanently and you will probably never again be the same as you were before you became a mother.

Later in this section, I deal with the factors that you may like to consider when making your decision. But before you turn to them,

1

subject yourself to a bit of character analysis. Do you think you have what it takes to succeed as a working mother?

- *Plenty of stamina and the ability to make do with very little sleep*
  Can you shine at a board meeting when you have been up all night with a feverish child and you are feeling light-headed and faintly sick from lack of sleep? Have you the energy to join the children in a game of cricket on the lawn before you have even had time to change out of your best suit? Will you be able to run for the train when you arrive late at the station because you have been searching for a missing plimsoll?
- *Good health*
  If you are the sort who needs a week off to recover from a touch of athlete's foot, forget it. Small children starting day nursery or nursery school catch one bug after another and you must be able to resist their generous attempts to pass each one on to you. And do not assume you will be able to treat yourself to a few restful days in bed when you do succumb. You will probably already have used up your sick leave nursing your suffering infant, having fobbed your employer off with an ambiguous tale of illness, patient unspecified ('Terribly sorry, won't be in for a couple of days,

2

awful bout of 'flu'). You will then have to struggle in to work with a roaring temperature or risk getting the sack for absenteeism.

● *Generosity*
Are you prepared to pour your spirit without stint into everybody else's projects without ever having leisure or energy for your own?

● *Perseverance and optimism*
Have you grit and determination and an infinite capacity to identify silver linings in clouds? Can you simulate satisfaction with your lot when it is quite plain that you are being put upon by all and sundry? Moan at work and your colleagues will take it as advance notice that you are about to slip up or shirk. Moan at home and your family will simply remind you forcefully that you are not the only one who has a hard life, that it was you who chose to work in the first place, and that you still have not made that clown costume for the school play on Monday.

In short, do you consider yourself to be saint and martyr material? If so, working motherhood may be a sensible option for you. Now consider the following factors:

● *Will it pay to go out to work?*
You may think this is a silly question, but the unfortunate fact is that working may not be worth your while from a financial point of view. If you have other motives for working, for instance to get out of the house or to preserve your career prospects, this may not concern you unduly. However, if money is a major incentive, before you make any firm arrangements about work, do some sums to make sure that it *will* pay. From the money you expect to earn after tax, you must deduct what it costs you to go out to work. You should not have much difficulty totting up the basic expenses (the cost of child care and travelling to work, possibly wages for a domestic help, etc.) but remember that there are also hidden extras. Clothes and shoes, for example – a couple of pairs of jeans and some trainers may do nicely when most of your time is spent at home looking after children, but you may have to upgrade your wardrobe when you go out to work, possibly at considerable expense. Lunches at work can be quite costly too, and you must make allowance for the temptation to splash out in the city centre shops in the lunch hour, for the extra expense of convenience foods for the family when you might otherwise have conjured up a tasty and economical casserole, and so on.

● *Are you cut out to stay at home?*
I love to be at home with the children, even for weeks at a stretch. However, I doubt whether I should get as much pleasure from the time I spend with them if that were my whole life. I need to go out to work to put family life into perspective, to prevent it becoming just the everyday grind.

Be honest with yourself about how well suited you are to make of children, husband and home your whole life. It is perfectly natural to be irritated and frustrated by constant exposure to children, whether they be egocentric, whingeing toddlers or critical, argumentative adolescents. Though your angelic sleeping baby may inspire nothing but love in you now, be assured that he will learn to stimulate the baser side of your nature before long. How well will you cope with the bad times? Would you cope better if you spent some of your time away from the family? I am not suggesting that you should go out and get a job just because you tend to fly off the bat handle every now and then, but if you are often bad-tempered and dissatisfied with your lot as a mother at home, you may feel happier working at least some of the time.

Many home-based mothers manage to make friends among other mothers of young children, but if you do not find that easy or sufficiently stimulating, you may feel bored, lonely and isolated at home and may wish to hang on to your contacts with the outside world at work.

● *Do you need to work to protect your career prospects?*
Like many working mothers, ideally I would have chosen to stay at home for several years whilst my children were young, returning to pick up where I left off once they were settled at school. For a lot of us, however, the world simply does not function that way. Imagine yourself attempting to return to work after five years at home with the children. Your job is gone or your business has ground to a halt and you have to venture once more into the labour market. You are at a disadvantage; whilst others have been progressing through the ranks gaining relevant experience, you have been gearing down your mental processes to the level of your pre-school children. Feeling out of date and out of practice, you face employers who label you 'only a housewife'; worse, you face employers who see women with children as potential shirkers and absentees, on a par with chronic back pain sufferers, the persistently late and the congenitally lazy. Is it any wonder that so many of us dare not risk being left behind and rush back to work to protect our career prospects at the earliest possible moment?

Whether you can afford to be more relaxed about taking time off will depend upon how desperately you care about your career. You may be happy for an excuse to escape from work, you may welcome the chance to change direction – perhaps working part time, starting your own business or retraining for another career. Remember though that it is not just the particular job of the moment that you are considering. You must look further ahead to the time when the children no longer need constant mothering and you may find yourself at a loose end and feeling rather purposeless.

● *Do you depend upon your work for your self-respect?*
I can remember going out to a business dinner with my husband three months after Charlotte was born. Normally I am quite confident about holding my own in such situations, but on this occasion I was timid and shy. After three months at home with a baby, I felt unable to elevate my conversation above the level of disposable nappies and mixed feeding and I could see that these high-powered business men found such topics less than riveting. Even such a short time in the comfortable and forgiving environment of home had narrowed my horizons and sapped my self-confidence. Although I did have serious doubts at that stage about going back to work, here was a timely reminder that I might not be happy staying at home for much longer.

Being needed by husband and children undeniably brings its own rewards, but it may not give you quite the boost that you get from being needed as an individual at work. If you have been used to being someone in your own right, it can be hard to accustom yourself to being simply 'Sophie's mummy' or 'James's wife'. You might also feel a loss of direction on giving up work entirely. Climbing a career ladder provides a ready-made goal in life. Before you kick away the ladder, think about whether you will be content with what is left when it is gone or whether you might feel stranded with nothing to strive after.

- *Can you bear to be parted from your baby/child?*
  Whatever the excitement and anticipation that precede the birth, many mothers are totally unprepared for the over-whelming love and protectiveness that they feel towards their child when he or she actually arrives. Cool, hard, rational career women turn into soppy, muddle-headed, doting parents overnight. You cannot guard against this or even anticipate what it will be like until it hits you. For this reason, decisions about going back to work should never be finalised until after your baby arrives.

  Even mothers of older children are unlikely to escape a sense of guilt and loss when they go back to work. If you have always been there to pick up your child from school and to supervise his homework, you are likely to miss this time with him and to feel guilty that you are no longer as available as other mums.

## What does your partner think?

To succeed as a working mother, you need at least a modicum of cooperation from your partner. Many single parents manage admirably on their own with work and family, so it is not that you require his active assistance (although it would be nice, of course). Your requirement is negative: no sabotage. Doing a double shift – home and work – and dealing with your own uncomfortable feelings about deserting the family will be quite bad enough with-out a disapproving husband or cohabitee haranguing you at every turn.

So, whilst the final decision must be yours, you must discuss the question of your work with your partner. Do not assume that an adverse initial reaction is necessarily a definitive indication of the shape of things to come. If your partner has got used to leaving household matters to you and to coming home to a blazing fire in the grate, his slippers on the hearth and a wonderful dinner on the table, naturally he may not give this up easily. Talk things over and, if you desperately want to work, make it clear to him just how important it is to you. Even the most determined objectors have been known to come round to the idea in the end.

However much support you have from your partner, take into account that working will affect your relationship with him. There will be disadvantages, for example:

☆ *Less free time together* – the pleasures of weekend outings *en famille* may well have to give way to the delights of a joint assault on the week's undone chores, and evenings out during the week lose their attraction when preceded by a mad dash home from the office and a frenzied hour subjugating the children.

☆ *Less flexibility* – you will not be able to provide dinner for the boss at short notice, nor will you necessarily be available to attend business functions with your partner. Holidays will have to be planned around both partners' leave entitlements.

☆ *A lower standard of service at home* – goodbye to the resident staff of gardener, housekeeper, interior decorator, handywoman, secretary and cordon bleu cook.

☆ *Arguments* – almost inevitable when both partners are working at full stretch.

☆ *Lack of energy* – for fun, for chat, for sympathising after he has had a bad day at the office, even for the bare necessities . . . when you crawl into bed at midnight after dealing with the final load of washing, you will be fast asleep before you even manage to mumble the headache excuse.

But there will also be all sorts of advantages. For example, you may be more contented and purposeful, have more confidence and more to talk about, be able to make a contribution to household finances.

## What do the children think?

One enormous advantage of returning to work whilst your child is still a baby is that he cannot argue with your decision. If he grows up with you working, that will seem to him perfectly natural and it will be some time before he realises that other families do things differently.

Unfortunately this period of acceptance does not go on for ever. As they become more articulate, even quite young children start to express opinions about mummy working. Do not let yourself be too much influenced by what they say; they are the most magnificent manipulators and very quick to realise that they can soften mummy up by getting at her about her work.

On the other hand, although you cannot afford to let them dictate, it may pay to involve your children (particularly teenagers) in your decision because, if you can get them on your side, life will be a lot easier. Do not assume that they will resent you going out to work.

When I was a teenager, my mother used to work part time, mostly mornings, and I loved it. I could get up at my own pace, leave my bed unmade until lunchtime and my nightclothes precisely where I stepped out of them, have peanut butter sandwiches and cake for breakfast if I wanted and watch TV all morning if I felt so inclined. Friends with older children have remarked on a welcome change in their children's attitude on learning that the old doormat has actually managed to get a job. Sudden awareness that mum is a person in her own right can lead to the growth of a healthy respect. And think of the swank value in classroom conversations: 'My mum's a brain surgeon; what does yours do?'

## Aunt Gertrude and other busybodies

Everybody seems to a have a view about whether mothers should work or not and you will probably be inundated with ill-informed, unsolicited advice.

Whether you work or not is your decision and what your Aunt Gertrude or your mother-in-law or Mrs Bloggs next door thinks could not matter less. However, unless you have a hide like an elephant, it always hurts to be told you are failing in your duty as a mother.

Just before I went back to work after Charlotte was born, we went to a New Year's Eve party. We knew few people there and were introduced to a pleasant enough lady with whom we chatted amicably. We discussed the baby for a while and then the conversation moved on to my impending return to work. Suddenly the pleasant lady changed. She seated herself firmly on her high horse and proceeded to tear strips off me. How could I contemplate leaving my baby to go back to work? Why did I have children if I was not going to look after them myself? According to her, it was people like me who were causing the problems in society today. Already overwrought at the prospect of being parted from my baby, I was the perfect target for her attack. She did not need to convince me – I knew, with a horrible certainty, that she was right. After all, were these not the very arguments with which I had tormented myself in my blackest moments? I turned my back on her and fled upstairs to the bedroom where we had parked the baby to shed tears of mortification over the carrycot.

It helps to be prepared against attack:

&#9734;Try to spot potential assailants before they can get their knives into you. One of the reasons I was so devastated was because I was taken completely by surprise.

&#9734;Whatever agonies of indecision you may be suffering, present an impression of supreme confidence to the world at large. Self-opinionated bullies are attracted by the weak and the vulnerable and should be frightened off if you radiate calm assurance.

☆Do not let yourself be drawn into discussion or argument. Change the subject or make a polite excuse to walk away.

☆If you cannot escape, take what is said with a generous pinch of salt. Ask yourself why your critic is so disapproving. Perhaps it is not so much a case of condemning you as of justifying his or her own way of life? A woman may not want you to manage to combine work and motherhood successfully because it implies that as a stay-at-home mother she is doing only half a job. Your career may seem to her to give you status, fulfilment and a sense of purpose and it may be envy making her bitter and belligerent. A man may feel his own wife belittled by your success or, worse still, may fear for his creature comforts should your example incite her to go out to work herself.

☆Remember that there is always another point of view. Magazines and newspapers are full of glamourised articles about combining careers and motherhood and the message from the colour supplements is that we are taking it easy if we have fewer than four children and a salary of under £100,000 p.a.

## Changing your working arrangements

Do not assume that your choice is necessarily between doing your old job and staying at home. You might be able to change your working arrangements to make life as a working mother more attractive and rather easier. There are various possibilities to explore.

### Flexitime

Flexitime (i.e. adjusting the timing of your work to suit yourself within limits set by your employer) can be a great boon for a working mother.

It can be a help with everyday arrangements. If you work a traditional 9 to 5 day, for instance, you can neither take your children to school in the morning nor collect them at teatime. But start work at 8, make up an hour by working through your lunch break and you can be away at 3 in time to meet the children at the school gate.

It can also be a lifesaver when it comes to disasters and emergencies – the afternoon that you take off to collect your vomiting child from the childminder can be made up by working longer hours later in the week.

If there is already a flexitime system at work, make sure you are using it to your best advantage. If there is not, ask your employer if he would mind you operating your own system. Obviously flexitime will not work for all jobs, but there is no harm in enquiring.

## Negotiating longer holidays/more time off

If, like the rest of us, you would like to spend more time at home with your children without prejudicing your job, why not ask your employer if he would allow you to take extra unpaid holiday over and above your annual paid leave? Even if he agrees to only a few extra days, this should take the pressure off if you have to stay at home to look after a child who is ill or because your nanny or childminder lets you down. And, who knows, he may even agree to several weeks. Similarly, if there are any other terms of your employment that cause you particular difficulties, why not take them up with your employer too? If you are a member of a union, they may be able to help you to negotiate.

## Job sharing

Job sharing (i.e. two people taking on one job and splitting the hours and responsibilities between them) can enable you to continue with a satisfying career whilst still having plenty of time with your children. It can also solve problems about who is to look after them whilst you are at work. You may, for example, be able to get away without employing a childminder or nanny if one job-sharing partner looks after both lots of children whilst the other is at work, and vice versa. If this does not appeal, you may still be able to cut childcare costs by sharing a nanny with the other half of your double act or with someone else who is working part time.

Some employers are used to job sharing but many others have never thought of it or are resistant to the idea, not realising that it can have advantages for employer as well as employee – maximum commitment from both participants because neither spends sufficiently long at work to become jaded, healthy competition between sharers, more flexibility to cover for ill children, absent nannies, etc. You may therefore have some persuading to do when you approach your employer. If you want to start to share your current job, you may find it most convenient to sound out your employer before looking for a job-sharing partner. However, if you are contemplating applying for new jobs, you may do better if you find someone to share with first so that you are able to present the prospective employer with a well thought out package from the very start.

Remember that you will need to sort out with your employer and your job-sharing partner what is to happen about holidays, periods of sickness, pension contributions and entitlements, dismissal, etc., and do be careful to think everything right through. What happens, for example, if your partner wants to give up the job and you do not

– will your employer let you try to find someone else to share with or is the whole arrangement dependent upon the two of you staying together? Are you happy to take your main holidays at the same time as your partner? Can odd days be taken individually? What happens about further periods of maternity leave?

Further information and advice are available from the Hackney Job Share Project and from New Ways to Work (addresses and phone numbers in the Address Book at the end of the Facts Section).

## Part-time work

Part-time work can offer the benefits of working without the bore of having to do it all the time. If what you want to do is to earn a bit of money and keep things ticking over at work whilst still having plenty of time to see the family growing up, part-time work may be ideal for you. However, even if you are able to get the right sort of part-time work (which is not always easy), you may find working part-time frustrating. Part-timers are often badly paid compared to similarly qualified colleagues in full-time jobs, conditions of employment can be poor (for example, no job security, no paid holidays, no maternity leave entitlement, no pension, etc.), status is low and opportunities for promotion virtually non-existent.

## Working from home

If all goes well, working from home can give you the best of all worlds, especially if you can be flexible about the hours when you actually do your work. You waste no time travelling. The children feel comfortable because you have not deserted them completely and you can keep in touch with what they are doing throughout the day and even break off for a walk or to watch Blue Peter with them if you get ahead of schedule. Because you are on hand to deal with emergencies, you can possibly economise on child care by settling for a mother's help or an au pair instead of the girl with training or experience that you might choose if you were going to leave her in sole charge whilst you went out to work.

Unfortunately though, working from home is often more won-derful in prospect than in reality. It *is* possible to do it successfully but it is something not to be undertaken lightly. You need to have the self-discipline to shut yourself away and keep at it even if the utility room is stuffed full of dirty washing and it sounds as if the nanny is murdering the baby. This is easier if you have a big and well-soundproofed house with a work room to call your own, but it still requires cooperation from the children and from whoever is looking after them. You will have to establish that there must be no visits from friendly toddlers (even if they do only want to tell you that they love you), that you do not wish to be summoned to advise upon whether the mince has gone off or to admonish the 4-year-old when he has defied nanny once too often, and that you would prefer it if they did not invite you to go with them to the park because you might not have the will-power to resist the invitation.

New mothers tend to think fondly that they will be able to rock the cradle with one hand whilst dialling long-distance business calls to America with the other, thus enjoying the benefits of a close motherly relationship with their infant and cutting costs by not employing anyone to look after him. I wonder how many of these same mothers are to be found only a few weeks later, long-distance calls to America abandoned but still rocking the cradle, desperately combing the 'Situations wanted' column of *The Lady* for nannies and mothers' helps? Some mothers do manage without a helper, fitting their work into their children's daytime sleeps/rests and visits to playschool or to play with friends, but I do not think any of them would describe their option as an easy one. The more children you have, the less likely you are to have them all quietly resting/out/otherwise engaged at the same time. So frequent are the interruptions to my own efforts to work during the day whilst the nanny is not on duty that I invariably give up after 20 minutes or so, resigning myself to the fact that I will yet again have to catch up late at night after the children have finally gone to bed.

## Becoming self-employed

Being your own boss can be a very sensible and flexible option for the working mother, but you need to be a fairly strong character to make a go of it. Some women are able to do more or less their old jobs on a freelance basis instead of as employees. For instance, I have a solicitor friend who resigned from her partnership and now hires herself out to other firms of solicitors on an hourly basis as and when it suits her. Other women take the opportunity to set up in a new business on their own or with a like-minded partner.

Do not assume that self-employment will necessarily be the answer to all your prayers. Remember that you will be giving up the benefits of being employed as well as the burdens. It will be your responsibility to ensure that the enterprise is economically viable and there will be no sick pay or paid holidays, no company pension scheme, no paid maternity leave. There will be a prodigious quantity of paperwork: contracts for particular jobs, contracts for any employees you may take on, tax returns and national insurance contributions, VAT returns, etc. And although in theory you will be able to take off as much time as you wish, do not be surprised if in practice you turn out to be the hardest taskmaster you have ever had. It will rarely be convenient to stay at home when children are ill or to take holidays when you want to, or at all, as there will always be the problem of who is going to mind the shop, the new customer you do not want to let down, the urgent order that has to be sent off.

# 2
# Guilt and other troublesome emotions

I always intended to go on working when we started a family. There were times, of course, when I pictured myself suffused in a rosy glow of motherhood, contentedly surrounded by gurgling babies and home baking, but I cannot say that the image ever troubled me for long. For the most part, I bulldozed blindly on with my master plan, obsessed with the practicalities of returning to work and never giving so much as a thought to whether I would *want* to go back to work when the time came and how I would feel about leaving my baby.

It was not until about half-way through my maternity leave that I began to have doubts. Such was my passionate attachment to the new baby that it was more than I could bear to leave her with my mother for a couple of hours whilst I went shopping – how, I began to wonder, was I going to cope with a whole day apart? How would anyone else distinguish the 'I'm lonely' cry from the 'I'm hungry' cry? What about maternal deprivation, lack of stimulation, emotional disturbance, baby battering, accidental injury, inadequate nutrition, gastro-enteritis? You name it, I worried about it.

I was due to start work again at the beginning of the New Year. Whilst everyone else counted down the shopping days to Christmas with agreeable anticipation, I morosely crossed off on my mental calendar my last few weeks as a real mother.

I tried to talk to my husband about how I was feeling. He put my agonisings down to post-natal perverseness and took a firm, sensible, thoroughly masculine approach, jollying me along. This was not what was required and our attempts at discussion would invariably end with me tearfully complaining that he did not understand. It was not his fault; who could expect him to understand that I needed to reopen the whole question of work and to talk interminably about whether I was making the right decision or whether I might be happier staying at home with the baby for longer or even for good?

I did not try to talk to anyone else about the problem and I felt very isolated. For all I knew I was the only mother ever to have suffered like this, a psychological freak.

In the end I went back to work as I had planned, I think for two reasons. First, and rather pathetically, it was easier to go ahead with the arrangements that I had made than it was to unscramble everything and stay at home with the baby. Second, and more fundamentally, I knew deep down that I would not be able to derive a lifetime's fulfilment from puréeing prunes, boiling nappies and knitting bed socks, and I recognised that I could not therefore afford to risk my career by gratifying my wish to prolong my time at home with the baby.

To begin with, making the break was almost as awful in reality as it had been in prospect, but as time went by I did get used to it and it became routine. I met other mothers who were leaving their children in order to work and we talked about how we felt. Nobody had a magic formula for healing the wounds, but each of us felt a lot better for having talked to others who understood and sympathised and for the realisation that we were not unique.

I hope you too will realise when you read this chapter that, whatever you may be feeling, you are not alone.

## The initial separation

Any mother making the initial break to return to work can expect to have very mixed emotions, but if you have delayed your return until after your children have started school, you have an important advantage over mothers of small babies or toddlers in that both you and your child have already had to become accustomed to separation in order to cope with school. This section is therefore directed not at you so much as at mothers of younger children for whom regular separation for a prolonged period (more than just a morning here or an afternoon there) is new, strange and often disconcertingly painful.

No one can tell you exactly what it will be like the first time you turn your back on your baby or toddler and go out to work. You may be lucky and take it in your stride, you may get away with a slight lump in the throat, or you may be absolutely flattened by the experience.

Leaving Charlotte behind for the first time, I felt a tremendous sense of loss. Not only did I miss her terribly whilst we were apart and worry about whether she would survive without me, for some weeks I also suffered from a troublesome feeling that I had forgotten something vital, much as if I had inadvertently come out without putting my skirt on.

With Andrew it was different. From the start, our relationship was much less claustrophobic. It was not just him and me: there was also Charlotte (then nearly 4 and anxious for more than her fair share of attention) and the nanny, Helen, who stayed on throughout my maternity leave. Whereas I had had no choice but to cart Charlotte

15

everywhere with me in a sling, I used to leave Andrew at home with Helen and get on with the jobs unencumbered. This I did with a clear conscience knowing that Andrew, even then a stickler for routine, preferred his regular snooze in his pram in the garden to the excitement of a trip with me to the supermarket or to collect Charlotte from nursery school. My absences, albeit short ones, were important for Helen too, giving her the chance to get to know the new baby and to get used to looking after him without an interfering mum looking over her shoulder all the time. With Charlotte I had insisted on breast milk only, making myself indispensable. With Andrew, total breastfeeding was out because he suffered from breast milk jaundice and had to be weaned temporarily on to formula milk when he was a few weeks old. Though I went back to breastfeeding again once the problems were over, I was much more relaxed about the whole affair than I had been with Charlotte and I did not worry if he was given the odd bottle of formula milk every now and then if I was out at feed time. These factors, together with the experience gained from my first innings, made the transition from home to work much easier second time round. Just as I had done with Charlotte, I counted down the last days of my maternity leave, eager for any excuse to postpone my return to work, but the dreadful feeling of black despondency that had wrecked the latter stages of my first maternity leave was not repeated.

How can you help yourself to survive the initial separation? Here are some tips:

- Try not to be too selfish about your relationship with your baby whilst you are at home on maternity leave. Deposit him with a friend or relation occasionally while you go out shopping or have some time to yourself at home so that you both get used to being apart.
- Be prepared for the first few days back at work to be almost unbearable. Brain atrophied through disuse, self-confidence at rock bottom, you may well find yourself quite unable to think about anything except the child you have left behind. Not only are you a rotten mother who has betrayed her child by leaving him in someone else's care, you are no longer any good as a worker either because you simply cannot keep your mind on the job. You will probably suffer a chronic sensation of bereavement punctuated by moments of acute anxiety – will the childminder remember that the baby will choke to death if he is not turned on his tummy for his sleep, has the nanny had an accident taking Sam to playgroup in the car, did you remember to lift the aspirins out of reach before you left home?
- Try to resist the temptation, at least during the very early days, to ring up to find out how things are going. You

can be sure that, if you do, you will have chosen the one moment when all hell has broken loose, shattering the peace and tranquility of an otherwise uneventful day. Unless you propose to rush home immediately to cope with the disaster (neither very practical nor, in the long run, a very helpful way of behaving), it is much better to remain in the dark about it until the end of the working day, by which time everything will almost certainly have returned to normal. If it has not, at least you will be in a position to do something about it. Let us face it, even if your childminder/the nanny/the nursery does reassure you when you telephone that everything is fine, for how long will that satisfy you? Give it a few minutes and the imagination will have dreamt up fresh horrors – perhaps the baby even rolled off the bed whilst the nanny was answering your telephone call? Are you going to ring back yet again to check?

- Do not make snap decisions about the future during these early days. This acutely difficult period *will* pass and it is better to wait until you are on a more even keel before you

evaluate whether you have got your childcare arrangements right or whether you should be working at all.

● Find someone who will listen patiently and talk to them about your feelings. It might be as well to avoid burdening your colleagues at the office with your doubts and fears unless you are very close to them and are sure that they will understand. They may already be wondering how you are going to shape up now that you are a working mother, and you will undermine their shaky faith in you still further if you tell them how desperately you are missing your baby and that you are not sure you are doing the right thing in coming back to work. And make sure that you do not pick on someone with a strong antipathy to working mothers who would be insensitive enough to treat your confidences as an invitation to deliver a homily on the subject of maternal deprivation. Another working mother ought to provide a sympathetic ear. If you do not already have a friend in the same boat, contact the Working Mothers' Association and/or the National Childbirth Trust (addresses and phone numbers in the Address Book at the end of the Facts Section) for details of local working mothers' groups which might be able to provide moral support. Alternatively, try a balanced and unprejudiced relative. If all else fails, pour out your troubles to the woman standing behind you in the supermarket queue or sitting next to you on the tube – anonymous strangers can make very good listeners.

## Guilt

If you are going to be a working mother, you must accept your share of the communal guilt. Only one working mother of my acquaintance claims to be free of guilt and she is atypical in so many other ways – impeccable hairdo, same coloured mascara on both eyes, no ladders in her tights, no sign of anyone else's breakfast smeared across her beautifully pressed suit – that, had I not seen her children with my own eyes, I would have been sure that she was a fraud. The rest of us are consumed by guilt much of the time and it makes us discontented, resentful, bad tempered and unsure of ourselves. It spoils our enjoyment of our jobs when we are at work and of our children when we are at home. It saps our energy. And, for the most part, it is wholly irrational and totally without foundation.

The average working mother's guilt complex seems to focus upon three particular concerns:

– that we are harming our children by going out to work,

- that we are letting down ourselves (and our employers and colleagues) in our jobs by dividing our loyalties between our work and our children, and
- that we are short-changing our husbands or cohabitees by not fulfilling the role of the perfect housewife at home.

Should we feel guilty? Are we harming our children? You may come across sociologists, psychiatrists, paediatricians and interfering old busybodies who mutter darkly about disturbance and deprivation, but they seem to be in the minority these days. On the basis of a wide range of studies, most experts seem to be in agreement that it does a child no harm if his mother works, provided of course that satisfactory alternative childcare arrangements are made. This is what Dr Christopher Green, a consultant paediatrician, has to say about it in his excellent book *Toddler Taming* (published by Century Hutchinson):

*The fact is that the children of good, working parents are just as happy and turn out equally well as those of parents who don't work. It is not the quantity of time you spend with your child that counts, it is the quality.*

And speaking with all the open-minded equilibrium of a committed working parent, I can endorse the findings of the professionals – my children are, it seems to me, just as well balanced and intelligent as the children of stay-at-home friends. In fact, were I not afraid of being accused of bias, I would say they were better in every respect!

Reassuring though it is to know that you have a vote of confidence from the experts, if you are like me, you will continue to feel guilty. For instance:

- You may blame yourself for every hiccup in your child's development from bed-wetting to tantrums, bad manners to reading difficulties. Good features, however, you will assume to be present by good luck rather than good management, considering it fortunate that they have survived despite your selfish pursuit of your career. An example of the over-excitability of my own conscience occurred during a particularly busy spell at work when Charlotte was nearly 5. For some weeks the 'quality time' with the children that is supposed to make up for all the rest of the time spent apart had been reduced to a bit of chivvying and a few choice words of chastisement designed to ensure that the bedtime routine was completed in record time so that I could get started on my brief for the following day. Andrew was becoming accustomed to being despatched, ebullient and wide-awake, to his cot on the pretext that he was tired and needed an early night and Charlotte was no longer surprised to be offered a chocolate biscuit and half an hour's television instead of her normal bedtime dose of Beatrix Potter or Teddy Robinson. Then she wet the bed one night, a thing she had not done more than a couple of times since she was potty trained at the age of 2. At once I blamed myself – here, I told myself, was the classic sign of a disturbed child and it was all my fault for putting my work first. I dare say I would immediately have embarked upon wholesale changes in my working life had it not been for my mother pointing out that Charlotte's last term at nursery school was drawing to a close and that, after two happy years there, if there was a problem, it might be apprehension about moving on to 'big school'. Sure enough, the very next day (completely unprompted) Charlotte announced that she did not really want to leave her little school. We talked about it until she felt happier and there were no more wet beds.

- You may feel guilty about not doing the things for your children that you imagine normal mothers do for theirs. Take school as an example: as all working mothers know, real mums (i.e. the stay-at-home variety) never, ever forget the school dinner money, the reading book or the breaktime biscuit, or send their children to school with dirty shoes or a button off their school coat, but I do – don't you? And, of course, they would never dream of condemning their child to the vagaries of the school run rota; they always do the taking and collecting in person so that they can pop in to admire the gold star for reading and discuss with the teacher the latest method of teaching differential calculus to 6-year-olds. You may find yourself going to any length to out-perform the real mums of your imagination. I went through a phase of baking my own bread. If I worked very hard for an entire day at the weekend I was able to provide a week's supply of leaden loaves – everybody preferred Mother's Pride but at least it proved I cared. And just last week I was lucky enough to be able to devote four or five hours to making marmalade. We do not actually eat much marmalade but it was nice to be able to renew my commitment to the family and perhaps I might even distribute a few surplus pots among the poor and needy of the parish together with a little calves' foot jelly . . . like normal mothers do.

- You may feel dreadful about having any time to yourself without the children. So obsessed was I about getting home from work to be with mine, that I would risk running out of petrol on the way rather than delay for 5 minutes to fill up at the garage. Though I resented the fact that I never had a moment to myself, I would take both children everywhere with me at weekends in order to compensate for all the time we had missed during the week. I am no longer quite so bad as I was, probably because Charlotte is now old enough to make it perfectly plain that she likes to have some time to herself too and would sooner do an hour's extra homework than traipse round town on a shopping spree with me. But even now, the only time I am really happy doing anything that does not involve the children is when they are in bed asleep. Nor can I bear to spend a night away from home without them – wherever I am working, I try to come home even if it means arriving after they have gone to sleep and setting off again before they wake up.

- You may feel guilty about the way you are doing (or not doing) your job, perhaps when you fall asleep over your desk after a particularly bad night or rush off early to attend the school sports. I feel guilty whenever I turn down work for reasons connected with the children, for example to take Andrew for his immunisations or to go to Charlotte's nativity play, and equally bad the other way round when I miss a school fete or the toddlers' Christmas party or I cannot be there to mop a fevered brow because I am tied up in court. This year I missed both sports day *and* speech day and, although Charlotte appeared hardly to notice my absence at either event, it will be a long time before I get over such a crushing double blow.
- You may suffer a few pangs about your failings as a house-keeper. Cobwebs do not bother me but I know that there are working mothers in whom they inspire remorse. And I do start to feel distinctly shifty when the dirty washing basket starts to overflow or we run out of lavatory paper or butter or resort to fishfingers for the third time in a week.
- Then there are your shortcomings as a wife/lover – always an easy target for the guilt complex. My idea of a treat is a weekday evening when I am free to get ahead with the wash-ing; the majority of evenings I spend poring over my work for the next day. Viewed in this context, my husband's tendency to work late or to go straight from the office to the pub or for a game of squash is entirely understandable. Why should he rush home to yet another mediocre take-away Chow Mein and a few hours watching television on his own?
- And what about your oppression of your overworked nan-ny/childminder/cleaner? My guilty feelings about my nanny focus on the dishwasher – she hates emptying it and I feel awful if she gets landed with the job more than once or twice in a row. Do not worry if you do not have a dishwasher or a nanny though, other situations will do equally well. For instance, you might worry about not wiping round the basin so that it is nice and clean when your domestic help comes to do the bathroom, or about asking your childminder to buy a few nappies because you have run out.

- And as if all that is not enough, perhaps you even feel guilty about feeling guilty? Or about *not* feeling guilty?

What can you do about guilt? The following suggestions may help:

☆ Analyse why you are feeling guilty. Silly complexes do not stand up to close scrutiny. They turn out to have been sparked off by some trifling little incident such as running out of cornflakes or not washing the kitchen floor, and I defy you to go on agonising about pinpricks such as these. Genuine worries will not be improved by sticking your head in the sand either – they need to be confronted and immediate action taken if appropriate. At least if your guilt feelings spur you on to do something about your serious suspicion that the childminder is consigning your infant to a cold and comfortless cot in a back room for most of the day, they will have served a useful purpose.

☆ Talk about the way you are feeling, swopping complexes with another working mother if you can. It helps to know that you are no different from anyone else.

☆ Hang on to your sense of humour and laugh at yourself whenever you can.

☆ Bear in mind that your emotional state is influenced by your physical state. For instance, you may be feeling particularly low because you are getting a cold or suffering from pre-menstrual tension. Or you may be worn out by a string of late or disturbed nights, in which case you can improve the situation by going to bed at the same time as the children for a while.

☆ Try to take a short holiday. A weekend away with the family can work wonders, or perhaps you could take a few days off and stay at home with the children.

☆ Look at the children. Do you like what you see? Do they seem contented and reasonably well-adjusted? If they are happy, there cannot be much to worry about.

## Other bad habits in otherwise well-balanced working mothers

### Spoiling

Spoiling can be a real problem. I catch myself at it all too frequently.

Sometimes the spoiling consists of sparing the rod. I want to part friends when I go to work, so I do not read the Riot Act about the felt tip on the duvet cover or the honey on the carpet. I tend to excuse bad behaviour on the ground that it is really my fault and not the child's. Charlotte, for instance, went through a phase of pestering me interminably for something special to eat (crisps perhaps, or a chocolate biscuit) as soon as I walked in through the door in the evening, even though she had just finished a big tea. If I had seen someone else's child behaving in the same way, I would have recognised it as flagrant manipulation but, because I felt rotten about having been out at work all day, I used to put it down to the difficult transition from nanny to mum and allow myself to be out-manoeuvred.

Sometimes the spoiling is material. For example, I used to spend my lunch hours buying extravagant quantities of books, toys and clothes for Charlotte. And I know I am not the only one at fault. My opponent in a recent case was another working mother. All sorts of last-minute crises cropped up so we had to work straight through the usual luncheon adjournment and she spent the afternoon distracted by anxiety as to whether she would manage to get to the shops before they closed to buy the melon she had promised her daughter.

Spoiling may make *you* feel a lot better but it is probably not doing your child any good at all, so watch your step. You may not even know you are doing it – a friend who recently returned to work when her youngest reached school age needed a prod from one of her older children before she realised that she was over-compensating the little one with treats.

## Feeling jealous of your child's carer

Helen has been with us for nearly four years. Both children look upon her as part of their everyday lives and love her dearly. This settled existence with lots of affection is, of course, exactly what I want for them but, if am absolutely honest, what I also want is to be sure that they love me best. There are times, therefore, when I feel hurt and threatened by the children's relationship with their nanny and jealous of her. I seize upon partisan gestures – Andrew collecting Helen's coat and handbag and propelling her towards the door the moment I arrive home from work; Andrew always crying for me in the night and when he is poorly; Charlotte invariably dedicating her school pictures 'To Mummy'. I conveniently ignore any evidence which suggests that I am dispensable – Andrew not even bothering to wave me goodbye in the morning; Charlotte remaining glued to the box rather than coming to greet me when I get in from work.

The sort of jealousy and insecurity that I feel is common among working mothers. Some mothers, for instance, are so concerned about being supplanted by a childminder or a nanny that they choose to send their child to a nursery where he will mix with a number of different adults and is less likely to become closely attached to any one person. Some find themselves behaving as if they were competing for their child's affection – if the nanny spends an afternoon making a mobile with the child during the week, they insist on spending the entire weekend constructing an elaborate matchstick model of the Eiffel Tower with him. Others seek reassurance directly from their child ('Who do you love best, me or Jane?'), sack the offending nanny or childminder in favour of a less popular replacement, or simply give up work in self-defence.

Whilst you probably will not be able to help feeling threatened from time to time, do try not to overreact. Have some confidence in your child. He may be too young to tell you, but he does know who his mother is and he does love you in a very special way; loving his childminder or his nanny is not *instead* of loving you, it is an extra bonus.

## Feeling bad tempered and resentful towards your partner

Every now and then, I am struck by how much easier it is to be a working father than a working mother.

There is no guilt on his gingerbread for a start. Ask a working father whether he feels guilty about playing a round of golf with his friends on a Saturday afternoon, about popping in for a swift half at the pub on the way home from work, about working late, about the tantrum that little Johnny had in the supermarket yesterday. He will look at you in amazement, quite unable to understand the question.

He has freedom from household chores too, at least in our household. My husband is proficient at noticing that we have run out of sugar or coffee and assiduously discharges his self-appointed responsibility to report shortages to me, but you will never catch him dashing to the supermarket in his lunch hour to stock up.

And freedom from responsibility for the day-to-day care of the children – it is taken for granted that it is my duty to cram my half-finished work into a briefcase and dash home from chambers to relieve the nanny, to administer baths, to read stories and to supervise homework. It is only on a Friday, by special arrangement (subject to weekly confirmation) and with obvious effort, that my husband manages to appear at or around 6 p.m. to babysit for Andrew whilst I take Charlotte for a music lesson.

Although I cannot help feeling put upon sometimes, it seems to me that there is very little to be done about these inequalities. You can campaign for more help if you think it will do any good (see Chapter 16) and blow your top occasionally as a safety-valve if you like, but do not expect dramatic results if your partner has been brought up to see work as his priority and the home and children as yours; and do not go around with a chip on your shoulder all the time or your relationship will suffer.

## Vying with your partner

If my husband has only had a quick sandwich at his desk for lunch, I have missed lunch altogether. If he has a rush job for a big client, I have an urgent case of the utmost importance. He is worn out, I am exhausted.

If you recognise this domestic one-upmanship, you too have probably been indulging in the type of competitive wrangle more suited to the infant school playground. It can happen for all sorts of reasons. You might, for instance, be trying to shame your partner into pulling his weight around the house, or it might be a way of justifying to him why you cannot fulfil the traditional woman's role or of convincing yourself that your work is sufficiently important to warrant you foresaking your duties as a full-time mother. Whatever the reason, bickering and tension will almost inevitably be the result.

## Divided loyalties at work

Having a baby plays havoc with your ambition. On the one hand, the desire to get on, to succeed, is just as strong as it ever was, but on the other there is the knowledge that success brings more responsibility and requires a greater commitment to the job, which in turn means less time for the family.

There are so many ways in which divided loyalties can make life difficult at work. Suppose there is a crisis just when you are about to leave for home – do you risk the wrath of the nanny and stay on to deal with it, or do you walk out, hoping that some long-suffering colleague will cope? The day you want to take off for the school play happens to be a day on which the office will be short staffed anyway – do you go ahead and take your holiday? In your particular job, important decisions are taken and vital contacts made in the pub after work – do you join in, missing out on a precious hour with the children before they go to bed, or do you dash home, knowing that you are prejudicing your chances of promotion?

Only you can decide your priorities. Some women make hard-and-fast rules for themselves, for instance that they will never take time off for school functions or childhood illnesses but will always leave work at 5 p.m. on the dot even if the boss is in mid-sentence. Others find rules too constraining and muddle along without any coherent policy.

## The office baby-bore

Your child may be brilliant and beautiful, but do not bore your colleagues rigid by going on and on about him or her at work. Do not spend the whole day on the telephone to the nanny talking about potty training. Think twice before you order a poster-size photograph of your baby for the wall of your office. And, although it can be a very good idea for your children to visit your place of work so that they can picture what you do all day, do not let visiting the office for a quick cuddle or to be shown off turn into a habit.

It is not only male colleagues who may be on the look out for signs that you are putting your infant before your productivity targets. Female colleagues (even those with children) may be critical too, particularly if they make a special effort not to mix home and work themselves. As one woman solicitor said of a partner who used to have her baby brought in to see her in the office at lunchtime: 'There I was telling this high-powered business man that we were an efficient and rapidly expanding commercial firm, when along she came with the baby in her arms, cooing and gurgling. I had to pretend she was a client.'

## If it all gets too much

Being a working mother does not suit everyone. If you are not happy, do not be afraid to admit it and to do something about it by cutting down your hours, rearranging the way you work or, if necessary, giving up altogether on a temporary basis or for good.

# 3

# Ante-natal
# survival tactics

As a would-be working mother, the chances are that you are not the type to give up work on the day after conception and spend your pregnancy reclining on a sofa knitting bootees. But, however healthy your attitude to your pregnancy, it *will* affect your working life. The aim of this chapter is to help you to survive the 9 months with the minimum of disruption to your normal working routine.

You will no doubt also be concerned to know what your rights are in relation to maternity leave, maternity pay, etc. You will find all the details in the Facts Section at the back of the book.

## Ante-natal care

Hospital ante-natal clinics are infamous. Each visit can easily consume several valuable hours out of your day. It is not the ante-natal care itself that takes up the time so much as travelling to the hospital and waiting your turn in the various queues for weighing, blood pressure, seeing the doctor, and so on. Although the staff will do their best to accommodate your commitments at work, clinics are held at set times only, so it will not necessarily be possible to get an appointment at a convenient time and, even if you do manage to secure a prime spot, there is no guarantee that the time on your appointment card means what it says.

If you see your ante-natal visits as a perfect opportunity to skive off work, you probably will not mind the hospital ante-natal routine and you are certainly entitled to paid time off to attend clinics (see page 163 in the Facts Section).

On the other hand, if you find it difficult to spare the time for ante-natal care, you may be interested to know that there are alternatives to that interminable wait in the hospital clinic. Arrangements vary from area to area so you must ask your own doctor what is on offer, but here are some options about which to enquire:

○ *Shared care*

Providing there are not likely to be complications with your pregnancy, it is often possible to have many of your ante-natal appointments with your GP rather than at the hospital, perhaps visiting the hospital clinic only once at the beginning of your pregnancy and a few times at the end. You will probably be able to schedule your appointments with the GP to fit in with your work. My GP used to let me attend normal evening surgery (even though he did run a special daytime ante-natal clinic) and I was in and out of the surgery in next to no time compared to a hospital visit. Your baby will still be born in hospital in the normal way unless you make special arrangements for delivery in a GP unit or at home.

○ *Private ante-natal care*

There is no doubt that private ante-natal care is very civilised and cuts out all that irritating waiting around at the clinic. The snag is that if you go the whole hog and have private ante-natal care, a private scan and a private delivery, along with your bouncing baby you will receive a big bill, which will not normally be covered by private health insurance. A cheaper alternative is to go partly private. I did this for both my pregnancies and found it a perfect compromise. After one visit to the hospital clinic in the very early stages of my pregnancy (to book in for my NHS delivery and scan), my care was shared between my GP on the NHS and the consultant obstetrician for whom I paid privately. Visits that would otherwise have been made to the hospital clinic were replaced by visits to the consultant's rooms (about once a month at the beginning of my pregnancy, more frequently towards the end). Appointments were available late in the day to suit me and usually took place more or less on time. What is more, I had the luxury of getting to know the consultant who was in charge of my care and never once felt hustled or deprived of the opportunity to talk over my anxieties or grumble about my discomforts.

## Maternity wear

Why do the manufacturers of maternity clothes cling so resolutely to the conviction that pregnant women want to wear badly made pinafore dresses in cheap and nasty fabric, flowery tents with broderie anglaise collars, elephantine T-shirts and voluminous trousers? Being in a profession that has stringent rules as to court dress (rules that barely acknowledge the existence of *women* barristers, let alone *pregnant* women barristers), how to cover the bump was a major problem for me, and I cannot believe it is much easier for any other expectant mother who wants to continue to look smart and stylish throughout her pregnancy. However, here are some ideas:

- *Make do without maternity wear*

  If you are inventive and the year's fashions are on your side, you may be able to get away without buying any true maternity wear at all if you shop around for big and baggy ordinary clothes and/or make a few modifications to your normal wardrobe. Laura Ashley, in particular, can be a fruitful source of roomy outfits and is worth a visit even if you do not usually shop there. Remember, though, that your top half will expand as well as your waistline. As designers of non-maternity wear tend not to allow enough room in the shoulders and bodice to accommodate this, however baggy the rest of the garment, you may find yourself busting out all over by the end of your pregnancy unless you have chosen very carefully.

  Expanding girth can be accommodated by a clever arrangement of elastic and safety pins at the waist of ordinary skirts and trousers. Braces can help to keep everything in place. I did not buy maternity trousers for either of my pregnancies. The first time round, I slashed the front of my ordinary close-fitting denim jeans and inserted two panels of very wide stretchy elastic, which I bought from the haberdashery department at John Lewis. The second time round, I simply let out the pleats at the waist of my trousers one by one as I got bigger and put them back in gain one by one as I got my figure back after the baby was born. Wear an oversized blouse, one of your husband's shirts or a long, loose jumper to cover whatever ingenious contraption you devise.

- *Borrow*

  Most people are glad to see the back of their maternity gear once the baby arrives and I had lots of generous offers from friends willing to lend their cast-offs. Alternatively, perhaps you might be able to buy second-hand from friends or acquaintances.

- *Hire*

  Bumpsadaisy has over 75 branches throughout the country which hire out maternity wear, plus three retail shops. Contact them to find out if there is an outlet near you (address and phone number in the Address Book at the end of the Facts Section).

- *Buy by mail order*

  Try Blooming Marvellous, for example (address and further details in the mail order part of the Facts Section). Look at the advertisements in magazines such as *Mother and Baby* for further possibilities.

- *Go to a specialist shop*
  Specialist shops such as Bumpsadaisy, Great Expectations, La Mama, Additions, Elegance Maternelle and Balloon carry a good range of better-quality (sometimes more expensive) maternity clothes (addresses and phone numbers in the Address Book at the end of the Facts Section).
- *Consider making you own maternity clothes or paying a dressmaker to make some for you.*

## When to give up work

Although I am a firm believer in ignoring pregnancy and carrying on as normal, I have to acknowledge that there comes a time, somewhere around the 29/30-week mark, when one can no longer turn a blind eye to the bump. Even the most basic everyday tasks become tests of endurance and ingenuity – just try cutting your toenails when you cannot even see them, let alone reach them.

Work can become something of a burden at this stage. The obvious problem is stamina. Rush hour tubes, bus queues, the walk from the car park, charging round the office, standing for prolonged periods, all present an unwelcome challenge when even a leisurely waddle round the garden necessitates a recuperative doze. What may surprise you more is to find your mental processes slowing down with your body, and your priorities changing. As the estimated date of delivery draws nearer, sales figures and deadlines begin to seem tedious and irrelevant in comparison to more pressing issues such as whether to stencil blue teddies or pink bunnies on the nursery walls and what to do if your membranes rupture at the supermarket checkout. Consequently it becomes harder to keep your mind on the job. So when do you give in and give up?

Subject to anything in your contract of employment and to any legal restrictions on you doing your particular job whilst pregnant, the decision is yours. The traditional choice is 29 weeks, probably because it ties in with the rules regarding maternity pay and leave (see the Facts Section). However, you do not have to give up then if you feel fit and you want to go on working. So:

> ☆ Calculate when you can afford to give up. Even if you are entitled to maternity pay or the state maternity allowance, your income will almost certainly suffer a drop when you stop work.
> ☆ Think about how long you can bear to spend at home crocheting bootees and monitoring your increasing bulk.

☆ Investigate whether, by taking less time off before the baby is born, you might be able to take more time off to enjoy it afterwards.

☆ Listen to medical advice and, if you are told firmly that you must stop work at a certain point, do so.

I worked to within two weeks of the birth of both my babies. With Charlotte, this was a bit of a cheat. I was working as a lecturer at a polytechnic at the time and she was a September baby so the last few weeks of my pregnancy coincided with the summer vacation. All I had to do was to pop in occasionally to interview new students or to invigilate resit exams. Far from being a hardship, this was a welcome diversion from nesting activities and breathing exercises.

By the time I had Andrew, I was back in practice as a barrister. As my pregnancy advanced, I began to find trips to distant courts exhausting and I did fall asleep over my desk in chambers one day, defeated by the uneven struggle with the three flights of stairs to my room. On the whole though, I felt relatively fit and everything progressed normally despite dire warnings from the medical profession about piles and varicose veins, low birth-weight babies and premature labour. At 35 weeks, I decided that the time had come to conform and exchanged my comparatively civilised and orderly working existence for a life of frenetic activity at home. After a fortnight of furniture shifting, spring cleaning, gardening and running round after an energetic 3-year-old, both the baby and I had had enough and, at 37 weeks, he arrived.

Do not be too rigid about your plans. You must make allowance for common problems such as high blood pressure, which can crop up at the most inconvenient moment and confine you to bed. Be warned also that it can be very difficult to sleep in the last few weeks of pregnancy – I planned the garden of our new house in minute detail during the sleepless nights before Charlotte was born. This, coupled with increasing bulk, can make you feel so tired that you simply have not got the energy to carry on at work, however good your intentions.

If you do go on with your job right up to the last minute, spare a thought for your colleagues who may be a lot more squeamish and apprehensive about the birth (and especially about the prospect that things might start to happen whilst you are at work) than you are. Deal patiently with the inevitable wisecracks about keeping a car handy for the dash to the delivery ward, and be careful not to permit yourself to emit the merest suggestion of a groan or you will be inundated with anxious enquiries as to the frequency of your contractions.

## Ante-natal classes

I am a great believer in ante-natal classes and found mine an enormous help in both my pregnancies. Hospitals and clinics, however, work on the assumption that every pregnant women downs tools at 29 weeks prompt, with the result that the majority of ante-natal classes take place during the day. If, like me, you do not feel able to take time off to attend a daytime class, do not just do nothing and hope for the best; you may be able to join a privately run class at a more convenient time.

I attended a course of evening classes run by the National Childbirth Trust. It was with some diffidence that I signed up, having picked up from somewhere the misguided impression that the NCT was an association of radical earth mothers. Would it matter that I was not particularly keen to give birth squatting on the living room floor?

In fact, as I soon discovered, the NCT is a perfectly ordinary organisation which simply aims to help women have their babies as easily as possible. There were seven other mothers in my group and we all intended to have our babies in hospital in the normal way. We did practise relaxation and breathing techniques during the classes, but more conventional forms of pain relief were discussed as well. Our teacher, a very experienced and slightly eccentric middle-aged lady, lent to the proceedings a pleasant air of comedy. We began each session by lurching for what seemed like miles down her extraordinarily long and narrow semi-detached back garden to an ancient colonial-style pavilion crammed full of beds, one of them a magnificent four poster. There we reclined in luxurious comfort while the teacher, sheathed in a skin-tight gymnastic outfit, incited us to push and to pant and to exercise the muscles of our pelvic floors and sustained us with coffee from a Thermos and chocolate biscuits. As the course progressed and the summer evenings lengthened, we were also able to spend some of each class propped in deckchairs outside the pavilion where, surrounded by the neighbours quietly enjoying the last of the evening sun in the adjoining gardens, we shared our most intimate doubts and fears and began to understand the finer points of delivery with the aid of a life-size baby doll which had got itself inextricably tangled up in a rather small string-bag womb.

The NCT's ante-natal classes tend to be very popular so you need to get your name down early on in your pregnancy. You may find a number for a local branch of the NCT in your phone book. Otherwise, contact the London headquarters (address and phone number in the Address Book at the end of the Facts Section) and ask to be put in touch with your nearest branch.

# 4

# Childcare options – look before you leap

W ell-planned childcare arrangements are the key to success as a working mother. Careful research, persistence and thoroughness really do pay.

Looking back on my own first experiments in arranging child care, I shudder at my cavalier approach. I could have written what I knew about nannies and nurseries on a sixpence but there I was, with all the discernment of a bargain hunter in the January sales, ready to grab the first half-decent nanny/childminder/nursery place I came across without so much as a thought as to how the arrangement might work out in practice.

It was not that I was lacking in love and concern. Part of my problem was sheer ignorance, part an irrational fear that there were only so many childcarers to go round and that, if I delayed, they would all be snapped up, leaving me holding the baby.

For starters, I interviewed a girl who had advertised in the local paper for a nannying job. It was a very short interview; I had no idea what to ask. I thought her a bit lacking in sparkle (very dull might have been a more honest verdict) but, on the basis of 20 minutes' acquaintance and no references, I felt qualified to pronounce her solid and dependable, if rather expensive. I would have had her, had it not been for a neighbour who came knocking on my door with an alternative proposal. Her children were both at school, she was looking for a job and she adored babies. Could she mind mine for me? With the confidence inspired by a few chats over the fence, I accepted immediately. Luckily my naive trust was not misplaced and, for over 18 months, Charlotte was very happy spending her days just down the road. Childminding did not suit me however, and when the arrangement came to a natural end because the neighbour's mother was ill, I decided to have a change.

Here was the opportunity for a comprehensive review of my requirements, but I still had not learnt sense. The familiar feeling of urgency and panic swamped me again and, with equally indecent haste, I took the first nursery place I was offered. The nursery was near to neither home nor work. It meant about 50 minutes in the car for Charlotte every day and an extra 40 minutes on top of that for me. All children had to be collected by 4.30 p.m. so I had to cut my working hours to be there in time. Worst of all, Charlotte hated it so much that she used to howl when I left her each morning and throw up in the car going home at night. How we stuck it for six months I cannot imagine, but it did at least provoke me into considering rationally what sort of child care we needed. The result was the engagement of our nanny, Helen, who has been with us ever since and has proved the answer to our prayers.

Fortunately, none of the family seem to have suffered in the long term from my initial lack of forward planning, but I now know how

much easier those first two years could have been had I appreciated the importance of careful groundwork.

So, before you leap, take the following basic precautions:

- Think out what your requirements are (when and for how long you need cover, whether you are prepared to take your child to a minder/nursery or would prefer to arrange for someone to look after him at home, whether you want your carer to do housework, etc.) and how much you can afford to pay.
- Find out what the various childcare options are from the summary in section 2 of the Facts Section and follow up the ones that interest you by arranging to see how they work in practice. Visit one or two nurseries and childminders, for instance. Talk over your requirements with a nanny agency. Contact an au pair bureau and ask about terms of employment, pay and availability.
- Ask other mothers how they manage, pressing them to tell you all the grisly details.

The pros and cons of the various childcare options are listed below. This is not intended to be a definitive catalogue of the factors for and against – every form of child care has its devotees, and what one mother considers to be an advantage of a particular arrangement, another may view as a distinct disadvantage. Nevertheless, skimming through my suggestions may help you to get your own ideas straight.

## The various childcare options – The Pros and the Cons

| Pros | Cons |
|---|---|
| **Relatives** | |
| ☆ Probably cheap | ☆ Will the debt of gratitude make you feel uncomfortable? |
| ☆ Already known, trusted and probably very experienced | ☆ Can you stand it when Granny insists on doing things her way and makes it plain she disapproves of your household arrangements? |
| ☆ Will provide your child with a normal family life whilst you are at work | |
| ☆ May be prepared to provide a comprehensive backup service in your own home | |

including cooking, cleaning, etc.
as well as childcare

☆ May be prepared to be
flexible

☆ May feel entitled to create
when you are 5 minutes late
home from work

☆ Family loyalty should make
for a settled arrangement
with few problems over last-
minute failure to clock on
for duty etc.

☆ Older relatives may suffer
quite frequent illnesses. Younger relatives may be hampered
by their own family commitments
☆ Can be too close for comfort,
leading to resentment and ill
feeling within the family

## Au pairs

☆ Reasonable cost
☆ Opportunity for older
children to practise languages

☆ Limited hours of work
☆ Communication difficulties

☆ Rarely possible to
interview an au pair before
engaging her
☆ May be short stay only
☆ May have no experience of
housework and childcare and
may find domestic duties
tedious – may be more
interested in learning English
and having a good time

☆ Lives in – on hand for
babysitting, early starts, etc.

☆ Lives in – loss of your spare
room, queues for the
bathroom and phone, close
contact with her social life, etc.
☆ You bear some responsibility
for her safety and welfare

☆ Successful au pairs can fit
in well and become lifelong
family friends

## Childminders

☆ Relatively economical, at
least if you only have one
child needing minding
☆ Often a mother herself – the
best sort of experience, some
say
☆ Can be a home from home
where your child is involved in
normal everyday activities

☆ Poorly paid for the minder –
do you get monkeys if you pay
peanuts?

* Can provide an opportunity for your child to enjoy the company of other children if the minder has her own young children or other charges
* Support systems such as the National Childminding Association, local authority toy libraries, etc. enable minder to get out and make life fun for self and charges
* A committed minder can be a very settled arrangement

* State of minder's home, own children, etc. give you something by which to judge her standards

* Compared to a nanny, less wear and tear and expense at your own house
* You can leave the house in a tip in the morning with the larder bare and no one but you will know or care

* Because she is working from home, may tolerate you arriving late to pick up occasionally

* Arrangement may have to end if minder's circumstances change, e.g. her husband's job moves
* Anything can go on behind closed doors once you leave and it can be difficult to check up
* Little control over way in which your child is cared for – the minder is likely to do things her way not yours
* Minders tend to offer care rather than education as they have their own housework to do and other children to look after – but then, is this not what you would offer yourself if you were at home full time?
* You have to hump child and belongings to and from minder's

* You cannot just walk out and leave your bleary-eyed pyjamad infant still munching his Frosties – he has to be ready to go when you go and it may mean a very early start to a long day

* The illness problem – an ill child cannot go to the minder's and an ill minder cannot mind. In addition, days may

37

be lost because the minder's own children are down with something nasty that you do not want yours to catch

☆ No administration – you just pay, she deals with her tax, NIC, etc.

☆ Will want her holiday to suit herself and her own family, not necessarily to suit you.

## Nurseries

☆ Often educate as well as caring for children
☆ Lots of social contact
☆ Good mix of children

☆ Particularly in local authority nurseries, may cater for underprivileged children and children with special difficulties who can disrupt routine and take up a lot of staff time
☆ Tend to be more institutional than other forms of child care and not as tailored to the individual child as a nanny or childminder

☆ Will not let you down because of illness, oversleeping or lack of enthusiasm

☆ May close down completely for annual holidays

☆ Bugs spread like wildfire. An ill child cannot attend nursery and will probably infect you whilst you stay off work to look after him

☆ Always a number of adults around – should be a safe-guard against secret maltreat-ment or neglect
☆ No need to be jealous of another adult stealing your child's affections

☆ No one loved and trusted adult to take your place whilst you are away
☆ Opening and closing times critical
☆ Can be very hard to get a place
☆ Not necessarily cheap,

especially if you are talking about more than one child

★ No administration – just pay the bill each week or month

★ Tend to be well equipped so you will probably have less clutter to transport to and fro than when using a child-minder . . .

but you still cannot depart for work leaving your child in his pyjamas, chomping Frosties

## Nannies and Mother's Helps

★ Will take charge, in your own home, of the pyjama-clad Frostie-chomping infant, leaving you free to travel to work unemcumbered and with no pitstops at the minder's or nursery on the way

★ One to one (or however many children you have)

★ If you leave her free from housework, a good nanny educates and stimulates as well as caring for your children

★ Theoretically more control over care than with minder or nursery

★ Can take the children wherever you want them to go providing transport is available

★ No problem when your child is poorly – the nanny copes and you hope she does not catch it too

★ Someone at home to let in the plumber, gas man, etc.

★ Can be an isolated life for your children unless the nanny chooses to get out and about

★ Lack of supervision – a bad nanny can get away with a great deal of no good

★ Wear and tear on house and higher fuel and food bills

★ Loss of privacy at home

★ Close contact with the nanny's social life

★ You may feel the need to keep the house in some sort of order so that the nanny will not be shocked at what a slut you are

☆ Doing the nanny's tax and national insurance is an awful bore

☆ What do you do if the nanny is ill or late?

☆ Expensive option for one child though not so bad if you have more than one

☆ Getting back exactly on time may not be so critical if nanny lives in

☆ Live-in nannies provide trouble – free babysitting and even daily nannies can be required to do some baby-sitting each week as part of their contracts

☆ Will probably want some of her holiday at a time you would not have chosen for your own holiday

☆ Can be settled long-term solution

☆ Will not necessarily stay very long and can walk out at short notice leaving you in the lurch

# 5

# Roping in relatives

## Mum and dad sharing the care

S ome couples organise their work so that they can take it in turns to look after the children. This can be a great success if one or the other parent only works part time, but if both parents have full-time jobs it probably means that they see very little of each other and one may have to work a night shift. Think carefully before you embark upon such an arrangement if you can avoid it. It may be nice for the children always to be looked after by one or the other parent and it is certainly cost effective, but it might prove to be disastrous for the parents if they only ever bump into each other for a few minutes when changing the guard. And what happens to family life?

## Using other relatives

On the face of it, a relative is the perfect solution to childcare problems – the price is usually right, the children feel comfortable and you can be confident that they are being loved and well cared for whilst you are away. Most working mothers would give their eye teeth for such an arrangement. However there can occasionally be difficulties too.

## The problem of the interfering busybody

Whoever looks after your child on a full-time basis will become very much part of your everyday life.

After 25 years of responsibility for her son's clean socks, grandma may find it hard not to criticise when she comes upon him urgently processing a pair through the tumble drier because you were too busy to deal with the washing at the weekend. Can you cope with her sniff of disapproval when she finds the remnants of a Chinese take-away in your kitchen bin for the third time in one week? Will you be able to stand up to her if she insists that potty training commences at 9 months when you know that bladder control cannot be learnt until well into the second year?

If your nanny or mother's help insists upon doing things her way rather than yours, at least you can use your clout as the employer to make sure that what you say goes. With a relative, you do not have this edge and it can be all to easy to allow yourself to be bossed about. This may not concern you unduly, indeed you might even welcome it if the disapproval can be channelled into constructive activity – perhaps if you forget those socks often enough, grandma will be motivated to deal with them herself? On the other hand, you may start to feel that your independence is being threatened and your privacy invaded, in which case you will need to be very diplomatic if you are to prevent serious resentment building up on both sides.

## The problem of the sanctimonious benefactor

Some relatives develop an irritating self-righteous glow designed to remind you at all times that they know they are doing you a favour.

The answer to this problem is to pay the going rate for the service (making sure that the relative appreciates that it *is* the going rate) or, if payment is not acceptable, to repay kindness with kindness whenever you can. But do not go to such lengths that you make it impossible for people to help you occasionally just for the love of it; some grandparents, in particular, like to be useful and get so much enjoyment from their grandchildren that they do not want payment.

## The problem of the discontented martyr

There may be trouble in store where a relative gives up other activities, for instance a job or a weekly bridge party, in order to look after your children.

A particularly trying day at home with a couple of crotchety toddlers highlights the attractions of the treat forgone and the martyr is born. Feelings of discontentment can then spill over into the relationship with you and with the children.

Make sure, therefore, that no irreversible steps are taken until the relative concerned has had a fair chance to sample the product, preferably on a rainy day after a disturbed night with a runny nose and back tooth coming through.

## The importance of making firm arrangements

There is a temptation to leave family arrangements very fluid and informal, particularly if more than one relative is helping out. However, I am sure it is worth agreeing a regular routine if you possibly can, as uncertainty and last-minute arrangements cause a lot of unnecessary stress and inconvenience to all concerned. A colleague of mine used to leave her child with one or the other granny while she went out to work. Nobody knew in advance which it was going to be and, not infrequently, both grannies made other arrangements and the colleague was left holding the baby.

## No need for relative to register as childminder

A relative who looks after your children in her own home is not classed as a childminder and need not be registered with the local authority, even if you pay her.

# 6

# Au pairs

An au pair is a single girl aged between 17 and 27 who comes to live with you as part of the family and, in return for pocket money, should help out around the house and lend a hand with the children. To comply with Home Office regulations (see further below), non-EC au pairs can only work an average of 5 hours a day and must have one full day off each week. EC au pairs expect to be employed on similar terms.

An au pair is not a cut-price alternative to a nanny, a childminder or a housekeeper. Many girls come over as au pairs to improve their English and to fill in time between school and college. You cannot really blame them, therefore, if they are more interested in attending their language courses, seeing the sights and generally having a bit of fun than in making your domestic life run smoothly. If all you want is someone to feed and supervise the kids for an hour or two after school, a responsible au pair may be the answer, providing you are not also expecting her to take sole charge for the entire school holidays or to step into the breach every time one of the children is off school ill. A good au pair may also fit the bill if you work part time and just need someone to mind a baby or toddler for a limited time each week. If, however, you are a full-timer with pre-school children and so in need of a pretty comprehensive childcare arrangement, an au pair is not the right choice.

## Home Office regulations

An au pair must conform to certain immigration rules. These are as follows:

* She must be aged between 17 and 27.
* She must be a national of a Western European country (this includes Malta, Cyprus and Turkey).
* She must not spend more than two years in this country as an au pair – if she has been over as an au pair before, she

can return for another stint but only if the *total* period is not more than two years.

☆ The period of time for which an au pair is admitted to this country will usually be stamped inside her passport. If she is admitted to this country for more than six months and she is not a national of a Commonwealth or an EC country, she will normally be required to register with the police. To do this, she has to take her passport and two passport-size photographs to a police station and pay the appropriate fee.

☆ If an au pair wants to stay for longer than the time stamped in her passport, she can apply to the Home Office Immigration and Nationality Department at Lunar House (address and phone number in the Address Book at the end of the Facts Section) or to one of six other immigration offices around the country. The Home Office leaflet *Information about au pairs* (see the end of the chapter) explains how the application should be made.

Nationals of EC countries (with the exception, until 1993, of Spain and Portugal) may take jobs in this country without a work permit. You can, therefore, employ an EC girl in the normal way as a nanny, mother's help or housekeeper, without complying with the immigration rules set out above. A girl employed in this way is not, strictly speaking, an au pair, though you may hear her described as an 'au pair plus'. She will normally have been admitted to this country for six months to begin with, but can apply for a residence permit if she wants to stay longer. Application forms can be obtained from the Home Office, the Department of Employment (look in your phone book under *Employment, Department of* for address and phone number) a Jobcentre or the police.

## Finding an au pair

There does not seem to be any shortage of girls wanting to do au pair jobs. In order to track them down, try:

● *Asking around*
   If you know someone with a satisfactory au pair, ask if the au pair can recommend a friend. If you know people who live abroad, ask them for contacts; they may even be prepared to interview possible girls for you.
   International organisations such as the Round Table might be able to help, and some churches have links abroad – I know of one family who have got hold of a number of successful au pairs this way. Once you have had one good au pair, things

should get easier as you can ask her to name her successor before she goes.

● *The agencies*

Some nanny/domestic help agencies have au pairs on their books and there are also a number of agencies that specialise in au pairs. Have a look at the agency adverts in *The Lady* magazine and the Yellow Pages. You can also find details of quite a number of au pair agencies in a book entitled *Working Holidays*, which is a guide to vacation jobs produced for students by the Central Bureau for Educational Visits and Exchanges (address and phone number in the Address Book). It is worth contacting London agencies even if you live outside London because they place au pairs all over the country.

Agencies must be licensed by the Department of Employment. Membership of the Federation of Recruitment and Employment Services (address and phone number in the Address Book) should give you an extra safeguard as to the bona fides of the agency; contact the Federation for addresses of member agencies.

A fee is payable for an agency introduction and the price can be quite steep, so make sure that you enquire about the agency's terms and conditions in advance. Do they, for example, permit you to have an initial trial period (a fortnight, say), undertaking to provide a replacement girl at no further cost if the original girl proves to be unsuitable during that time?

Whereas most au pairs come direct from their home country to start their first job, agencies may be able to offer girls who are already in the UK. Taking one of these girls can have pros and cons. The great advantage is that you can interview the girl in person and, if she has been here long enough to pick up some English, there ought to be less of a language barrier than there can be with an au pair who comes straight to you from overseas. On the debit side, she will have had time to find her feet and may therefore be less flexible than a new arrival; you may have to fit your requirements around her English classes and her already thriving social life.

● *Adverts*

*The Lady* carries adverts from families wanting au pairs and from au pairs wanting families. Keep your eyes open for adverts from prospective au pairs in other English magazines, newspapers and journals as well.

Another possibility is to advertise abroad. If you do not know how to go about this yourself, see the Facts Section at the back for details of Publicitas, an international advertising agency. Alternatively, you will find information on advertising jobs abroad in the Central Bureau's *Working Holidays* guide.

● *Other organisations*

There are a number of organisations that exist to look after the welfare of au pair girls and other young foreigners in this country. Some of these may be able to help you to get in touch with prospective au pairs. You might try, for example, International Youth Welfare or St Patrick's International Youth Centre (addresses and phone numbers in the Address Book).

## Selecting the right girl

Selecting an au pair always seems to me to be more a matter of good luck than of good judgement. Very rarely will you be able to meet her before she actually arrives to start the job and, even when she does turn up on the doorstep, it may be several weeks before she learns sufficient English to communicate with you. Her written references may be unintelligible and her own letters to you not much better.

I am amazed and encouraged to see how relaxed and optimistic old hands at au pairing are about the whole affair notwithstanding. I know families who seem able to find plenty of charming, well-balanced, helpful girls and employ au pair after au pair with very few disasters, some of the girls becoming lifelong family friends.

Here are some tips to improve the odds in favour of success:

☆ If you can, choose a girl who has been personally recommended by someone you trust.

☆ Supply full details about yourself, your family and your lifestyle by letter and request her to do the same.

☆ Set out plainly for her what the job involves. Do not succumb to the temptation to omit the grotty bits.

☆ Request a photo of her and her home and reciprocate with some of your own photos.

☆ Insist on written references even if you are doubtful whether you will understand them; someone may be able to translate for you.

☆ Speak to the girl, her family and referees by telephone, language permitting. International calls are so simple and not expensive compared to the cost of an early flight home for a disastrous mistake.

☆ If the girl has already been employed in this country, insist on speaking to the family for whom she worked to find out how she got on and why she left.

☆ Do not fall into the trap of assuming that a girl from a 'good family' will make a good au pair. She may well be a social asset, mind her Ps and Qs and hold her knife and fork correctly, but she may not be terribly useful if she has not been accustomed to mucking in with the domestic chores at home. A friend of mine lives in a Georgian rectory which is riddled with dry rot and constantly overrun by builders and all their attendant mess and muddle. Everything is frequently coated in a quantity of dust and dirt from the renovation work and for a considerable period there was no hot water for baths or washing. As the friend says, most girls would not have put up with the conditions for more than a week, but she has kept her girl for two years. Obviously luck has played a part but she also attributes the success of the arrangement to the fact that, having been brought up in a house with only an outside loo, the girl thought nothing of the upheaval!

## What your au pair will need to gain entry to this country

On arrival in Britain, your au pair will need to produce to the Immigration Officer a letter of invitation from you setting out the au pair arrangements including the duties you expect her to fulfil, free time, the amount of pocket money you have agreed to pay, the accommodation provided, details of your family and house, etc. Your au pair may also be required to produce a return ticket or evidence of sufficient funds to get herself back home. Once she has satisfied the Immigration Officer that she should be allowed into this country, the period of time for which she can stay will be stamped in her passport. This may only be six months in the first instance but it may be possible for her to apply later for an extension (see page 45).

## Explaining the house rules

Your au pair is not *employed* by you so she will not expect to have a formal contract. However, upon her arrival:

- Reiterate what you have already told her in correspondence about her hours and duties, preferably handing her a written resumé which she can translate and study at her leisure.
- Make sure that you explain the rules of the house clearly to her (no boyfriends in the bedroom, use of the bathroom confined to half an hour at peak time, telephone calls only with permission, etc.).
- Let her know what day of the week will be pocket money day so that she can budget.

- If you want to be sure that she is available at certain times of the day, say so at once before she organises a daily English class just when you wanted her to mind the children for you.

## Getting your money's worth

Providing your au pair agrees, you can juggle her 5 hours a day to suit your own requirements. She might, for example, do a full day for you once a week in return for having the whole of each weekend completely free.

When she is on duty, it is quite in order to expect the au pair to do light household tasks such as cleaning, tidying and bed making,

though you cannot assume that she will be particularly good at them. It may not be enough to explain six times in words of one syllable how to work the vacuum cleaner – you may also have to explain what a vacuum cleaner is for and in what circumstances it might be a good idea to use one, particularly if she has been used to having a devoted mother/domestic help to look after her every need.

Cooking seems to be an accepted part of the au pair's province but do not look forward to haute cuisine. Whilst you may be making a brave attempt to acquire a taste for the special Spanish paella, the au pair may be under the impression that she is making a very creditable try at English rice pudding. Indeed, one friend of mine has suffered so many culinary disasters at the hands of her au pairs that she now administers cookery lessons to each new girl as a matter of course.

Babysitting for children who are safely tucked up in bed is fair game, several times a week if you want. Judge for yourself whether your particular au pair is also capable of looking after children who are not safely tucked up in bed. Some girls are sufficiently responsible to be left in sole charge of the household day or night; others cannot even take care of themselves without supervision, let alone keep a menagerie of lively youngsters out of trouble.

If the au pair has a driving licence, she may be prepared to help out by chauffeuring the children around for you. Check that she is a competent driver and can cope with your car before you turn her loose. You cannot afford to risk her careering off on the right-hand side of the road and attempting to operate some bizarre rule of priority at your nearest roundabout. It might even be worth requiring her to have a driving lesson before she can use the car. A friend who did insist on this was relieved that she had when the driving instructor returned from the lesson white and shaking, issuing stern warnings never to allow the girl to get behind the wheel again, let alone to drive the children anywhere.

Encourage older children to practise their languages on the au pair – this is one way in which she can be very useful without a lot of effort on her part.

Whenever you feel the au pair is not pulling her weight, prod her into activity. You may not be paying her much, but you *are* paying her and you are entitled to feel peeved if she sits around reading *Paris-Match* while you do all the work. Even when she is not on official duty, she can be expected to keep her room tidy, to wipe her spilt toothpaste off the washbasin and to help set the table or wash up at mealtimes just like any other member of the family.

The reverse of the idle au pair is the rather over-zealous one who appears to find English habits sloppy and distasteful. The French au pair we had when I was a child used to get out the brush and pointedly sweep the kitchen floor after breakfast each morning. Given half a chance, I think she might also have started to hang our blankets and eiderdowns out of the bedroom windows to air. Take a robust attitude in the face of such superiority; if the au pair wants to scrub the back doorstep every day, do not take it as an implied criticism of your way of life, just let her get on with it provided it does not disrupt family life too much.

## Your role as a substitute family

Do not treat the au pair as a guest. She comes to live as family and will be with you for several months, so life must go on as normal. I remember we saw little of my mother whilst our au pair was with us. Knowing that all French families have at least one gourmet meal each day and not wishing to let the British side down, she spent her entire time in the kitchen with one of Elizabeth David's French cookery books, producing babas au rhum, soufflés and coqs au vin. We never had another au pair – it was too hard work.

Having the au pair to live as family also means taking some responsibility for her whilst she is with you. Be on the look out for attacks of the weepies; however robust the au pair is, she *is* in a foreign country a long way from home, and it would not be unnatural for her to be a bit homesick and miserable until she settles in. It is up to you to cheer her up and make her feel someone cares. You may also find that she needs your help in practical matters from time to time, for instance in organising her language classes, arranging to see a doctor or a dentist or fixing up her travel arrangements for a weekend away. Whether or not you appoint yourself guardian of her morals is up to you but remember that it could be embarrassing to have to send her home to mummy and daddy pregnant or suffering from a venereal disease. A lot depends on the au pair's age, but most people would consider it reasonable to impose a curfew and to forbid boyfriends in the bedroom.

## Further information and advice

The Home Office Immigration and Nationality Department at Lunar House (see the Address Book for address and phone number) produces a free leaflet entitled *Information about au pairs*.

Staff at Lunar House will also answer individual queries about au pairs, but I found that some of the independent organisations listed in the Home Office leaflet were more helpful. I also got a lot of good advice from the Catholic Advisory Group for Au Pairs (address and phone number in the Address Book). This is a multinational welfare organisation looking after the interests of au pairs in this country (Catholics and non-Catholics alike). Many countries also have welfare offices in the UK that can help au pairs in distress.

# 7

# Using a
# childminder

A childminder looks after your child in her own home. There is no training for the job though some childminders are able to attend short courses or group training sessions occasionally. Most childminders are mothers themselves and well used to all aspects of childcare. Some have experience of working with children in other capacities, for instance as nursery nurses, nannies or school teachers. My sister-in-law is an example. She started off as a nurse but when she had her first child (now aged 5), she decided that she wanted to be at home with the baby so registered as a childminder instead. One of her original childminding charges is still with her.

## Tracking down possible childminders

Finding a childminder who can take your child is not always easy. Here are some suggestions as to how to go about it:

- *Contact your local Social Services Department*
  All childminders who look after one or more under-fives for 2 hours or more per day for pay are required by law to register with Social Services unless the child/children is a close relative. Social Services therefore have a list of registered minders in the area and may know whether any of them are likely to have vacancies for a child the age of yours. You want to have as much choice as possible so press them to give you whatever names they have on the list rather than just one or two that they think might be suitable.
  If you are not sure how to get in touch with Social Services, refer to the Address Book at the end of the Facts Section.
- *Contact the National Childminding Association (NCMA)*
  The NCMA (address and phone number in the Address

Book) is an organisation set up in 1977 by a group of childminders, daycare workers and parents which offers support and practical advice to minders and parents. They may be able to put you in touch with a local group of childminders with information about vacancies in your area.

● *Track down adverts from childminders with vacancies*
Try the noticeboards in post offices, newsagents, corner shops and supermarkets. Also try the doctor's surgery, the child health clinic and places where mother and toddler groups or playgroups meet. Look in the local newspaper too under Employment Wanted and also under Prams and Nursery, Mother and Baby, etc.

● *Consider advertising locally yourself*

● *Ask around*
Tell everyone you are looking for a childminder and I mean everyone – the milkman, the vicar, the health visitor, parents at playgroup, neighbours, etc. If you know other mothers who use childminders, ask them if their minder has a vacancy or can recommend someone.

● *Set up your own childminding arrangement*
You may find someone who is willing to look after your child in her own home and who would be perfect for the job save that she has never minded children before and is not a registered childminder. It may, for example, be someone who answers your advert, a relative, a neighbour, a friend or an acquaintance you have met through the National Childbirth Trust (NCT) or at a mother and toddler group. There is no need for a close relative to register as a childminder even if you pay for her services, but in all other cases either you or your prospective minder should contact your local Social Services Department to find out whether she needs to be registered and, if so, how to go about getting this done. The bureaucratic wheels can grind exceeding slow, so get in touch with Social Services as soon as you can.

● *Other possibilities*
In my area there is an enterprising working mother's group, (part of our branch of the NCT) who are setting up their own register of local childcare facilities including childminders. There may be something similar where you live or you may have a branch of the Working Mothers' Association that could help (see the Address Book for addresses).

# When to start looking

There seem to be two schools of thought about how soon to start looking for a childminder. Vacancies come and go at short notice and some childminders prefer not to plan too far ahead, so there is something to be said for leaving it until shortly before you are aiming to go back to work. It is rather tempting to take this line if you have your head stuck firmly in the sand because you are not looking forward to your return to work, if you do not really know where to begin with your search for a minder or if you never seem to find enough hours in the day to get cracking. On the other hand, not knowing until the last minute what your arrangements are going to be can be a considerable strain and you might miss out on some desirable vacancies with minders who do like to plan ahead. At worst, you may be forced into leaving your child with a minder with whom you are distinctly unhappy because you are returning to work the following week and you are desperate.

My firm advice would be to start looking several months before you want to go back to work. If you are too early, the minders you contact will soon tell you and you can take their advice as to when to try again. In the meantime, they may be prepared for you to visit them to see for yourself whether a childminder is likely to be the right option for you. Seize the opportunity to do this. Visit several minders – the more you see, the better you will be at choosing the right set-up for your child when the time comes. And if you have got altogether the wrong idea about childminders and ought to be investigating the possibility of a nanny or a nursery instead, at least you will find out before the eleventh hour when it is too late to change tack.

## Choosing the right minder

It goes without saying that it is vital to choose your minder very carefully.

The fact that a minder is registered with Social Services is a valuable safeguard because it means that an independent professional has visited her to check that she is a fit person to look after children, that she and the rest of the household are in good health and that she has the appropriate equipment such as fireguards and stair gates to make her house safe for children. Social Services may also take up references before registering a prospective minder and can make enquiries within the Social Services Department and with police and health visitors as to whether she has a criminal record or has had any children who have been taken into care or placed under the Social Services' supervision. However, you cannot assume that, just because a particular minder has been registered by Social Services, she will be the sort of person whom you want to look after your child. It is quite clear from talking to social workers that some registered minders are first-rate by anybody's standards but that there are other registered minders who might seem to many of us to be barely adequate. Even though a representative from Social Services should visit regularly –

every few months or so – he or she will not be able to spend sufficient time with the minder to see whether she plays regularly with her charges and chatters to them, whether she cares more about keeping her carpets clean than she does about the children having fun, and whether those promised trips to the park actually materialise.

So, when it comes to the crunch, the responsibility for picking a good minder is yours and yours alone. Turn to Chapter 9 for advice on how to go about it.

## Your contract with your childminder

When you have decided on your childminder, the two of you ought to enter into a written agreement. The NCMA produces a contract form which covers all the main points. A copy is reproduced in section 3 of the Facts Section.

## Fees

The minder is free to charge whatever she thinks fit, but the NCMA does issue guidelines on pay and conditions and recommends certain minimum charges. Members can obtain a copy of their leaflet *Guidelines on Pay and Conditions*, which is re-issued with up-to-date figures each April. If you are not a member, simply contact the NCMA by phone and they will tell you what you need to know.

Depending on what suits you and the minder best, you can agree on a flat weekly rate or pay by the hour. Meals provided by the minder will normally be included in the price, but some things may be classed as extras and charged for separately – for instance, outings and special items for babies such as baby milk or disposable nappies if the minder provides them.

Weekends, bank holidays and unsocial hours (before 8 a.m. and after 6 p.m.) cost more than standard weekday minding as you might anticipate. The minder may want to agree an hourly rate for overtime which will come into operation if you are late picking up. It is worth asking if there is any discount on fees if you have more than one child with the minder.

Do not fall into the trap of thinking that, if your child is away from the minder's for some reason, you will not have to pay. If your minder goes by the guidelines, you can expect to be charged as follows for absences:

> ☆ No charge for absences due to
> – the minder's illness
> – the minder's holiday when it does not coincide with your own.
> ☆ Full fee when absence is due to

  - your own or your child's illness when you are being paid (half fee when you are not being paid)
  - your occasional days off (unless you give the minder at least 48 hours' notice, in which case she may charge half fee)
  - bank holidays and other statutory holidays when the minder is available for work.

☆ At least half fee when absence is due to your holiday when this does not coincide with the childminder's holiday and at any other time when the childminder is available for work and you do not use her. This covers, for example, school teachers and university lecturers who do not take their children to the minder during the vacation.

If your child attends playgroup or nursery in the course of a day at the minder's, expect to have to pay the minder the full fee for the day and any charge for the nursery/playgroup on top.

## Information your childminder needs about you and your child

There are certain things your childminder needs to know. The NCMA produces a record form which your childminder may use if she is a member. A copy is reproduced in section 4 of the Facts Section. If the minder does not ask you for the information necessary to fill in the form, make sure that you write down the relevant details and hand them to her yourself.

The childminder will probably find it helpful to know something about your child's general family background as well, such as how many other children you have and what you and your partner both do for a living. She will be able to help him to settle in more quickly if you pass on some personal details about him such as special words he uses, particular fears and food fads, behaviour problems, whether he is used to being parted from you, what experience he has had of nurseries/minders, etc.

If you feel strongly that you do not want the childminder to smack your child, spell this out to her at the outset. In theory she should not smack him without your permission but this is not always appreciated and there is no harm in making your position plain.

## Settling your child in

Try to accustom your child gradually to the idea of the childminder. Chat to him about it and let him know that going to the minder's is something nice and that you think it is a good idea. If the minder can come to your house to meet your child, this can ease the introductions.

Accompany your child to the minder's for one or two short preliminary visits, staying the whole time with him. Then, when he is familiar with her and her house, leave him for a short while on his own. You can expect a few tears at first but, provided he is not unduly distressed, he should settle quickly into a routine. Try not to linger over the goodbyes – assure your child that you will be back at teatime or whenever, say goodbye firmly and go. The usual pattern is for the shrieks to stop the minute you walk down the path.

If your child enjoys books, you might like to read *My Childminder* by Althea (Dinosaur Publications) and/or *Mummy goes to work* by Patsy Hutchinson (a NCMA publication) with him. The NCMA can supply copies by mail order.

## Keeping in touch with the minder

Take the time to have a word with the minder morning and evening.

She needs to know what your child has been doing whilst he has been with you – for instance that he is a bit upset because Daddy is away on business or that he is very excited because Granny is coming to stay – and you will naturally want a blow-by-blow account of your child's day with the minder.

Do not let anxieties and grievances fester. Talk problems over with the minder and make sure she feels free to do the same with you.

## Everyday problems

Every childminding arrangement has its problems. Here are some of the common ones.

### Illness

Illness is a problem for any working mother, but the mother who uses a childminder probably comes off worst. She has so many people's illness to worry about – her own, her child's, the minder's, the minder's children's, the minder's extended family's . . .

It seemed to be one thing after another when I used a childminder. There was a prolonged period when the minder's children had measles (consecutively). I took time off to look after Charlotte myself because I did not want her catching measles at less than a year old. Then one of the minder's children broke a leg and an arm in two separate accidents. This did not prevent Charlotte going to the minder's but it did mean that she spent rather more of her time than I would have liked trekking backwards and forwards to casualty and outpatients departments. And of course there were all her own colds, coughs and viruses, most of which involved frequent vomiting which put going to the minder's quite out of the question. Hence more time off or an SOS to Granny who would have to drop everything and dash to the rescue. Finally, the minder's mother unfortunately became quite seriously ill and she decided that she could no longer carry on doing the job.

Discuss with the minder the sort of bugs she will put up with and the sort she will not entertain – coughs and runny noses will probably be acceptable, diarrhoea, vomiting and high temperatures will probably not. What about infectious diseases such as chickenpox or German measles?

If you want to have the option of keeping your child away if someone in the minder's family is poorly, ask her to let you know of the illness as soon as she can. Make contingency plans in advance so that you are not caught short. If it is your child who is ill, the responsibility for making alternative arrangements is yours alone (consult Chapter 12 for what to do in an emergency if you get really stuck). If the illness is on the childminder's side, she might be able to find a stand-in amongst her childminding friends or through her local childminding group; the NCMA suggests that, *in extremis,* it might be worth contacting the childminding worker at the Social Services Department.

## The packhorse syndrome

The packhorse syndrome is a complaint that afflicts the mothers of babies and toddlers who go to childminders. It is caused by carting immense quantities of clutter backwards and forwards from the minder's, and sufferers (as I discovered) quickly become jaded, bad tempered and rebellious. Each morning I loaded up the big pram with steriliser, bottles, small portion of casserole in plastic container, a potato, a vegetable, a piece of fruit or similar for pudding, pushchair, nappy bucket, spare nappies, spare clothes and favourite toys. Off I would go down the road to the minder's with the whole lot precariously balanced on top of the baby. Cargo deposited, I would dash back home to pick up the car to drive to work, sometimes stopping again at the minder's on the way to deliver the carrycot or some other essential item forgotten on the first trip. In the evening, the whole process would be reversed, except that by this time the nappy bucket that had been empty in the morning would be full of dirty nappies and nappy cleansing solution would slop out all over me and the pram every time we hit a rut in the dark.

The cure for the complaint is often simple, provided that the sufferer can lay her hands on a bit of spare cash. The first step on the road to recovery is to sit down and think. When I did this, it dawned upon me for the first time that terry nappies and childminders did not go together. The NCMA does not recommend that childminders get into the habit of washing terry nappies, apart from rinsing dirty ones through, and I certainly do not recommend transporting used terry nappies home to be washed, so the obvious answer is to change to disposables. If your childminder has room, buy in bulk and let her have 40 or 60 at a time so that you do not have to think about nappies more than once every fortnight or so. You might even arrange for a month's supply to be delivered direct to her if she is agreeable (Boots and Mothercare will deliver – see page 213 in the Facts Section).

Consider the other bits of equipment you transport to and fro – could you afford to buy or improvise duplicates so that you could have one at each home? Sterilising units do not cost very much for instance, or a plastic box will do nicely instead if you happen to have one the right size. A few extra feeding bottles and teats will not break the bank. Even bigger pieces of equipment can sometimes be bought quite cheaply second hand. As for the things that cannot be duplicated, such as favourite toys, clothing, etc., write yourself a list so that you can check you have everything before you set off – that should save having to go back for teddy or the wellington boots.

If you are providing meals, as I was, perhaps you could agree with the childminder that she will cater? Quite apart from the improvement you should see in the appearance of your files when you give up carrying leaky containers of stew about in your briefcase, it will be one less thing for you to think about.

## Niggles over picking up

Anticipate hostility if you are persistently late picking up. Childminders have their own family responsibilities and are entitled to expect you to stick to the hours agreed. Minimise problems by being brutally honest when you first meet the minder, resisting the temptation to make the job seem more attractive than it is. Do not say 'I'm often home by 4 p.m. so I'd be picking little Johnny up early several times a week' if the true position is that you rarely leave the office before 4 p.m., or 'I know you do not want to work after 5 and I am sure that I can always be there on the dot' if you really mean 'I am regularly late leaving work but you are perfect for my requirements and I will say anything to make sure of you'. You may get the childminder to agree to take on your child this way, but it is not a recipe for long-term success and harmony.

## An unsettled child

Always pay attention to out-of-character behaviour that might indicate that your child is not happy with the minder – for instance, if he seems unusually quiet or aggressive or unexpectedly starts to wet the bed or to cling when you leave for work.

Do not be too quick to blame the minder for minor upsets though. Working mothers have a tendency to blame their childcare arrangements for every undesirable quirk of their child's development when in fact the child may not be feeling awfully well or may just be going through a grisly phase. However, if you are still worried when you have talked things over with the minder, investigate further, perhaps even calling in during the day unexpectedly to find out what is going on. Should you decide that things have gone badly awry and that your child may be at risk at the minder's, either physically or emotionally, do not hesitate to terminate the arrangement.

## Finding out more about childminding

The best source of further information is the NCMA. It produces a publications list detailing all the literature it can supply. *I need a childminder* is a helpful inexpensive pamphlet. *How to survive as a childminder* is a handbook written for childminders but equally informative for parents. Non-members can order books so why not send for the publications list and see what is on offer?

For a small charge, you can support the NCMA by becoming a member and you will then receive a copy of the Association's newsletter automatically every two months. The office staff are always willing to answer queries from members and from the general public and the Association will take up problems for members.

# 8

# Nurseries

Day nurseries provide a full-time childcare service. Opening hours usually coincide roughly with the normal working day plus a little bit extra at either end to allow parents time to drop off and collect. Some nurseries stay open all year round apart from bank holidays, others close for a few weeks' annual holiday. Age limits vary, with some nurseries even taking babies.

Going to nursery means plenty of company from children of a similar age. It can also be a lot of fun, with most nurseries offering a good blend of activities for the children each day – singing, outside play, craft work, stories, quiet periods with books and jigsaws, messy play with sand and water, etc. Some nurseries may offer pre-school education, possibly employing a qualified infant teacher. If the nursery caters for babies and toddlers, staff will expect to change nappies and to tackle potty training when the time comes.

## Finding a nursery

All nurseries must register with the local authority, so contact the Social Services Department of your local authority for a list of registered nurseries (for how to get in touch with Social Services, see the Address Book at the end of the Facts Section). Nurseries may be grouped together according to type. The main categories are:

- *Local authority nurseries*
  Local authority run. Priority given to underprivileged and needy families so not an option for most working mothers, which is a pity as facilities tend to be good and charges modest or even nil in special cases. Single-parent working mums may have a chance of a place in some areas.
- *Workplace nurseries or crèches*
  Provided by some large employers/educational establishments for the children of employees/students. Other children sometimes accepted as well. Can be good value

if subsidised, but beware the taxman – if your earnings (*including* the amount of the subsidy) are £8,500 or above, the subsidy will be treated as a benefit in kind and you will be taxed on it. Usually situated near the workplace, making daytime visits possible (e.g. to breastfeed).

● *Private day nurseries*
Funding and management differ from nursery to nursery. Some run as commercial enterprises, some on a charitable basis, others as cooperatives with substantial parental involvement. Some (sometimes labelled 'community nurseries') are community based, accepting children only from the vicinity of the nursery.

## Start looking well ahead

Tracking down a nursery may not be difficult but finding a nursery *with a vacancy* often is, so you need to get geared up in good time in order to secure a prime position on the waiting list. If you think you may want a place for a new baby, begin to make enquiries as early as possible during your pregnancy – not all nurseries cater for very tiny babies, which adds to the pressure on places.

Should you need a nursery at short notice however, do not be defeatist. Pester each and every local nursery and you may well find that a place materialises mysteriously at the last minute. This is what happened with Charlotte, although the nursery was a very popular and busy one. I never understood how it was done, but I was very grateful to the Matron for getting me out of a tight spot.

## Choosing a nursery

Compulsory registration with the local authority means that all nurseries are subjected to a certain amount of supervision by Social Services. There is a limit to how much checking the Social Services Department can do however, so do not assume that registration is a guarantee of quality. It is up to you to investigate for yourself by looking round and asking questions and to decide which establishment will fulfil the particular needs of your child best.

You will notice marked differences between nurseries both in the standard of care provided and in the individual 'feel' of the nursery. All sorts of factors may influence your reaction to a particular establishment – the colour of the walls, the menu, whether the children are grouped according to age, in family groups with a spread of ages or not at all, what the philosophy is about discipline, etc., etc.

Chapter 9 should help you to look out for the right things and to evaluate what you see. Clearly most of your time and energy

will go into working out which of the nurseries on offer is most likely to provide your child with a happy, settled and stimulating environment, but do consider yourself as well. Do not, for example, take up a place in a community-based nursery that requires heavy parental involvement if you cannot stand fund-raising barn dances or if, with the best will in the world, you simply will not have time to pull your weight.

## Your contract with the nursery

You should have a written agreement with the nursery you choose. The nursery will probably have its own standard contract form detailing all the important points, such as when your child is to start, what days he will attend each week, annual nursery holidays and bank holiday arrangements, fees and notice requirements.

Read through the completed contract form before you sign to make sure that it is an accurate representation of your agreement with the nursery and ask for your own copy of the signed form so that you know where you stand.

## Information the nursery needs about you and your child

The nursery needs to be supplied with various details about you and your child (for example, where you can be contacted in case of emergency and whether your child has any health problems or allergies) and will probably ask you for whatever information it considers relevant. If you are not asked to provide any details, write down the most important facts and hand a copy to the person in charge. Use the NCMA form in section 4 of the Facts Section as a guide to what to include.

## Settling your child in

Take advice from the nursery as to how to settle your child in – having gone through the process dozens of times before the staff should know what usually works best. A gradual progression may be recommended, starting with short accompanied visits, moving on to short visits alone and building up to whole sessions unaccompanied. Some children are so beguiled by the wonderful array of nursery equipment and all the potential playmates that they find progress *too* gradual, not wanting to leave at the end of the first visit. Although this is very encouraging, do not rush things – there is a world of difference between a happy hour playing with the nursery toys with Mummy comfortably close for reassurance and an 8–10-hour day on your own in strange surroundings.

Consult the nursery staff about how to deal with tears on parting as well. Charlotte's nursery advocated the clean break approach. I would be disentangled from the bawling bundle by a kind and friendly nursery nurse and would then ostentatiously let myself out of the door and hover out of sight on the threshold anxiously waiting for the cries to stop. Someone must have been very skilful at distraction because the screams always did stop within a matter of minutes.

Whatever you do, do not let your child sense any uneasiness that you may have about leaving him at the nursery. I have often wondered whether this is where I slipped up with Charlotte. She relished every minute of the trial session despite cutting her lip in a nasty tumble from a tricycle (whilst under my supervision, of course). Yet before very long she was unsettled, reluctant to go in each morning, tense and anxious each evening. Looking back it seems quite possible that I conveyed to her my own uncertainties about the nursery and undermined her confidence.

## Problems

No childcare arrangement is perfect and problems are bound to crop up from time to time. Whatever they may be – persistent/extreme distress over parting, uncharacteristic behaviour by your child such as bed-wetting, aggression or excessive tiredness, or just dislike of the Spam served at lunchtime – talk them over with the nursery staff without delay. Perhaps they can reassure you by explaining the symptoms; for instance, the reason your child has suddenly become reluctant to go to nursery may be because a special friend has moved on or a favourite nursery nurse has been replaced. Or maybe you can agree that your child has an extra rest so that he finds his day less exhausting, or sort out a combined approach to a particular discipline problem to avoid the confusion of double standards at home and nursery.

Unfortunately there is one problem that cannot be solved by talking and that is illness. As bug-breeding grounds, nurseries are unparalleled and young children with little accumulated immunity tend to catch anything and everything that is going. As a family, we had more tummy upsets and virus infections while Charlotte was at the nursery than ever before or since. Once you know that your child is ill, you cannot send him to nursery, so you must have contingency plans – in our case a hand-to-mouth affair which involved both of us taking a limited amount of time off work and Granny filling in the gaps.

# 9

# Choosing a nursery or childminder

C hoosing a nursery or a childminder is a tremendous responsibility and one for which most working mothers are totally
unprepared.

How can you ensure that you make the right choice?

## General tips

- *Shop around*
  Try to visit several nurseries/childminders before you make
  up your mind. Comparing one with another will highlight
  good and bad features and help you to evaluate what you
  see.
- *Be brazen*
  Put whatever questions you want and ask to be shown every
  nook and cranny of the premises if you feel it necessary.
  Take with you a list of the things that you particularly want
  to check.
- *Make several visits*
  If you are seriously interested in a minder or a nursery,
  visit more than once. Try to make one of your visits an
  unscheduled stop at an unexpected time so that you can
  see what the regime is like when no parents are around. Do
  not just breeze in and out; the longer you stay, the more you
  will learn.
- *Consider asking for a second opinion*
  If you are not sure about a particular set-up, take someone
  else along to see it – for instance, your mother or a friend
  who has experience of using a nursery/childminder.
- *Keep your own child's needs firmly in mind*
  Nobody knows your child like you do and it is up to you to
  select the care that will be most appropriate for him as an
  individual. If he hates dogs, do not choose a minder with

a Great Dane. If he loves outdoor play, choose a nursery with a garden or playground. If he is car sick, do not make arrangements that will involve him in a long and winding car journey at the beginning and end of each day.

- *Take your child along*
  Take your child along with you to meet the minder/the nursery staff before you sign on the dotted line. You can learn a lot by watching how the minder or the staff relate to him, how well they cope with shyness and make him feel at home, whether he appears to warm to them. I can remember interviewing cleaners when Charlotte was about 2 years old. Most of the ladies came and went with hardly a glance from her but one perfectly ordinary lady, who (so far as *I* could tell) was indistinguishable from the rest, provoked an astonishing reaction – screams, tears, cowering behind my skirts. There was no way I could have employed that lady even if she had been the best cleaner in Yorkshire.

- *Follow up references if you can*
  Ask if you can be put in touch with other parents who use the nursery/childminder. If this is not possible, ask for other references and contact the referees by phone to give them the chance to furnish you with the true picture off the record.

- *Be guided by intuition as well as by what you see and what you are told*
  However cool and rational you try to be about your choice of carer, intuition is bound to play a part and it is very difficult to know how much weight to give to your instinctive feelings. Most of us feel a bit unsure about our childcare arrangements until they have been tried and tested, and this natural diffidence (which you can afford to ignore) has to be distinguished from the intuitive feeling that all is not right with a particular nursery or childminder (which you cannot).

- *Do not be rushed into making a decision.* On the other hand, if you have made up your mind, do not risk losing a good minder or nursery place by dithering.

## What to watch out for

Here are some of the things to look out for when you visit a particular minder or nursery:

- *Contented children involved in their play*
  Make due allowances for children who are having an off day, but steer clear if the minder/nursery seems to have more

than its fair share of bored, irritable, miserable or withdrawn children.

● *A minder/staff who seem to enjoy the job and to have a good relationship with the children*

Enthusiasm and a genuine interest in children are big pluses. You will not necessarily be able to judge the calibre of the staff by talking to them yourself. Adults who are good with children are not always good with other adults and may not shine in conversation. You need to watch how they get on with their charges. Do the children get plenty of cuddles and individual attention? Do they approach the minder/staff freely? Does someone listen to what they have to say and respond appropriately? Are crises averted, disputes over toys settled before they result in blows? Do not be too influenced by personal appearance. Round and cuddly motherly types are not guaranteed to be good with children, nor do they have a monopoly on maternal instinct. Charlotte got on particularly well at nursery with a teenage nursery nurse with a rather repellent shock of spiky punk rock hair.

● *A satisfactory approach to discipline*

Is discipline a lot of shouting, culminating in a hefty smack, or a more sophisticated process, tailored to the individual child? Is there consistency of approach? Do you agree with the standards that are being taught?

● *The right amount of supervision*

It can be very hard to strike a sensible balance between over-protectiveness and over-permissiveness, especially when you are looking after someone else's child. Babies obviously need fairly close supervision, particularly when they start to crawl, but they also need freedom to experiment safely. Older children need to be allowed to enjoy their own company and that of their peers, to quarrel and to indulge in minor skirmishes over toys, to try out new manoeuvres on the climbing frame and to fall over on roller skates. But they still need an observant adult around to make sure that things do not get out of hand – exploring to the far end of the playground alone is character forming, climbing over the wall to explore the road outside the nursery is dangerous.

● *Sensitive handover arrangements*

Handover times are potentially disastrous so you must check carefully how dropping off and picking up are handled. You will get the best idea of how things work if you are able to be present one day, but, if this is not possible, at least ask what the arrangements are.

At Charlotte's nursery, the outside door was kept locked. Obviously this was necessary to prevent intruders and escapees, but it meant an uncomfortable wait in the mornings while a member of staff came to greet us. However stoical she was during the journey to the nursery, Charlotte always used to lose her nerve whilst we stood on the doorstep and, by the time we parted, she would invariably be howling. Picking-up time was equally difficult. Many of the children were collected early by parents who were teachers. If I did not arrive with the first posse of pickers up, Charlotte (who naturally had no idea of time) would think that the end of the day had come and would work herself up into a frightful state, convinced that she had been abandoned. This impression was compounded by the nursery routine at the end of the day. Had the nursery been a shop, it would have been the sort of shop where the assistants cease normal trading half an hour before closing time in order to start cashing up so that they can get away the minute the doors close. Translated into nursery terms this meant packing away toys and games and getting all the children into hats and coats in advance ready to be transferred to the collecting parent with a minimum of delay. It was not long before I found myself leaving work when the afternoon had barely started in an effort to win the collection race and save Charlotte from the late afternoon turmoil.

Try to make sure that the staff/minder will be able and willing to spare the time to have a chat with you about your child when you drop off and when you collect. They need to know if he has had a bad night and might be crotchety from lack of sleep or if he complained of a tummy-ache at breakfast. You want to know how he has got on during the day.

● *Good facilities*

Look for a good selection of toys, books, craft activities, etc. Obviously you can expect more from a nursery than from a childminder. Not many homes have a full-size indoor sand tray, a slide in the living room or an unlimited supply of gummed paper and art materials. On the other hand, if all the minder can show you is a small cardboard carton containing a forlorn jumble of battered and broken toys, go elsewhere.

Safe toys should be readily accessible to children, subject to any reasonable house rules that there may be – for instance, about tidiness or about not riding bikes during storytime. Messy or potentially dangerous toys and activities such as poster paints, scissors, clay, etc. should be under adult control.

There should be somewhere quiet for reading or colouring or just winding down.

I would go for somewhere with facilities for outside play if you can – a safe garden or a playground with outdoor toys. If that is not possible, ask whether children are taken on trips to the park or to the shops.

Do not overlook the basics such as loos, washbasins and food. I diligently inspected the toilet facilities and the dining room at Charlotte's nursery but I never thought to ask *when* the children were fed; it turned out that meals, although of the nourishing school food variety, were served at bizarre times – lunch not long after 11 a.m. and a sort of snack tea at around 3 p.m. We were home in time for a real tea so it did not matter much but, had I not been picking up until 5 p.m. or later, I might have preferred a nursery that provided a proper tea at teatime so that I did not have to start cooking for a desperately hungry toddler the minute I got into the house.

If your child still has a rest during the day, ask about rest facilities too. At Charlotte's nursery, resting was a timetabled activity. When the appointed hour arrived, tiny camp beds were brought out and all the children lay down and went to sleep. How the staff managed to induce universal somnolence to order defeats me, but I do not remember Charlotte suffering any particular problems over tiredness so the system must have worked fairly well for her. On the other hand, children's resting and sleeping needs do tend to vary and I would have been happier with a flexible system that allowed for rests as and when needed.

● *Safety*

Look for all the usual things – stair gates, garden gates, fireguards, window locks, potentially dangerous substances such as medicines, cleaning materials and weedkillers safely closeted away, etc.

● *Order and cleanliness*

You want a minder/nursery with a balanced attitude to order, cleanliness and hygiene. Avoid the sort of set-up where the toddler's unchanged nappies are so wet and heavy that they droop on the floor, where snotty noses are left unwiped for hours on end and hands never washed, where nobody ever bothers to clear up yesterday's projects and spilt milk, and children have to root through the accumulated clutter of weeks or even months in order to find the particular toy that they want. Beware also of childminders who are obsessionally houseproud and might view your child as a potential source of mess rather than an interesting and creative human being; will they have time to squeeze a cuddle and a visit to the library into that tight schedule of rug beating and window polishing?

● *Geographical situation*

Obviously geography is not the most important factor in choosing a nursery or minder but it can have quite a significant influence on how well a particular arrangement works out, so be sure to check how long it takes to get from home to nursery and nursery to work, whether there are buses and trains at convenient times, whether there is somewhere to park whilst you drop off, etc. You may have special reasons for wanting a carer near to your place of work (for example, if you want to call in to breastfeed in your lunch hour), but otherwise I recommend picking somewhere near to home if you can. Charlotte demanded a non-stop cabaret act during the long journey to and from nursery: stories, nursery rhymes, community singing, the lot. When the entertainment failed to come up to scratch, she would liven things up by wriggling out of her car seat and rolling about on the rear parcel shelf. On occasions, she marked her disapproval particularly forcefully by throwing up all over everything – hardly an auspicious beginning or end to anyone's day.

# Things to talk over

Have a long chat with the minder or nursery staff, particularly the person in charge. The following list should give you an idea of the sort of areas to cover.

* Opening hours – what are they and is there any flexibility if you have to work late or start early occasionally?
* Holiday arrangements – does the nursery close for bank holidays or for a fixed annual holiday? How much holiday does the childminder take? Does she take the same weeks every year? Would she be willing to consult you before fixing anything?
* Fees.
* Registered with Social Services?
* Training/experience of minder/nursery staff and understanding of young children.
* Views of minder/nursery staff on any matters that are particularly important to you such as pre-school education, discipline, potty training, manners, etc.
* Daily routine – is there one and do you like the sound of it if there is?
* Staff/child ratio – DHSS guidelines recommend that there should be one member of staff for every two under-2s and one member of staff for every four 2–5 year olds.
* Staff turnover – ask yourself whether a rapid turnover of staff can be put down to the natural flightiness of young nursery nurses or whether it might point to something wrong with the particular nursery. Remember that children can find frequent changes of staff unsettling whatever the cause.
* Turnover of children – of course children leave for all sorts of reasons (for instance, to go on to nursery school or because the family moves out of the area or mum stops work) so it is difficult to assess the significance of a rapid turnover of children. It might, however, be a good sign if children seem to stay for a long time and it might be a bad sign if they are always chopping and changing.
* Relationships between staff/minder and parents – can you come any time for a chat about problems or progress? Are there any regular meetings between staff and parents and/or open days?
* Rules about ill children – obviously you will not expect a nursery or minder to take your child when he is really ill, but what about the days when he is just a bit under the weather with a cold? What if he becomes unwell during a day at nursery? Is there somewhere he can rest until you are able to get there to take him home?

☆ Insurance – check that the minder/nursery has insurance to cover any damage that your child may do to someone else's property whilst he is in the care of the nursery/minder (for example, the football through next door's conservatory window) and any personal injury that he may suffer through the fault of the nursery or minder (for example, a serious burn from falling into an unguarded fire).

Extra matters to raise with a childminder include:

☆ Minder's personal circumstances. All sorts of things can come under this heading: marital status, husband's job, ages and circumstances of own children, state of health, smoker or non-smoker, etc. It is also worth asking whether there are any changes in the pipeline that might mean her having to give up childminding, such as another baby of her own, a job move for her husband or a move to a new house in a different area.

☆ Regular and emergency backup. Does anyone help the minder out on a regular basis or if she has to visit the doctor or dentist? Ask for details and consider whether you should ask to meet the person concerned. Who holds the fort if there is an emergency – for example, if one of the children has a bad fall and has to be taken to Casualty? Is there anyone to take over when the minder is ill?

☆ Pets. My childminder had pets and, though it did not put me off using her, I always felt uncomfortable about the dog sniffing my baby and I have vivid recollections of the crisis that affected the whole household when the hamster began to eat its own babies in a fit of post-natal depression. Even if you find the idea of a pet-owning childminder acceptable in principle, do take the trouble to do a spot check on Tabitha and Fido before you expose your child to their tender mercies. Your good-natured labrador may not mind when the baby pokes a Bickipeg in his ear, but will Fido? Does Tabitha have a penchant for sitting on babies in their prams? Is that Fido's dinner in which the childminder's toddler is dabbling his Mothercare spoon?

☆ Transport. The general rule is that you deliver to and collect from the minder's house but, if some other arrangement would suit you better, ask if the minder would be prepared to go along with it. Could she, for instance, collect your child from your house on her way to drop her own children off at school? Would she take your child to playgroup for you and to the clinic for weighing, injections and check-ups? Ask if the minder has a car and whether she would want to take your child out in it. Has she got appropriate safety restraints for a child the age of yours or would she agree to having carrycot straps/child's seat/harness/safety belt fitted at her cost or yours? Has she got a clean driving licence? Does her car insurance cover her to take minded children out in the car?

# 10

# Nannies and
# mother's helps

The very mention of a nanny conjures up all sorts of images, most of them totally at odds with the reality of today's nannies. These days the young master has exchanged his sailor suit for a pair of Osh-Kosh dungarees and his spinning top for a personal computer. Nursery tea has given way to a couple of fishfingers and a tin of beans downed in front of the telly, and the grey-haired, starched-aproned disciplinarian nanny of yesteryear has been replaced by one of a new breed.

Of course, modern nannies still do basically the same job they have always done – they look after your children for you in your own home. But by far the majority of modern nannies are young and a lot more fun than the old-fashioned sort.

Normal duties include all the routine care of the children (making their beds, looking after their clothes, feeding them, etc). However, Nanny is just as likely to be found organising some thoroughly messy finger painting and water play (the sort you can never face yourself because of the appalling aftermath which takes hours to clear up), doing the school run, enjoying a tea party with other nannies and their charges, or scaling the assault course at the sports centre with the children.

Mother's helps are similar to nannies but, having no training and relatively little experience, have rather less dignity on which to stand. The average nanny will do housework only in so far as it relates to the children, if necessary spending 20 minutes sorting through the family's dirty clothing in order to ensure that not so much as one adult sock should find its way into a load of the children's washing. The average mother's help accepts that she is there to provide general household assistance and has no choice but to do whatever light domestic duties are asked of her. On the other hand, whereas you can expect the average nanny to have sufficient training and/or experience to take sole charge of the children right from the word go, there is no guarantee that the average mother's help will be up to this straight away or, in some cases, at all.

For most of this chapter, I have used the term 'nanny' as shorthand for any girl who comes to look after your children in your own home, be she a qualified nanny, a mother's help or whatever. The one or two places where the term is used in a narrower sense should be clear from the context.

## Nannying qualifications

- *The NNEB certificate*
  The most common nannying qualification is the National Nursery Examination Board's certificate in Nursery Nursing, often referred to simply as 'the NNEB'. NNEB courses usually last two years. Part of the time is spent in college, where students are given a general education (home economics, art and craft, etc.) and taught about the growth, development and care of children. A fair amount of time is spent gaining practical experience working with children outside the college – for example, with a family and in day nurseries, nursery and infant schools, maternity hospitals and special schools. Performance is continuously assessed and, in order to get a certificate, students have to come up to scratch in their practical and written coursework as well as passing the final examination.

  Many local authority colleges of further education run approved NNEB courses, and there are three well-established private nursery training colleges, Norland, Chiltern and Princess Christian (more detail later in this chapter). These private colleges award their own qualifications as well as preparing girls for the NNEB.
- *The Royal Society of Health Diploma in Nursery Nursing*
  In addition to the NNEB and a certificate from their college, girls who have attended Norland, Chiltern or Princess Christian may have this diploma, which is simply another qualification in nursery nursing.
- *Other certificates, diplomas and training*
  Some colleges of further education offer other courses that help to prepare students for work with children, old people, the handicapped, etc. For instance, my local college of arts and technology offers a course leading to a Preliminary Certificate in Social Care and also a Family and Community Care course.

  If you want to know what a particular qualification means, contact the college that ran the course.

## Norland, Chiltern and Princess Christian colleges

Norland, Chiltern, and Princess Christian colleges are nanny-training establishments in a class of their own. Like the Mercedes Estate, the portable phone and the weekend cottage in the country, a nanny from one of the big three (preferably one who can be relied upon to wear her uniform when collecting her young charges from their private school and on all other public occasions) will greatly enhance the status of any upwardly mobile mother.

However, quite apart from their snob appeal, there are other features that make the nannies from these colleges different. These are the only *residential* nursery training establishments in Britain. They can take their pick from an enormous number of applicants, who must have at least three O-level passes (not necessarily required at local authority colleges). Entrants on the course must be at least 18 (as opposed to 16 for local authority courses), so girls are that little bit older when they qualify, which can be an advantage.

The colleges all have their own childcare facilities where students can gain experience with children in addition to their practical experience in the community in hospitals and schools and with families. Norland has a residential nursery where students can learn to look after children round the clock.

Each college has its own individual system of training and its own rules and quirks. Norland, for example, has a two-stage graduation process. After six terms training at the college and a term working with children in hospital, students are eligible for the Norland Preliminary Certificate, provided they have passed the NNEB examination and the final Norland Assessment. However, they are not awarded the full Norland Diploma and Badge until they have completed a further nine months' satisfactory work as a 'probationer nurse' in a private residential post.

All the colleges maintain a protective interest in their students after they have qualified and play an active part in helping them to obtain suitable employment.

> ☆ Norland has its own employment agency (The Norland Registry). Probationers *must* be employed through the agency and Norland takes up a reference on *you* before letting you loose on one. Qualified Norlanders can use the agency if they want to, but are not compelled to do so. All prospective employers are charged a registration fee. An engagement fee is charged if the agency finds a nurse to fill the post (by no means a foregone conclusion, as demand for nurses far exceeds supply). Norland produces a booklet giving no-nonsense guidance as to the conditions of employment of Norland nurses. Definitely no nursery tea for any parent who suggests some housework whilst Junior has his nap. And whatever you

do, do not ask Nurse to indulge in a bit of spanking – mere mortal mums may need to resort to violence every now and then, but the steely glint in Nurse's eye is all that is required to keep even the most unspeakable villain in check.

☆ Chiltern and Princess Christian do not have agencies as such but, if you contact them, details of the job will be entered in their records and passed on to girls who are looking for employment. For the first two years after qualifying, Princess Christian girls wanting private posts are obliged to find employment through the college lists.

For more details or to register a vacancy, contact the colleges direct. You will find addresses and phone numbers in the Address Book at the end of the Facts Section.

## What sort of help do you require?

Do not waste time dreaming of the perfect nanny. If she exists at all, she is undoubtedly happily ensconced in someone else's household and quite impervious to blackmail.

Take a realistic approach from the very beginning. Sit down and work out exactly what the job will involve. There is a checklist in section 5 of the Facts Section to help you.

Consider your priorities – would you be prepared to do without walking the dog/family ironing/mowing the lawn if an applicant were right in every other respect? Is it fair to ask one person to perform all the tasks on your list? Perhaps, finances permitting, you should be thinking of employing a part-time cleaner as well?

## Live-in or live-out?

Many mothers agonise over whether to go for a live-in girl or for one who comes in daily. Both arrangements have their pros and cons.

○ *Live-in*:
Advantages:    Never late for work – even the most dedicated oversleeper can be booted out of bed to clock on in her dressing gown if necessary.

Cannot take days off for imaginary illnesses.

May be able to soldier on when slightly off colour.

79

Built-in babysitter.

May be more tolerant about you arriving home late from work occasionally.

More likely to agree to do breakfasts and bathtimes.

Available to cope with nightmares, wet beds, and other nocturnal disasters.

Normally paid less than a daily nanny (but allow for hidden costs of board, lodging, phone calls, etc.).

Disadvantages: Loss of privacy (though a mature, sensitive nanny can do much to alleviate the problem by making herself scarce when she is not wanted and, despite serious misgivings, we did not feel that our live-in nanny intruded at all).

Close contact with her social life – how will you feel if she rolls home in the early hours or extends your hospitality to her unsavoury suitors?

Less chance to have your child entirely to yourself.

Takes up a bedroom.

May hog the bathroom, phone, etc.

May burden you with her emotional problems.

Little niggles can get out of proportion when you are living with each other 24 hours a day.

○ **Daily:**

Advantages: Less of an intrusion.

Easier to keep your distance and maintain a proper employer/employee relationship.

Overnight breathing space helps keep minor grumbles in proportion.

Does not take up a bedroom.

Disadvantages: May be late for work.

Can get away with time off sick for phantom or minor illnesses.

No on-the-spot babysitter (though, if she

agrees, you can make it part of her contract that she does one or two evenings a week).

Less likely to tolerate you arriving home late from work.

More obviously expensive in cash terms.

## The search for the right girl

To make contact in the first place, try:

- *Word of mouth*
  The nanny grapevine is tremendously effective and, though originally designed to transmit intimate titbits about employers' personal habits and finances, can be used to good effect to spread the word that you are looking for a nanny. To set things in motion, just ask a friend with a nanny to mention your requirements in conversation with the nanny (preferably confidentially), then sit back and wait for results.
- *Advertising*
  If you live outside London and you want a daily nanny rather than a live-in, it is probably best to concentrate on local

advertising. A card in a shop window/supermarket/community centre, etc. is cheap but it does not spread the word very widely. Local papers may be a better bet.

If you live in the London area or you live outside London but you are prepared to take a live-in girl, use *The Lady* (a weekly general interest magazine/newspaper) and/or *Nursery World* (a fortnightly childcare magazine bought by nannies and others working with children). Of the two publications, *The Lady* seems to be the more popular place to advertise. Instructions are only accepted by post (address in the Address Book). *Nursery World* will accept copy by post, phone or fax (phone/fax numbers and address in the Address Book). For how to word your advert, see the next section.

Do not overlook 'Situations Wanted' columns. *The Lady* in particular carries quite a few adverts from nannies/housekeepers/mother's helps looking for work.

● *Agencies*

All employment agencies must be licensed by the Department of Employment. There are licensed nanny/mother's agencies all over the country. You will have to pay a fee for their services so enquire about precise terms before you get involved. Using an agency can save you time and trouble in the long run. For example:

- The agency should only send you girls who meet your basic requirements. This saves you the task of weeding out the no-hopers yourself and makes interviewing less of a burden.
- Good agencies realise that it is bad for trade if their nannies make a habit of beating up the baby or walking out after a week and therefore screen girls before sending them out by interviewing them and taking up their references. This is a useful backup to your own screening procedures.
- The agency may be privy to information not available to you and may be able to help you informally when it comes to making a decision about a particular girl. For instance, if you like a girl and you feel she is suitable but you are worried because she walked out of her last job after three weeks, the agency might be prepared to let slip (very discreetly of course) that they have never known a nanny to stick with that particular employer for more than a month.
- An agency will be able to give you a guide as to the going rate for the sort of job you are offering and probably to advise you on other terms of employment as well. This is useful, though you must treat such advice with a modicum of caution (see below).

You should find local agencies listed in the Yellow Pages and there are lots of agency adverts in *The Lady* and *Nursery World*. Because girls tend to approach an agency in the area where they want to work, try agencies in your own immediate area first. Go for an outfit that has been personally recommended if you can. Otherwise make some enquiries about the way the particular agency operates before you enlist their help. Is it their practice to meet girls before taking them on to their books? What is their screening procedure? Be wary of an agency that simply sends you the briefest of forms to fill in without having a chat about your requirements – how can they decide which girls might be suitable without finding out a bit about you, and do they really care that much anyway? Membership of the Federation of Recruitment and Employment Services (address and phone number in the Address Book) should give you an extra safeguard as to the bona fides of an agency; contact the Federation for addresses of member agencies.

If you ask for advice from an agency (for example, about salary or about whether a particular girl is likely to be suitable), always remember that the agency has a financial interest in getting you fixed up and that the fee payable to the agency may be governed by the level of salary that you agree to pay. Even with the best will in the world, it may therefore be difficult for the agency to be completely impartial.

● *Approaching colleges and schools*
Norland, Chiltern and Princess Christian will all do their best to fix you up with a suitable girl. See pages 78-9 for further details.

Local authority colleges of further education that run the NNEB course also have an interest in placing their students in jobs and may be prepared to keep an eye out for someone who might fit the bill. To find out which colleges run an NNEB course, try the careers section at the library or contact the NNEB (address and phone number in the Address Book).

Schools may put you in touch with leavers who want jobs as mother's helps.

● *Jobcentre*
A possible source of mother's helps. Not the traditional place to find a nanny but there is no charge for the service, so why not register your vacancy just on the off chance?

● *Careers offices*
Worth a try perhaps?

## Wording your advert

It is important to word your advert carefully in order to ensure that you get the best possible response. Buy yourself a copy of *The Lady* and of *Nursery World* so that you can crib from everyone else.

Apart from a few families who want a 'person', a 'girl' or a 'Girl Friday', most adverts are for a 'nanny', a 'mother's help' or a 'nanny/mother's help'. Make sure you label your job correctly:

- ○ 'Nanny' generally implies training or a decent amount of experience (though note that some agencies and employers will call a girl a nanny only if she actually has the NNEB), sole charge at least some of the time, no housework except 'nursery duties' (i.e. looking after the children's rooms, washing their clothes, feeding them, etc.) and a generous wage packet.
- ○ 'Mother's help' generally implies youngish (for example, a school leaver), no training and not much experience, willing to help with the kids but not necessarily to take sole charge, prepared to do housework, and content to accept a more modest wage packet.
- ○ 'Nanny/mother's help' is a vague term that covers a multitude of sins. Some applicants will interpret it as an indication that you are flexible and would be prepared to take on either a nanny or a mother's help. Some will assume that you want a sort of halfway house between an experienced nanny and an average mother's help – for example, a nanny fresh from training college with no post-qualifying experience, or a mother's help with a bit of experience of sole charge. Others will take it that you want the best of all worlds, i.e. a nanny who does housework. A friend's recent experience suggests that the response to a nanny/mother's help advert can be disappointing. What she wanted was a versatile and easy-going nanny, brilliant with the children but also prepared to answer the office phone, turn out a room, or conjure up a casserole for supper – as she put it, 'someone to be me when I'm not around'. She had no shortage of replies to her advert in *The Lady* but, although she had stipulated that experience and references were essential, most of the applicants were raw mother's helps and did not even merit an interview. When I asked my own nanny about this, she was not surprised. With training, experience and good references under her belt, she would not even consider a nanny/mother's help job. Why risk being landed with the housework when there are plenty of mothers prepared to guarantee nursery duties only?

Stipulate in your advert:

- – whether the post is residential;
- – where it is based;
- – how applicants should contact you. I give my phone number, partly because I am impatient for results and partly because

I find it valuable to carry out a preliminary selection procedure over the phone. Totally unsuitable candidates can be eliminated after a short chat, very promising ones invited for immediate interview, and the rest asked to send in written applications. However, if you do give a telephone number, you will have to accept that you may be inundated with enquiries, some of them prompted by nothing more than idle curiosity. Stipulating written enquiries and applications will limit the number of casual enquiries, but good applicants may also be put off if they cannot do a preliminary recce without putting pen to paper. Go for a box number if you would prefer not to disclose either your address or phone number.

It is probably a good idea also to mention the following:

- how many children you have and their ages (*The Lady* advises that you do not include the children's names if you are also giving your address or telephone number);
- family pets – perhaps not the goldfish but think about including dogs, cats, reptiles, etc.;
- whether the job involves sole charge;
- if you are asking for a nanny, whether it is nursery duties only or whether you require housework. Mother's helps will assume as a matter of course that some housework is included;
- non-smoker if smoking is a definite no-no in your household;
- any particular transport requirements, e.g. 'must have clean driving licence/own car'.

Extra flannel about fringe benefits and a happy atmosphere may make your ad more attractive but can be quite costly. I got my nanny to skim through *The Lady* and *Nursery World* marking the adverts that attracted her. Here are the features she went for, together with her reasons:

- 'Present nanny recommends' (sounds promising and there might be a possibility of discussing the post with the outgoing nanny before deciding whether to take it);
- 'No weekends' (reduces the days of the week on which you can be put upon from seven to five);
- 'Cleaner employed' (as an insurance against housework);
- 'Car provided' (a considerable perk and she has got used to the luxury of having one).

Nauseating adverts purporting to be the work of 9-month-old Willikins or Baby Jemima in person should surely be avoided, if only out of a sense of duty to other readers of the classified ads.

## Arranging interviews

* ☆ Once you start to receive applications, arrange interviews with promising candidates immediately. If you leave it, good applicants will get fixed up with other jobs.
* ☆ Take down basic details such as name, address and phone number when you first make contact so that you can alter arrangements if necessary. Give interviewees your phone number if they do not already have it so that they can get in touch with you quickly if something prevents them from attending at the appointed time.
* ☆ If you will be seeing a number of applicants on one day, space out the appointments – allow at least an hour for each candidate so that you will not be rushed, even if one or two are a bit late.
* ☆ Do not forget to tell each interviewee where you live and to give directions for getting there if it is out of the way. You may be asked to pay travelling expenses if the interviewee has to come any distance. If you agree to do so, you might think it sensible to hand over the money at the interview, not in advance.
* ☆ Ask interviewees to send you or bring to the interview a written curriculum vitae setting out their training and experience. No need for anything very formal – a simple handwritten list will save you wasting valuable interview time extracting technical details from the candidate and will give you enough information about her to enable you to put her at her ease at the beginning of the interview.

## The actual interview

Interviewing is a very personal thing and it would be misguided of me to lay down the law about how to do it. It does pay, however, to think about your approach in advance and the following tips might help:

* • *Interview promising candidates at least twice*
  An interview has two main purposes. It is your chance to form an impression of the interviewee – her personality, appearance, experience, etc. – and it is an opportunity for the two of you to compare notes about the job you are offering to make sure that she would be prepared to operate on your terms. If you try to cram everything into one interview, there is a danger that you will become so bogged down with whether or not the particular girl would be prepared to wash your husband's socks that you never even consider whether you

*like* her and whether the children would take to her. So think about arranging a preliminary screening interview at which you can give a very general picture of the job and have a relaxed chat to see if you would get on. If she seems promising and is interested in the post, give her a copy of your job profile (see section 5 of the Facts Section) to take home with her and arrange for a second interview at which you can get down to the nitty-gritty of sock washing if you want.

● *Have someone else on hand to look after the children*

You cannot interview properly with young children around, so preliminary interviews should, if possible, be held when they are in bed or when there is someone else around to take care of them. You *will* need to arrange for them to meet prospective nannies before you make a final decision, but there will be time enough for this when you have got down to a shortlist.

● *Notes and lists*

A list of points that you want to cover can be helpful (see below for topics) but be prepared to depart from your formula if it is making the interview difficult and unproductive. It is a good idea to make notes about the interview, particularly if you are seeing several applicants. Organised interviewers have a clipboard or notebook with a separate pre-headed page for each girl. I use the back of an envelope and one of the children's wax crayons. Do not spend the whole interview writing, just jot down one or two things and complete your

notes immediately after the girl has gone. I have found that the most useful notes are the very personal ones that remind me what a particular applicant was like. You know the sort of thing – 'blousy peroxide-blonde barmaid type, lovely smile and brilliant ideas for entertaining kids, second interview? But do be careful not to leave your libellous scribbles lying around for the unfortunate subject to find on her first day at work.

- *Get a second opinion*

  Try to arrange for your partner to meet applicants in whom you are seriously interested. The object of this exercise is largely, of course, to get a second opinion. However, it is also comforting to think that, if you make the wrong choice and the new nanny keeps the whole family awake with rowdy parties in her room every night, it is just as much his fault as yours.

- *Take nerves into account*

  Interviewees may well be tense, so try not to pay too much attention to silly giggles, shyness, nervous nail-biting and the like. Pedestrian chat about the weather, her journey, whether she knows the area, etc. will give the interviewee a chance to settle down before you move on to more serious questions.

Here are some of the topics you might like to cover:

○ Personal circumstances (age, married, steady boyfriend, own children, etc.) and health.

  A friend stressed the importance of personal questions of this sort after her quiet and apparently innocent nanny discovered sex in a big way and finished up having frequent injections at a clinic for sexually transmitted diseases. Fortunately it was not Aids, but perhaps one should ask if the interviewee has it/has been tested for it? Should one (dare one?) also ask whether the candidate has any criminal convictions or any children in care?

○ Family background.

  Tells you a lot about what you can expect from a girl. I actually met our nanny's family when she first started to work for us and found it reassuring that I liked them and that they were interested in what she was doing and cared enough to do an hour's round trip to pick her up every Friday evening so that she could spend the weekend at home. When interviewing a girl who will be leaving home for the first time, try to find out how she will react and whether she has considered the possibility that she will be homesick.

○ Smoker?

○ Religion and politics if they matter to you.

○ Long-term plans.

One nanny I know of through the nanny grapevine makes no secret of the fact that she has always intended to move on after a year in her present post. Her employer does not know this, presumably because she has never asked the right question.

○ Training.

○ Previous experience.

Do not just stick to the basic facts; ask her what she liked and did not like about her last job and why she left – it can be revealing.

○ What does she think about discipline, potty training, nutrition, daytime rests, fresh air, routine, pets, etc.?

○ What ideas does she have for entertaining a child of the age of your child?

○ Is she clued up on first aid and safety?

○ Clean driving licence and car (if you want her to chauffeur for you).

○ Does she swim/play the piano/speak Esperanto or whatever is important in your family?

○ References (see below).

Make your terms perfectly plain. Deal with:

✰ Hours
✰ Pay
✰ Accommodation and living arrangements if she is to live-in (including rules about boyfriends visiting, phoning, etc.) or arrangements for meals at work if she is living out
✰ Holidays and sick pay
✰ Trial period (see below)
✰ Notice
✰ Exactly what the job involves – warts, lavatory cleaning, dishwasher emptying and all.

Provide an opportunity for the candidate to ask you questions. She is interviewing you too and she will no doubt want to see the children's rooms and the living areas and kitchen, plus (is she is to live in) the bedroom she would have. She may also want to view the children themselves at an early stage before she decides whether or not she is interested in the job – she may not find the little monsters as attractive as you do.

## Trial periods

However good you are at interviewing, there is a limit to what you can find out about someone during a conventional interview. It is therefore worth arranging, if you can, for your chosen candidate to spend a whole day with the family or perhaps even a trial week, so that you can get to know her better before you finally take her on. It would not be unreasonable of her to expect you to pay her for the trial period whether or not she gets the job, but it will be money well spent if it helps you to make the right choice.

## References

Always take up references, preferably from the applicant's last employer or, in the case of a girl fresh from school or college, from a teacher or tutor.

Follow up written references by speaking to the referee in person so that he or she has the opportunity to talk freely, off the record. Be blunt and ask exactly what you want to know.

If your enquiries reveal skeletons in the cupboard but you are still keen on the girl concerned, have her back for another interview and sound her out about the difficulties – it is always possible that it was the employer who was unreasonable rather than the girl herself who was at fault.

## Once you have made your decision

Do not hang about once you have made up your mind. Contact your chosen nanny immediately and, if she confirms that she would like to take the job, arrange to meet to go over the finer details of the contract.

Do not forget to write to the applicants who were unsuccessful to let them off the hook. Hang on to the names and addresses on your shortlist for a few weeks though, until you see how things work out. That way you can always contact them to see if they are still interested should you find yourself unexpectedly nannyless again.

## The contract

It makes sense to record the terms of your nanny's employment right at the start and the law says that you *must* provide a written contract once your employee has worked for you for a period of 13 weeks or more. I must confess immediately that this is a case of 'Do as I say, not as I do' – my nanny has no written contract and I know of only one nanny who does.

You will find a suggested form of contract in section 6 of the Facts Section, together with some notes for guidance. Bearing in mind how bad we all are at paperwork, I have deliberately kept the contract very basic. You can dress it up and incorporate as much detail as you like. Prepare two copies, sign each one yourself and get the nanny to sign them both too. Keep a copy each for future reference.

## Insurance

### Household insurance

Notify your household insurers that you are employing a nanny. They may need to make some adjustment to your policy to ensure that you are still fully covered. Confirm specifically that you will be covered if your nanny has an accident at work and you have to pay her damages.

### Motor insurance

If your nanny will be driving *your* car, check that she is covered on your policy. She will be driving in the course of her business and this needs to be made plain to the insurers.

If she will be driving your children around in her *own* car, get her to notify her insurers of the position so that her cover can be extended if necessary.

### Personal accident insurance

You might want to take out some cover in case your child has an accident whilst in the nanny's care.

For children of 5 and over, you can take out personal accident cover, which entitles you to a fixed lump sum payment in the event of the child suffering a serious disability. This will, incidentally, also cover the child whilst he is at school or in your own care.

Alternatively, the nanny can take out insurance that will cover her for any damages she has to pay as a result of an injury your child suffers through her negligence. If she is a member of the Professional Association of Nursery Nurses (see Address Book), she will automatically be covered – this is a free perk of membership. If not, you or she could contact the Lyall Eason & Dudley Division of Robert Barrow Ltd (address and phone number in the Address Book), who may be able to arrange cover. The nanny could fairly look to you to pay the insurance premium for her if the policy is your idea.

## Tax, national insurance and sick pay

As your nanny's employer, you will have to deal with her tax and national insurance contributions. This is a nightmare for the uninitiated and a bore even when you know how. Turn to section 8 of the Facts Section for help and also for information about sick pay.

## The initial handover

Let your child accustom himself gradually to the idea of a new nanny. If he is old enough to understand, talk to him about your plans. If he has never had a nanny before, tell him what it will be like. If he is an old hand, do not underrate his attachment to his existing nanny, even if she has been an unmitigated disaster from your point of view (Chapter 12 offers some suggestions as to how to ease the parting).

Try to arrange for the new nanny to start at least a week before she will be required to take sole charge so that she has time to learn the ropes from you or from your existing nanny and so that your child has an opportunity to get to know her. During this period, make sure that the new nanny spends some time with the child on her own. On Helen's first day in the job, I sent her off to the library with Charlotte, then aged 2¼. Charlotte was not keen on the idea at all and I watched as she indulged in the most horrific tantrum, kicking and screaming in the middle of the road and refusing either to walk or to get into her pushchair. Helen waited calmly for the outburst to subside, dumped the body unceremoniously into the pushchair and departed at top speed in the direction of the village. Nobody ever looked back from the incident – Charlotte and Helen returned from the library friends (but with Charlotte in no doubt as to who was boss), and, having seen for myself that Helen could cope with Charlotte at her very worst, I felt confident about leaving her in charge when I returned to work the following week.

Draw up a list of useful facts for the new nanny (see the Information Sheet in section 7 of the Facts Section). Provide her with her own copy to digest in advance and display another copy prominently, perhaps near the phone so that it is handy for emergencies.

If you can avoid it, do not make other changes in your child's life (such as introducing solid food, swopping from a bottle to a feeding cup or moving him from his cot to a big bed) at the same time as introducing a new nanny.

Anticipate a few tears when you initially hand over sole charge but do not allow yourself to be unduly impressed by them; they will probably stop the moment you are out of sight.

## Keeping your nanny/mother's help

No working mother ever really escapes from the fear that the nanny might walk out. However reasonable you are, however well paid the job and angelic the children, you can never be absolutely sure that it will not happen. There is always the pull of the boyfriend in Aberdeen, the once-in-a-lifetime opportunity to go to America, the prospect of working for someone richer or more famous than you, the need for a change.

There is no doubt that some employers are better at keeping their helpers than others, just as some girls are better at staying than others. I suggest the following 'dos' and 'don'ts':

- *Do establish and maintain your status as the friendly employer*
  It is quite a shock to the system to have someone who is neither family nor a guest around the house full time, and many of us find ourselves at a loss as to how to treat the newcomer. It is so important to strike the right balance from the start. You cannot afford to become over-friendly because you need to remain firmly in charge and you must be able to put your foot down effectively if something is going wrong. On the other hand, you have got to realise that a girl in a new household can feel extremely isolated and lonely and needs to be made welcome and comfortable. Introducing her to other nannies will help her to settle and to be less dependent on you for company, making it easier for you to keep a friendly distance, so go out of your way to help her to make friends with your friends' nannies or through toddler groups or similar. This will also have the further advantage that you may be able to get some feedback on how she is shaping up – nannies are inveterate gossips and it should not be long before you hear about any shortcomings and disasters on the grapevine.
- *Do deal with grievances straight away*
  If you do not like the way the nanny is doing something or feel she is not pulling her weight, take it up with her immediately. Providing everything else is right about your relationship, she will not pack her bags just because you tell her that you would prefer her not to put the baby's jumpers in the tumble drier or that you would like her to clean out the bath after she uses it.

  Similarly, encourage her to raise with you anything about which she is unhappy. If you can tell there is a problem but she soldiers on silently, ask her point blank what is the matter – a good mutual grouse can serve to release a lot of tension and may be all that is needed to get things on an even keel again. Watch out for token strikes and demonstrations – I know something is up when I find that the dishwasher has been emptied and exactly half the clean pots have been put away, my share being left ostentatiously on the worktop for my attention.
- *Do stick to the terms of employment you originally agreed*
  This means letting the nanny go on time, not expecting her to do your housework if she contracted to do only nursery duties, always paying wages on the nail, etc. If you are as good as your word, you may find that she is rather better than hers, perhaps voluntarily ironing the odd shirt for you

or doing a bit of shopping when she can see you are under pressure.

● *Do sort out the question of household finance in advance*
Niggly gripes over cash can cause a lot of discontent. You ask the nanny to buy you a copy of the evening paper and then forget to pay her back, you give her a £5 note to get some sausages for the children's lunch and she forgets to give you the change . . . To avoid this sort of difficulty, we have a household purse which I keep stocked with a modest amount of money for use on household items, children's food, outings (Helen's expenses as well as the children's), things which I specially ask Helen to buy, etc. Because Helen is careful, there is never any need for formal accounting, but you could always ask for receipts to be kept if the purse turns into a drain.

● *Do try to provide treats every now and then*
The occasional special treat works wonders. Anything from a weekend away to a bottle of wine, an unexpected half-day or something nice from the perfume counter will do. It is fun for the nanny and it shows you care.

● *Do give praise where praise is due*

● *Do not pry into the nanny's private life unless it is impinging on your own or your children's.*

● *Do not blame the nanny when life does not seem to be running quite as smoothly as you would like* – it is not fair to tear a strip off her because you have had a rotten day at work or a row with your husband.

● *Do not organise your nanny's life for her without asking first*
There is no reason why you should not ask your nanny to stay in for the gas man or the carpet fitter occasionally, but do not just book the appointment on the assumption that she will be there; do her the courtesy of asking her first. And always clear it with her first before offering her services as a babysitter or agreeing to let a friend's child spend the day with yours in her care.

● *Do not undermine her confidence*
You will not see eye to eye with the nanny over everything. Some things really matter – you cannot, for instance, let the nanny go on leaving the baby in the house alone while she pops to the post box. Other things – for example, the way the nanny folds the baby's nappy or cooks his carrots – are not terribly important and should really be ignored in the interests of good labour relations. If you pick the nanny up every time she does something her way rather than yours, you will irritate her and undermine her confidence.

● *Do not undermine her authority*
Inevitably the children will try to play nanny and mum off against each other. It is bad enough to find yourself acting

as a Court of Appeal from one of the nanny's less popular decisions the minute you come in from the office and the problem can become a nightmare if you work from home. So plot tactics with the nanny in advance, make it clear to the children whose word goes when, and stick to your guns.

- *Do not force her to come to you for a rise* – get in just before she does.

# 11

# School-age children

W orking mothers with under-5s dream that when the children are at school their childcare problems will be over. In fact, making arrangements for out-of-school hours and school holidays can be every bit as taxing as making arrangements for someone to look after your children full time.

In this chapter I mention some of the options. With ingenuity you will no doubt come up with others.

## Term time

For term time, you need a two-tier support system:

○ a routine arrangement for taking and collecting and to plug any gaps before and after school; and
○ a safety net for the days when school is cancelled because there is a blizzard or a teachers' strike or the heating has broken down, for the days when your child is so poorly that you really cannot send him to school and for the days when, having sent him to school when you should not have done, you are summoned to collect him mid-morning because he has fulfilled all his earlier promise and thrown up on the classroom floor.

### Normal termtime routine

You and your partner may be able to cope with routine arrangements between you by juggling your normal timetable around. Some schools will receive children quite a while before morning school actually starts (about 25 minutes in our case). This may be enough to enable one of you to drop your child off and still be at work on time. If the other partner has flexible working hours, perhaps he or she could start and finish early in order to be able to pick up at the other end of the day?

If you cannot manage between you, try:

* *Mothers of school friends*

  Insist on putting things on a commercial basis if you can. This should prevent you from feeling you are taking advantage of the other mother and might help the arrangement to survive when the novelty wears off or the children fall out.

* *Neighbours with children*

  Not an answer to the problem of transport to and from school unless your child and the neighbour's children are at the same school or the neighbour can make a combined journey to both schools. However, a neighbour can be a useful stopgap, say between you setting off for work and the school run rota collecting your child to take him to school.

* *School run rota*

  May be the solution to school transport problems. Ask at school whether any other children live in your area or whether you are likely to be on anyone else's route to school. Do not be frightened to ask if you can join an existing rota simply because the help you can give will be restricted by your working hours. A friend of mine hesitated because her job as a teacher meant she was unable to do any weekday school runs. In the end, she did pluck up the courage to approach the other parents and found she was welcomed with open arms because she offered to do Saturday mornings which everyone else hated.

  If there are enough of you in the rota, your day/week may come round only once every four days/four weeks or so. If your husband shares the job, your turns will be even less frequent and you may find your employer amenable to you adjusting your hours for the occasional day/week even if he would not be prepared to let you rearrange them on a permanent basis.

* *Taxis*

  Another possible solution to school transport problems. Obviously entrusting your children to a taxidriver is not something to be done lightly. However, taxis regularly collect children from my daughter's school and I know that my sister, who is a taxidriver, does a school run each morning and afternoon. Go for a firm that can guarantee the same driver every day so that you can check him or her out carefully before making the arrangement. Try to find a woman driver if it would make you feel more secure. School may be able to tell you of a taxi firm that other parents have used successfully.

* *Staying on at school*

  Just as some schools accept children quite a while before morning school begins, certain schools make provision for children to stay on at the end of the day until parents can pick them up – ask if there are any such arrangements at your school.

☆ *Out-of-school and latchkey schemes*

In term time these schemes provide someone to collect children from school and look after them until the end of the working day. They offer an all-day service during the holidays. Enquire of your local authority about schemes in your area or contact The National Out of School Alliance (address and phone number in the Address Book at the end of the Facts Section). Londoners may find useful NOOSA'S directory of out-of-school schemes in London (called *Out of School in London*). As well as advising on the existing schemes available, NOOSA will help anyone interested in setting up a new scheme.

☆ *Childminders*

Childminders do not just look after the under-5s. Some will mind older children before and/or after school and during the holidays, and some will also take responsibility for taking your child to school and/or picking him up. See Chapter 7 for more details.

☆ *Au pairs*

May be just the job during term time – see Chapter 6 for details.

☆ *Relatives*

I often come across grandparents, aunts and other relatives at the school gate. Maybe yours might be prepared to help out?

☆ *Waiting with you at work*

If your child can get himself to your place of work after school, an easygoing employer might be prepared to let him stay quietly with you until going home time.

☆ *Advertising for help*

If you get stuck, consider advertising. The local paper or a shop window would probably be the best place. Alternatively ask around to see whether anyone knows someone who might be interested in the job. Vet any applicants carefully of course, and be sure to take up references.

☆ *Agencies*

Some domestic help/nanny agencies can provide part-time helpers for out-of-school hours and/or an escort service (car and driver) for collecting children from school. You can find out more about using an agency in Chapter 10.

Older children are often left to cope on their own. I always thought that it was illegal to leave a child of less than 14 in the house alone. In fact, there is no minimum age. The law leaves it up to you to decide whether you can trust your child in the house alone, although it *is* a criminal offence to wilfully neglect a child in a manner likely to cause unnecessary suffering and, in addition, in an extreme case, if social services felt that you were putting him at risk, they could seek to take him into care. Do not forget that, however mature and capable your child is, he may still be lonely in an empty house on his own and might be frightened, particularly on dark winter nights.

If you do decide to risk it:

- Reiterate all the usual warnings about not talking to strangers, not accepting lifts, not making detours on the way home etc. Issue frequent reminders and go out of your way to make it plain that women can be just as dangerous as men and to stress that even those who appear to be respectable and who claim to be doctors, teachers, fathers of school friends, etc. are not to be trusted. Despite many careful briefings from my parents, when I was 11 I accepted a lift from a stranger who said he was a headmaster attending a conference at my school and asked for directions to the main school building. I had difficulty in explaining which way he should go and it seemed simpler to climb into his car, as he suggested, and direct him stage by stage. Fortunately for me, we did not disappear together into the sunset but I shudder now to think of the risk I ran.
- Make sure your child had road sense and can cope with the route to and from school and with public transport.
- Find a safe place for your child to carry his door key. Keys stuffed in pockets or school bags get lost. Leave a spare set with a neighbour just in case.
- Find a safe place for bus money.
- Make sure that your child has your telephone number at work and preferably at least one other number of someone close at hand upon whom he can call if he has problems.
- Post up emergency numbers such as the police and doctor by the phone and drill into your child what he must do in a crisis.
- Consider asking him to check in by ringing you as soon as he gets home.
- Let trusted neighbours know that he will be in on his own. This is one situation in which nosy and interfering neighbours could be a blessing as they will probably keep a close eye on the child for their own entertainment!
- Establish the ground rules clearly – no gangs of friends to call, microwave cooking only, outside doors always to be kept locked, no strangers to be admitted, etc.

- Do not overburden older children with the responsibility of looking after younger brothers and sisters too often or for too long – it is not fair.
- Be on the alert for signs that your child is getting upset by the arrangement.

## Termtime safety net

This is very much a hand-to-mouth affair for many parents. See Chapter 12 for suggestions as to how to cope.

# Holidays

If you thought termtime arrangements required Machiavellian cunning, try the holidays. Here are some possibilities:

☆ *Mum and/or Dad take time off*

It always seems a pity for parents to stagger their holiday entitlement but it does ease the burden of school holidays. If you are each entitled to, say, four weeks' holiday, you might decide to have a family holiday for a fortnight and then to take the remaining two weeks separately so that, between you, you can cover a further four weeks of your

child's holidays. Add to this bank holidays and time off at Christmas that does not count towards your holiday entitlement and you might find that you can cope with at least half the school holidays.

☆ *Visits to relatives and friends*

School holidays provide an excellent opportunity for the children to go to stay with doting relatives and with school friends. The children love it. The problem is not getting them to go but getting them to come home. Grannies and grandpas, in particular, love it (provided it does not go on for too long). Cousins and school friends love it and their mothers welcome it as ready-made company for their children. The only people who might not love it are the parents, rattling around in an empty house every evening, wracked with misplaced guilt at condemning their children to two parentless weeks. If you cannot bear to be parted, try inviting grandparents to stay with you instead.

☆ *Holiday playschemes*

Comb the community centres, sports centres, libraries, health centres, local papers, council information office, etc. for information about any school holiday playschemes that there may be in your area. Playschemes tend to operate during the long summer holiday and offer children the chance to participate in supervised activities and outings, sometimes on an all-day basis. This summer my daughter learnt fabric printing and attended an arts and crafts class. If she had been so inclined, she could have learnt circus skills, bounced on an inflatable castle, visited a stately home or two, had tennis coaching and done a dozen other things besides. Some schools open during the holidays offering a similar sort of thing, not necessarily restricted to their own pupils. If you cannot find anything to fit the bill, you could always consider setting up your own scheme. The National Playing Fields Association and NOOSA (see the Address Book) will advise and supply books on how to go about it.

☆ *Holiday camps*

Well established in America for many years and now becoming popular in this country too. Options can range from the old-fashioned Brownie or Guide camp to much more trendy camps run on a commercial basis. Some camps are residential, with children being accommodated in boarding school premises or under canvas, for example; others operate on a daily basis. All sorts of activities are offered – camping, sports and outward bound, walking, pony trekking, etc. There are several books available giving details, for example *Adventure Holidays* by Simon Calder published by Vacation-Work (address in the Address Book). Your travel agent may also be able to help. Do as much as you can (by asking questions and, wherever possible, inspecting facilities) to check on the standard of supervision and instruction before you book your child in. Fairly recently the British Activity Holiday Association (address and telephone number in the Address Book) was set up with the aim of establishing a code of conduct for operators. They should be able to put you in touch with members of the association.

☆ *Temporary nanny/childminder*

You may be able to employ someone to look after the children temporarily during the school holidays. School leavers waiting to go up to university or polytechnic and students on vacation are possibles. Whilst I have not actually tried to get hold of a student to do childcare work, I did register a vacancy for a temporary gardener with the local Jobcentre at the beginning of last summer and I was inundated with applications from students looking for vacation jobs. For a very reasonable wage, I got a keen and responsible postgraduate, prepared to turn his hand to anything. I think he might even have looked after the children for me had I asked him to do so – certainly they spent many happy hours 'helping' him in the garden. As an alternative to the Jobcentre, you could advertise at a few universities during the summer term or ask your local schools and colleges if they can put you in touch with likely candidates. If you have a local college of further education that runs the NNEB course (a nannying qualification – see Chapter 10), you might like to make this your first port of call. You can find out which colleges do run such a course from the careers section of your library or by enquiring directly of the NNEB (address and phone number in the Address Book).

If you want cover for only a limited number of hours each day, a short-term au pair might be worth considering (see Chapter 6). Make sure you arrange for her to start work some time before the holidays begin or the combination of her newness and the language barrier could prove to be a complete disaster.

Alternatively you might find a childminder willing to do school holidays only or a nanny or mother's help looking for a temporary post.

☆ *Sharing/borrowing a nanny*

A friend of mine used to bring her little boy to be looked after by my nanny on occasional days during the school holidays. This sort of system can work to everyone's advantage. In our case, the cost to the friend was rather less than a childminder and she knew that her child was safe and settled in familiar surroundings, the money gave a welcome boost to my nanny's salary and Charlotte loved having a friend to keep her company.

Another idea is to try to pair up with a working mother who has school holidays off (for instance, a teacher or lecturer) and wants to save money by doing without her nanny/mother's help while she is at home herself. She could employ the nanny/mother's help during term time and you could be responsible for her wages during the holidays.

☆ *Sharing the load with another working mother*

Do you know another working mother who might be prepared to look after your children for the first half of the school holidays if you take care of hers for the second half?

☆ *Nurseries*

Some nurseries take older children in the school holidays, particularly if the family already has a link with the nursery because a younger brother or sister attends or the child himself used to do so.

## The easy option

If all this sounds too complicated for you and you can afford to pay for an easier option, the answer to your problems is almost certainly a full-time permanent employee who will be there to take responsibility for the children whenever they need it, be it before or after school, during the holidays or when they are ill.

You are unlikely to want to go on employing a full-time nanny once all your children are at school – it is not an economical use of your money and it is a dead-end job for the nanny, who will sooner or later get bored with spending her days drinking coffee and watching Neighbours. So why not consider employing a full-time or nearly full-time housekeeper instead? Just think of the luxury – all the shopping, cleaning, washing and ironing done, a casserole simmering in the oven when you get home from work, and child care thrown in! Apart from the cost (and that may not seem prohibitive when you take into account that you will no longer be paying for a nanny/nursery/childminder and will be able to dispense with the cleaner), the main difficulty is likely to be tracking down a suitable person to do the job. Go about it the same way as you would if you were looking for a nanny or mother's help (see Chapter 10).

# 12
# Help!

As working mothers, most of us are uncomfortably aware of how near we are to the danger line. Just as you are congratulating yourself on the fact that at long last you seem to have got life under control, your mother-in-law descends unexpectedly for an extended visit, the nanny hands in her notice, the school contacts you to ask what you are going to do about your eldest child who has started to disrupt lessons with his unruly behaviour, and you find yourself once more hurtling towards disaster. It does not take much to upset the balance – I can remember coming home from work to find a note from the cleaner stuffed through the letter box. All it said was, 'Sorry, I won't be able to come any more.' I just sat in the kitchen and cried.

So how do you cope when disaster strikes? The two most important pieces of general advice are probably 'Don't panic' and 'Don't despair'. Most problems *are* capable of resolution and what seems at first to be a complete catastrophe can turn out to be exactly the spur you need to reorganise your arrangements and make them work.

Certain crises recur with monotonous regularity and I offer what help I can with them in the following paragraphs.

## When you think something is going wrong with your childcare arrangements

All sorts of things can start the alarm bells ringing – your happy-go-lucky child starts to cling to you, screaming, when you leave him with his minder, your 5-year-old asks what that man was doing to nanny in her bedroom yesterday afternoon, the neighbour complains about the rowdy party the night you were away on business . . .

Naturally, if you discover that the childminder locks your child in a back room and goes out to bingo or that the nanny has been swiping the silver and beating the baby, you will fire her right away. But, generally, it is best not to over-react. First, make sure it is not just the old guilt complex rearing its ugly head and making a mountain out of a molehill (see Chapter 2). Then, if you are still concerned, investigate further:

- Listen carefully to what your child is saying.
- Sound out neighbours/friends/other nannies/other parents who use the same nursery or childminder/anyone else who may be able to tell you what is going on.
- Take an hour or two off work and drop in unexpectedly yourself.
- Face the nanny/nursery/childminder with your worries – there may be a perfectly reasonable explanation.

Should your worst fears be confirmed, do not hesitate to move your child from the unsatisfactory nursery or, in the case of a childminder or nanny, to get rid of the offending carer. Give notice if you feel you can do so without putting your child at risk; otherwise, terminate the arrangement with immediate effect. You are not liable for any pay in lieu or notice if there has been serious misconduct. However, where you dismiss a live-in nanny/mother's help/au pair out of hand, it might be charitable to check that she has her fare home.

## Coping with a change of childcare

Even the best of childcare arrangements come to an end eventually and, quite apart from the headache of finding a replacement nanny or nursery, you may have to cope with a reaction from your child when he realises that the days of the old regime are numbered.

Children tend to be very conservative. They grow fond of their carers and do not welcome change. They may blame themselves for the departure of a nanny or mother's help or when a childminder gives up, and they may become anxious that you too will let them down.

You can help by talking to your child about his feelings if he is old enough. Explain why the change is necessary. This can be tricky if you have just sacked the nanny. In this case, it is probably as well to stick to a fairly bland explanation, avoiding a recitation of the unfortunate girl's faults. 'Nannies do move on after a year or so' is a fairly neutral formula. Where the change is instigated by the carer for a good reason, tell the child what it is – for example, 'You don't need her now you're at school all day', 'Her husband is changing his job and she is going to be moving to Scotland', 'She is going to have a baby of her own', or whatever. Make sure that the carer explains too, giving the same reason.

Let your child know that you understand that he misses his carer and reassure him that this is a perfectly normal way to feel when one has grown fond of someone. Many carers want to keep in touch and this can make it easier for the child to accept the parting. Judge for yourself whether a short period without contact might be advisable first, so that the child can settle in with the replacement.

Though there are bound to be changes in the child's daily life when his carer changes, keep as much as you can the same. Stick to routine and make sure that you always do what you say you will and turn up on the dot of when you are expected so that he does not start to feel generally insecure.

## When your normal childcare arrangements temporarily cease to function

We have all experienced the panic that sets in when there is a hiccup in our normal arrangements – the baby is ill and cannot go to the minder, the heating breaks down at school and classes are cancelled at short notice, the nanny rings in sick. What are the options at a time like this?

- *Help from relatives*
  Brilliant if you happen to have a useful relative living nearby. When we lived a bit closer to my parents, I frequently rang for last-minute assistance or called to dump a feverish child at their house on my way to work.
- *Help from neighbours and friends*
  Provided you do not make a habit of getting in a mess, you may be pleasantly surprised at how neighbours and friends rally round when they know you are in difficulties. Shrewd working mothers set things up in advance. For instance, if you and a friend each have a nanny, you could (nannies permitting) come to an arrangement whereby your nanny looks after the friend's children if her nanny is away on holiday or off sick and vice versa.

  Grab opportunities to build up credit with non-working mothers. Have their child to play for the day occasionally, help them out of a hole by babysitting at short notice, invite their children to stay for a weekend so that they can have a short break away and keep your fingers crossed that they will feel disposed to repay the favours if you have to ask in an emergency. Try to have plenty of possibilities lined up and to spread the load as thinly as you can. I have heard one non-working mother complain bitterly about working friends who seem to think she has nothing better to do than to assist them in times of crisis.
- *Trading on the goodwill of your employer*
  Quite a few employers will turn a blind eye if a well-behaved child is brought to work for an hour or two in an extreme

emergency. I used to share a room with another working mother when I worked at the polytechnic. Normally her daughter was at school but occasionally, when school was cancelled or closed early, she would bring her crayons and get on quietly with some writing or drawing in our room. I certainly did not mind and I do not think anyone else did either, if they even knew.

Taking the children to work is not on for me – judges, however understanding, simply do not tolerate counsel appearing in front of them with two kids in tow. However, the children *have* accompanied my husband to work. His office staff seem to be only too ready to turn childminder, the children come home contentedly full of sweeties and proudly clutching printouts of their efforts on the word-processor, and my husband suffers no interruption to his normal working pattern.

If taking your child to work with you is out of the question, perhaps you could take your work home instead? I work from home frequently. If there are problems, my chambers can get in touch with me immediately by phone and urgent calls can be rerouted to my home number. It is not just women with sick children or childcare problems who work from home occasionally – my male accountant works at home on one day every week and no one seems to think anything of it.

What if your children cannot come to work and your work cannot come to your children? Could you take some holiday at short notice? Alternatively, would your employer be prepared to grant you some last-minute unpaid leave if you tell him exactly what the difficulty is and throw yourself on his mercy?

● *Local support groups*

Another source of emergency support might be a local working mothers' group. In my area, there is a working mothers' branch of the National Childbirth Trust and I know that groups of the Working Mothers' Association have also been established throughout the country. Addresses and phone numbers for both organisations can be found in the Address Book at the end of the Facts Section. No doubt you will get a better reception if you make the effort to participate *before* you have a problem rather than waiting until you are on your knees.

● *Paid help*

Not perhaps the best solution, bearing in mind that it is a bit much to expect your children to take to a complete stranger virtually overnight, but the only way out in some circumstances.

Many domestic/nanny employment agencies will do their

utmost to fix you up with someone temporary at short notice. Trace local agencies through the Yellow Pages (where they will probably be listed under 'Employment agencies and consultants'). If they cannot help you, ask them to suggest who might. Some agencies do place people on a countrywide basis so, if you have no success locally, spread the net a bit further by working through the agency adverts in *The Lady* magazine. A long-established agency that is very used to providing emergency cover nationwide at the drop of a hat is Universal Aunts (address and phone number in the Address Book).

# 13

# Breastfeeding for working mothers

G oing back to work should not prevent you from breastfeeding your baby. Many mothers manage to combine feeding and working very successfully.

## Is it worth the bother?

There is no doubt that continuing to breastfeed once you have returned to work does require a certain amount of dedication, at least until you have got into a routine. You may wonder whether it is worth the bother.

In fact, there is a lot to be said for making the effort:

☆ All new working mothers worry that their baby will transfer his affections from them to his nanny or minder or a favourite nursery nurse. It is tremendously reassuring to know that you have something special to offer your baby, something that only you can give.

☆ Most working mothers suffer from misguided feelings of guilt much of the time. Giving up breastfeeding in order to go back to work is the stuff of which complexes are made.

☆ There is a great temptation to give priority to household chores when you arrive home from work and it is all too easy to find yourself racing round laying fires, making supper and doing the washing up from breakfast rather than spending time with the baby. Breastfeeding mothers *have* to allow themselves the luxury of putting the baby first.

☆ However much you miss your baby while you are at work, you will almost certainly find that it takes a little time to adjust to being a mother again when you come home. Giving a breastfeed somehow makes up for the time you have been apart and can help you to feel close to your baby again and to start functioning on his wavelength.

* Once you have got used to the ease of breastfeeding, bottlefeeding can seem a real burden – all that paraphernalia of teats and sterilisers and bottle-warmers and the wait for the milk to come to just the right temperature while the baby howls the house down.

However, should you decide that you are going to give up breastfeeding, do not let anyone make you feel bad about it. Swopping to a bottle certainly has its attractions – not for you the ravages of the breast pump, the embarrassment of soggy blouses ruined by leaking milk, or the lunch hours in the office broom cupboard collecting the next day's feeds. Even if you have breastfed your baby for only a few weeks, you will have done a worthwhile job and got him off to a good start, and it is better that he should now move on to a bottle than that you should start to resent breastfeeding.

## Advance planning

If you do want to continue to breastfeed when you go back to work, it pays to start planning early, as a little bit of advance organisation during your maternity leave can make it a lot easier to combine breastfeeding and work. For example:

- The timing of your return has a bearing on your chances of successfully continuing to breastfeed. Delay until feeding is well established if you possibly can. For instance, the La Leche League (more details at the end of the chapter) recommend that you do not return sooner than three months after your baby is born.

- Some mothers like to be able to breastfeed their baby during the working day, at least in the very early stages after returning to work. If you aim to do this, you will have to tailor your childcare arrangements so that you can go to your baby or he can be brought to you for his daytime feed. This means looking for a minder or nursery close to your place of work or employing someone willing and able to take your baby on a milk run once or twice a day.

- If you decide that you do not want your baby to be given formula milk when you are at work (see the next section), you will have to provide an adequate supply of expressed breast milk. This will be considerably less of a burden if you build up a bank of frozen breast milk whilst you are on maternity leave. With time on your side, you should be able to avoid last-minute panics over introducing the baby to a bottle as well.

## Breast milk only?

Some mothers like their baby to continue to receive exclusively breast milk, others decide to introduce formula milk for feeds during the working day. Your choice may well depend upon the age of your baby when you go back to work and how conscientious you are prepared to be about expressing your milk. At 6 months, a baby can be given ordinary cow's milk from the dairy if you wish (boiled if your health visitor advises it) and many mothers, working or not, do seem to introduce cow's milk at this stage even if their baby has been wholly breastfed up to then. There is therefore no need to express breast milk for a baby of 6 months plus unless you are particularly concerned about allergies, etc. At the other end of the scale, you may want to stick to breast milk exclusively if your baby is very tiny and still on a milk-only diet.

Soya milk formula is an alternative to ordinary formula milk. It comes powdered in tins, just like other baby milks, and is marketed under brand names such as Wysoy. Before you seize on it as the perfect compromise however, you should be aware that nobody is offering any guarantees that it is any better for babies than modified cow's milk formula. It may turn out to cause its own problems, albeit different ones from those caused by normal formula milks, and has recently been cited as having high aluminium levels.

There is plenty of literature about the pros and cons of breast milk and formula milk which you can read if you are not sure what to do (you will find some suggestions at the end of the chapter). Alternatively, you could consult your doctor and/or health visitor and/or a breastfeeding counsellor. Do keep things in perspective though – this is not a life and death issue.

Should you decide to introduce formula milk, bear in mind that each brand is slightly different and that some babies do not seem to like the taste of certain brands. So if your baby spits out his feed, try another brand. However, once you have found a brand that suits him, it makes sense not to offend him by chopping and changing, so do not let yourself be seduced by clever advertising from rival manufacturers.

## When to introduce a bottle

Although I would always choose to breastfeed, there is one respect in which I do envy the mother who bottlefeeds right from the start. She may have niggly worries about whether the nanny or the childminder will warm the milk to the correct temperature or burp the baby properly, but she will at least be secure in the knowledge that her infant will not starve when she returns to work. Not so the breastfeeding mother, as I found with my first child.

Wanting to give breastfeeding the best possible chance, I made sure from the outset that Charlotte was never given so much as a sniff of a bottle. I did not anticipate any problems and left it until the week before my return to work to introduce the new regime. I laboriously expressed the required quantity of milk, filled a bottle and offered it to her. I could tell from her cries that she was ravenous, but could I get her to take that bottle? Each time I poked the teat into her screaming mouth, she spat it out. I rubbed a little breast milk on the teat and offered it again but she simply howled louder. In the end, worn down by her determined opposition, I gave in and offered her the breast. 'Never mind,' everybody said, 'she'll be fine when you are not around and she knows that it is the bottle or nothing.' But she remained resolute in her opposition and she would not take the milk from a cup or a spoon either. My first week or so back at work was a nightmare, punctuated by 30-mile round trips back to the childminder's to deliver the goods in person.

How do you avoid getting into this sort of a mess? You may think that the answer is to make sure that the baby gets used to both the bottle and the breast from the start. There is not doubt that you will not then have to worry about the bottle being rejected when you go back to work. The difficulty is that the arrangement may play havoc with your breastfeeding. Too much bottle in the early days means that your breasts may not be stimulated to make sufficient milk and you may have problems establishing your milk supply. What is more, drinking from a bottle requires a totally different technique from breastfeeding. The baby may therefore become confused and, because drinking from a bottle is easier, may forget how to breastfeed or lose interest in it. Not wanting to be caught out twice, I introduced bottles to my second child from the very beginning. Even one bottle was enough to knock him off his stride for the next few breastfeeds and, as I discovered to my cost, once a baby has lost the knack of breastfeeding, it can take a lot of patience and perseverence before he relearns the technique.

As far as I can tell, nobody has yet come up with a foolproof solution to the problem. If I had another baby, I think I would be inclined to breastfeed exclusively for the first few weeks until the baby had thoroughly mastered the technique but to introduce a bottle as early as I dared, certainly well before he became totally devoted to the breast at the 3- or 4-month stage. This is only my own personal view – I have not tried it and, even if I had, that would be no guarantee that it would work for your baby because they are all different. Nor does my view coincide with the views of the experts, who tend to advocate banning the bottle completely until a few days before returning to work, blithely assuring the mother that her hungry baby will soon learn new tricks when he knows she is not around. In the end, you will have to make your own plans using trial and error and a little imagination. Remember that there are no *rules*; it all depends on what works for your baby, and your own ideas will be at least as good as anyone else's and probably rather better in some respects since you know exactly what you are up against.

## How to introduce a bottle

Again there are no rules but the following suggestions might help:

- Do not try to give the baby his first few bottles yourself. Elect a fond and very patient adult with whom the baby is familiar and make yourself scarce. You may be lucky and have a baby who takes to the bottle straight away, but it is safer to look on the black side and assume that there will be a few problems to start off with. As it is almost impossible to resist the cries of a hungry and frustrated infant if you are within earshot, go out for at least half an hour when the feed is due so that you are not tempted to come to the rescue with a breastfeed. This tactic also makes it clear to the baby that the only choice is bottle or starve, leaving him less scope to manipulate the situation. Find yourself something riveting to do whilst you are out, or I guarantee that within the first 10 minutes or so you will be back outside the front door listening for howls.

- Express your own milk for the first few bottles, even if you intend the baby to have powdered milk in the long run. Breast milk and powdered milk taste different and you risk increasing the baby's confusion if you change both his method of feeding and the taste of his food at the same time. The time to introduce powdered milk is when he has learned to accept the bottle.
- If the baby steadfastly refuses to take a bottle, try changing to another type of teat. Charlotte finally gave up her opposition to the bottle when the childminder tried a Playtex teat which has a much more natural, nipple shape. Playtex teats are part of the special Playtex Nurser system. The milk is poured into a disposable, pre-sterilised plastic bottle liner (available in rolls of 50) which sits inside a rigid plastic holder. The teat fits over the top of the holder and a retaining ring keeps everything in place. Once I got used to it, I found the system worked very well and it saved me the job of washing and sterilising bottles. The only snag is that it is not always easy to get hold of the bits and pieces that you need. If you have difficulty, try the bigger branches of Boots.
- If the baby remains resolutely anti-bottle, you could try breastfeeding wearing a nipple shield for a few sessions so that he gets used to the taste and feel of rubber or silicon but without having to forgo all the joys of a breastfeed as well. Once he is prepared to put up with the nipple shield, try him again on a bottle.
- If your baby's refusal to take a bottle is absolute, milk can be given by teaspoon, cup or eye dropper. So they say! Do not expect the innovation to be popular – you (or your child carer) will need lots of patience.
- Do not assume that an initial failure to interest the baby in a bottle means he will never come round to it. I am sure that no baby could be more determinedly anti than Charlotte and even she did eventually give in. Keep calm and keep trying.

## Expressing milk – some general tips

Expressing is a useful technique to learn. You will need to do a lot of it if you want to leave breast milk for your baby to have whilst you are at work and, even if you decide he should have formula milk, you will need to express from time to time for your own comfort and possibly also to keep your milk supply going. Do not worry if you seem to have to express frequently at the beginning to relieve overfull or leaking breasts. Your body will get used to the new regime and you may soon find that if you are expressing for comfort only, you can get by with once a day at most and possibly not at all except after a weekend or a day off when your supply has been increased because you have feeding the baby more frequently than normal.

It will help you to express successfully if you know a little about how the breasts work. Breast milk is made in the milk glands, which are distributed through the breast tissue, and travels by means of ducts to the nipple. Some milk is stored in the ducts under the areola (the dark area of the breast around the nipple). The rest of the milk is stored in the milk glands and is only made available in spurts when the let-down reflex operates. You may feel the let-down reflex as a sort of tense, tingling sensation in your breasts at the beginning of a feed and you may know that it is working because the breast from which the baby is not feeding starts to leak or spray milk. The let-down reflex is very temperamental. It is controlled not only by physical stimuli but by emotional factors as well. So, for example, you may find that you start to leak milk whenever you hear a baby cry (even if it is not your own and you have no intention of feeding it) and you may also find that the let-down reflex is inhibited if you are uncomfortable or worried or not completely relaxed for any other reason.

There are two ways of expressing breast milk: by hand or with a pump. Whichever method you intend to use, there are some general tips that may assist:

- Wear a nursing bra and the sort of clothes that you would wear if you were actually going to breastfeed a baby. You do not want to have to get undressed before you can begin.
- Tuck a breast pad into your bra on the side from which you are not expressing to catch any leaks.
- Have a cloth handy to cover up your clothes. Unless you are very good at expressing, you will probably find that you get drips of milk all over the place. Something like a gauze nappy will do perfectly and is not too bulky to carry around. Alternatively, some women find that leaning over a washbasin prevents milk dripping on their clothes. I have never tried this, but would have thought that it might be fairly uncomfortable, especially after a quarter of an hour or so. Not terribly private either if you happen to be using the office loos.
- Try to allow plenty of time to express. A feed normally takes around 20 minutes, so it is unlikely to take much less time to express the same quantity of milk, although you will get away with a shorter time if all you want to do is to relieve uncomfortable and overfull breasts.
- Wash your hands before you start to express, particularly if you are going to collect the milk to save for your baby.
- Make yourself as comfortable as possible. This should not be too difficult when you are expressing at home but conditions at work can be far from ideal. Although you may feel quite

happy to breastfeed a baby in public, pumping away at your breasts in front of every Tom, Dick and Harry is a totally different proposition and certainly not one that has ever appealed to me. The problem is that, if you want privacy at work, you will probably have to settle for the ladies' loo and all ladies' lavatories were surely designed by men. There is normally not so much as a hook for a handbag, let alone a shelf big enough to hold a sterile breast pump, a mopping-up cloth, a sterile container for the milk. . . Even if you manage to install yourself in a cubicle (the lavatory itself usually being the only seat in sight) and to balance all your tackle precariously on the top of the cistern, you can be sure that the strain of the whole occasion will have played havoc with your let-down reflex and it will take at least 5 minutes of relaxation exercises before you manage to extract anything at all. As one who has breast-pumped in a British Rail lavatory on a moving high-speed train, I speak with the voice of experience.

- Relax and think about feeding the baby even though he is not there – it will help the let-down reflex. Gently massaging your breasts can also help to get the milk flowing.
- Do not panic if you do not seem to be having much success at first. It can take several minutes before the milk lets down and until then you will only be able to express a few drops. If you get upset you will inhibit the let-down reflex, so just keep calm and wait. Even once the milk has started to flow, it will probably not come out in a constant stream but in spurts. Carry on expressing during the intervals between spurts, but if the supply seems to have dried up temporarily try changing to the other breast for a while.
- Try not to be embarrassed and secretive about the whole affair. If you sneak off to the lavatory to do a bit of surreptitious expressing without telling anyone first, you may find yourself harassed alternately by irritated prospective users of the facilities and anxious enquirers after your health. If you use a breast pump, the bewilderment of the growing queue outside will no doubt be increased considerably by the loud slurping and slopping noises which it will almost certainly emit. I can remember emerging from one of the ladies' lavatories at the Birmingham Crown Court after an emergency pumping session to find two members of the court staff staring at me in amazement. It was quite clear from the looks on their faces as I washed out my breast pump in the basin that they had not the least idea what I had been doing and feared the worst. In retrospect I think it might have been better had I explained – a word in the right ear ought to save awkwardness.

## Expressing by hand

I have never been very successful at expressing any quantity of milk by hand, but hand expressing can be extremely efficient if you have the knack and is recommended by some (for example the La Leche League) in preference to using a pump. There are a number of reasons why you might find it better; for instance:

☆ It is gentler than a pump and less likely to lead to sore nipples.
☆ It is more selective in that you can feel which part of the breast is full and express the milk from that part rather than pumping away at the whole breast all the time.
☆ It does not involve as much clutter.
☆ It is quieter than using a breast pump, which will save embarrassment if you do not have much privacy for expressing at work.

Hand expressing techniques seem to vary slightly. The NCT suggest that you proceed as follows. Start by gently stroking the breast towards the nipple. If you have access to warm water, you will find that warm compresses (a flannel wrung out in hot water) will help the milk to flow. Support your left breast with your right hand, with your thumb at the top of the areola, and the rest of your hand underneath. Press your thumb and hand into the breast towards your ribcage, then squeeze them rhythmically together. Repeat this movement around the circle of the breast, being careful not to slide your fingers down towards the nipple. Gently massage the breast from time to time to help move milk down to the nipple.

## Expressing with a breast pump

There are several types of breast pump. The ones that look rather like an old-fashioned perfume spray with a rubber bulb to squeeze are not recommended. They do not work very well – in fact I have never got one to work at all – and they are not easy to keep sterile.

The other commonly available type of hand pump is the syringe variety. I have found this sort of pump basic and fairly brutal but effective. You can feed milk back to the baby direct from the pump if you want as it doubles as a feeding bottle, and there are no cleaning problems as the whole pump can be submerged in the steriliser after each use.

Big heavy-duty electric breast pumps are also available. The Egnell Breast Pump, for instance, can be hired through the NCT and some chemists. It is efficient, easy to use and not unpleasant once you get over feeling like a cow in a milking parlour, but it is far too expensive to contemplate buying and not cheap to hire (although the NCT do special rates for long-term hire) so it may not be feasible to use as your regular means of expressing milk. Some local groups of the

Association of Breastfeeding Mothers (see the end of the chapter) also hire out hospital-quality electric pumps.

A fairly recent innovation is the battery-operated breast pump. Hand pumping can be quite tiring and a battery pump ought to be a boon. Unfortunately I have had a poor report from a friend who has tried one, but I do not consider this to be a sufficient sample on which to judge.

If you have difficulty getting hold of the sort of pump you want, contact the NCT or the Association of Breastfeeding Mothers, both of whom supply hand pumps by post.

## Collecting milk for your baby

Breast milk is best collected (and stored) in plastic containers, which should be sterilised before use. Glass containers are not recommended because certain of the ingredients in the milk stick to the glass and are lost and also, of course, because they are easily broken. If you use a breast pump, all the components of that will also need to be sterilised.

Try to avoid having to collect milk whilst you are at work if you possibly can. It required a high degree of organisation and it is a bore.

Some mothers start stashing away milk in the freezer when the baby is very tiny and build up a considerable hoard by the time they go back to work. Used in conjunction with whatever they manage to express morning and/or evening, this provides an ample supply for even the greediest baby.

Even if you have no reserve supplies, you may still be able to express sufficient milk outside working hours. Much will depend upon the stage your baby is at and how copious your milk is. Experiment with the timings of your expressing sessions. You may be able to get in a particularly productive session immediately after an early morning feed, for instance, as you will have plenty of milk after a night's rest (especially if the baby has slept right through) and it should be flowing freely because it has already let down for the baby. Another good time is after the weekend when the extra stimulation of feeding the baby will have stepped up the quantity of milk you produce. Alternatively, if the baby has started to sleep through from the early evening, fit in a session just before you go to bed.

If you are saddled with collecting milk at work, you will have to work out a system for keeping the equipment (breast pump, collecting container, etc.) scrupulously clean. Perhaps you might keep a steriliser at work for your pump and your collecting bottles? You will also need somewhere to keep the milk cool until you are able to get it into the fridge or freezer at home. If you have a fridge at work, this should make life considerably easier, although you may still have to make special arrangements for your journey home if you have a long way to go or the weather is exceptionally hot. You can use a Thermos flask if you have no fridge at work and during your journey home, but it is rather a palaver. Choose a large flask with a wide neck and get it thoroughly cold before you go to work by putting ice in it. When you have collected your milk, pour the-ice out of the Thermos and put in the milk (in its container). Providing your milk container is watertight, there is no reason why you should not then re-pack any space around it with ice if the ice has not melted. It is not practical to put the milk directly into the Thermos because of the difficulties of sterilising the Thermos. As an alternative to a Thermos, you might consider using an insulated bag or box of the sort people use for picnics and camping. These are quite effective at keeping things cool if used in conjunction with one or two ice packs (plastic containers of liquid which you can freeze and then leave in the bag with the container of milk).

## Storing breast milk

Breast milk can be stored in the fridge or freezer. However, if you are striving for perfection, use the fridge as freezing apparently harms the living cells in the milk.

### Storing milk in the fridge

Milk that is stored in the fridge should be kept covered. The NCT say that it should be used within 24 hours, the La Leche League advise that it should be used within 48 hours. Keep each batch of expressed milk separate and label it with the date and time of expressing so that there is no confusion as to what it is and how long it will last. Buy a roll of small self-adhesive labels for the job. You can, of course, combine batches for a feed.

The milk will separate out in the fridge and can look rather unpalatable – all it needs is a shake. Warm it by holding the container under warm running water for a few minutes until it reaches the right temperature or by standing the container in a jug of very hot water. Alternatively, you can stand the container in a pan of water on the stove, but do not warm the milk by putting it directly into a pan on the stove as it is too easy to overheat it and destroy important ingredients. Do not keep warmed milk hanging around for longer than about half an hour. If you have problems over giving the feed or the baby dawdles excessively, you will have to throw it away and start again.

## Freezing milk

Freeze milk in small quantities, say 2–4 ounces. It defrosts more quickly this way and there is less waste as it is possible to defrost varying amounts according to the baby's appetite at each feed. Cover the container securely, leaving room for the milk to expand as it freezes, and label it with what it is and the date. Some mothers freeze their milk in plastic bottle liners (such as the ones you can buy to go with the Playtex Nurser system) which can be sealed particularly efficiently using a heat sealing machine. The La Leche League does, however, draw attention to the fact that there is some concern about using plastic nurser bags for long-term storage, although they do not specify why. The League say that frozen milk will keep for up to two weeks in the freezer compartment of a fridge or for up to two years in a separate freezer where the temperature is 0 degrees Fahrenheit. The NCT say that milk should be kept frozen for up to three months only. You will have to decide whose advice to follow for yourself, although I cannot see many mothers wanting to store frozen breast milk for years in any event.

Frozen milk can be thawed and warmed quickly for immediate use by holding the container under running water, cool at first but gradually getting warmer as the milk thaws. Do not keep it once you have thawed it this way – throw it away if you do not use it immediately. If you do not need the feed straight away, you can thaw it by leaving it in the fridge for a few hours. If you defrost in the fridge, remember that you should not leave the milk sitting there for too long before you give it to the baby – the total time that it spends out of the freezer should not exceed the recommended storage time for milk that has never been frozen. As it is easy to forget how long the milk sat in the fridge before you originally froze it, the safest course is probably to defrost one feed at a time so that you know the milk will be used up in a few hours at most.

The NCT say that you should not defrost milk in a microwave oven because, as with boiling, some of the important ingredients of the milk are destroyed; also it is too easy to be misled into giving the baby a burning hot feed, as the container tends to remain cooler than its contents in microwave cookery – I am not sure that all mothers obey this advice.

Never re-freeze thawed milk.

## Arrangements with your nanny/nursery/childminder

Take the time to talk to the person who will be looking after your child about feeding so that she knows what your plans are. If you have decided that you do not want your baby to have formula milk, make this absolutely plain and make sure that she knows how to deal with the supplies of breast milk that you have left and understands that it is important not to waste any.

Discuss what you want her to do towards the end of the day – should she try to distract the baby or to tide him over with an ounce or two of milk or some juice instead of a full feed so that you can feed when you get in? There is nothing worse than arriving home full to bursting and desperate to feed the baby only to find him already replete. Let her talk about any problems she is having over feeding too; there may be ways in which you can help.

## Not enough milk

You may find that you are a bit short of milk after you go back to work. There are various reasons why this might be so, for instance:

☆ You may be getting over-tired – most of us do. Although it may be well-nigh impossible to get more rest, do try. Attempt to get a few early nights, stop racing round doing chores at home, and ease up at work for a little while.

☆ You may not be expressing sufficient milk when you are apart from the baby and your breasts may be getting the message that you want to cut down the supply. Try to express more frequently and, if you have been stopping when there is still plenty of milk, go on for a bit longer at each session.

When you are at home, put the baby to the breast as often as he wants and for as long as it suits him. His sucking will stimulate your milk supply. Make sure that you are eating sensibly and drinking whenever you are thirsty, but not too much because, surprisingly, there is evidence that this can inhibit milk production. Smoking can also reduce your milk supply, so be careful that you have not increased your tobacco consumption now that you are back at work. Do not have too much caffeine either (coffee, tea, etc.) as this can produce a reaction in the baby.

## Leaking milk

Most mothers who breastfeed find that their breasts leak milk when the baby is tiny, but that the problem gets less as breast feeding is established. It is therefore annoying when the leaking starts all over again when you go back to work. Just thinking about the baby can be enough to cause the milk to let down and it is not always easy to staunch the flow, particularly if your breasts are rather full. Save embarrassment and ruined clothing by wearing disposable breast pads inside the cups of your bra and keep some spares with you so that you can change them frequently. Escaping milk will show less on dark or patterned clothes. Some mothers are able to put a stop to the leaking by applying pressure directly on the nipple for a minute or two. You do not need to make a big song and dance about this as it can be done by folding your arms across the breasts. I have to say, though, that I am dubious about this tip, having spent an entire afternoon at a wedding with my arms firmly folded without making the slightest impression upon the great pools of milk spreading inexorably and very obviously across the front of my best dress. Perhaps you will have more success.

## Sore breasts

Soreness of the nipples can be caused by using a breast pump. If you have this problem, you might have to try another sort of pump or learn to express my hand.

You might develop a red, tender lump or area on one of your breasts from a blocked milk duct. This can happen if the breasts become overfull, as they may, for instance, if you are not very successful at expressing or do not do it often enough or after a weekend when you change over from frequent breastfeeding to expressing. You can usually clear the blocked duct yourself, but do take action as soon as possible as an untreated blockage can lead to infection. Take the following steps:

- Feed or express (or both) often. At each session, carry on until the affected breast is as empty as you can get it. If the baby gives up when there is still milk there, express whatever is left.
- Give the baby the affected breast first each time he feeds because he is likely to suck hardest at the beginning of his feed. Put him back on that breast again later in the feed as well.
- Change the position in which the baby feeds so that he works on a different part of the breast. For example, if you normally cradle him in your arms in the conventional nursing position, try holding him like a rugby ball with his legs sticking out under your arm at the side from which he is feeding and his body supported by a pillow or cushion.
- Gently massage the red area/lump towards the nipple whilst the baby is feeding or whilst you are expressing to help free the blockage. This can be particularly effective if you bathe the breast in warm water before you start – I used to do this by having a long soak in a deep, warm bath.

If the breast does not go back to normal fairly quickly, say within 24 hours or so, make an appointment to see your doctor as he may want to give you antibiotics to prevent infection. It is especially important to consult your doctor without delay if you start to have flu-like symptoms or a temperature, as this can indicate that an infection has already set in.

If you have repeated problems with blocked ducts, have a look at the fit of your bras. I seemed to be getting more than my fair share of trouble when I was feeding Andrew and it was quite a long time before I realised that the culprit was zip-cupped nursing bra with elastic sides which was applying pressure in all the wrong places.

## Stopping breastfeeding

Pills used to be given to stop a mother's milk supply when she decided that she wanted to give up breastfeeding. These days, the milk supply is usually left to dry up naturally as the demand for milk decreases. It is advisable not to try to give up overnight; this can be asking for trouble such as engorgement of the breasts, blocked ducts and breast infections. Phase out breast feeding gradually by first reducing the length of time the baby spends on the breast and then cutting out feeds altogether, one by one. Be careful to make sure that the baby gets sufficient milk from his cup or bottle to make up for the breast milk he is no longer having. The process may take several weeks, but if your breasts adjust rapidly and you do not get any discomfort it might be accomplished sooner, particularly if your baby is already partially weaned by the time you start.

## Help and advice

Do not hesitate to ask for help if you get into difficulties. I found my general practitioner very sympathetic. However, I know that not all GPs feel confident about advising on breastfeeding, although they will, of course, deal with problems of a physical nature (such as a breast infection). For practical help and advice, it may be better to approach your health visitor or, better still:

- *An NCT breastfeeding counsellor*
  The NCT has a network of trained breastfeeding counsellors who offer non-medical support and advice. Some queries can be dealt with over the phone or you can visit the counsellor with the baby if you need practical help. If you are in special need, the counsellor might be able to come out to you. Counsellors are open all hours. I have pestered mine late at

night as well as during the day and I have always had a helpful response.

You should be able to get the telephone number of your local NCT branch from the telephone directory and they will put you in touch with your nearest breastfeeding counsellor if her telephone number is not listed separately in the directory. Otherwise contact the NCT in London (address and phone number in the Address Book at the end of the Facts Section).

● *The La Leche League*

The La Leche League is an international organisation set up in the 1950s to help with breastfeeding (address and phone number in the Address Book).

The League has local leaders who hold meetings for breastfeeding mothers and will offer advice and support on an individual basis. They stress that they are available to talk to mothers at any time.

● *The Association of Breastfeeding Mothers*

The Association (address and phone number in the Address Book) provides information, encouragement and practical mother-to-mother support for breastfeeders. They have counsellors throughout the country who are ready to share their experiences of breastfeeding with other mothers.

There are many useful publications about breastfeeding, some of which are written specifically with working mothers in mind. The NCT, the La Leche League and the Association of Breastfeeding Mothers all have publications lists. You might find particularly useful:

☆ *Breastfeeding – Returning to work* (NCT booklet)
☆ *Practical Hints for Working and Breastfeeding* (La Leche League leaflet).

*Breast is Best* by Doctors Penny and Andrew Stanway (Pan) is a much-used general book on breastfeeding. However, although the book is good on most aspects of breastfeeding, I should warn you that the chapter on working mothers is depressing reading. Mothers who take to mothering naturally don't want to leave their babies; they'll go through all sorts of hardships to stay at home, declare the authors, implying that those of us who do choose to go out to work do not really love our babies and are not prepared to suffer for them. If you are in the least bit sensitive about your decision to go back to work, I counsel you to miss out the first two and a half pages of the chapter and concentrate on the practical information about expressing milk etc.

Century Books publish *The Breastfeeding Guide for the Working Mother* by Anne Price and Nancy Bamford.

# 14

# First steps on the road to domestic sanity

I do not pretend to have discovered the secret of trouble-free day-to-day living – far from it. There are times when things do run quite smoothly, but we are just as likely to lurch from crisis to crisis with no food for supper, no shirt for work and inches of dust everywhere.

What I *have* discovered since I began life as a working mother is that there is no end to the good ideas that might help to oil the wheels. All that is lacking is the energy to put them into practice.

In case you have more stamina than I do, I offer some suggestions in this chapter and the chapters that follow. I make no apology for the fact that many of the ideas are simply common sense – a lot of the best ideas are. Take them or leave them, but do at least seize the opportunity to think about the way in which you get through each day and to consider whether it could be improved.

## Labour-saving equipment

The first step on the road to domestic sanity and order is to kit yourself out with as much labour-saving equipment as you can afford. If it helps you to justify the expenditure, see it as a necessary expense of working, on a par with the day-nursery bill and the cost of travelling to work.

## Top-priority items

My own nominations for the top-priority category are as follows:

- *Car (or use of one)*
  I need my car to do my job, but even if I did not it would come first on my list of priority equipment. There are so

many things that are easier with a car – shopping (from mammoth bulk-buying expeditions to a last-minute panic purchase of a couple of chops for supper), travelling to work (except perhaps in Central London), dropping off at nursery or the childminder's, spur of the moment outings to the park with the children after work, etc.

● *Automatic washing machine*

Twin tubs, launderettes and handwashing are all labour intensive and therefore out of the question for working mothers, so an automatic washer is a must.

Make sure the machine you choose has a fast spin speed, 1000 rpm or faster. This cuts down drying time enormously and is much more important than lots of elaborate wash programmes.

● *Tumble drier*

A tumble drier was one of my earliest purchases after we got married and my mother viewed it as a sure sign of extravagance, sloth and general moral degeneration. I do still hang the clothes out on the line if the weather is fine, but I cannot postpone my washing day until the rain holds off and I cannot cope with festoons of damp towels and socks all over the house, so, whenever conditions do not look promising, I bung the lot in the drier.

Be careful to stop tumbling *just before* the wash is bone dry (particularly if you are dealing with 100% cotton items) otherwise ironing will be a nightmare. Try to lift out the dry clothes as soon as the programme has finished. Towels, terry nappies and stretch towelling should emerge beautifully fluffy and soft, ready to be folded and put away immediately. People say you can also get away without ironing polyester/cotton items such as shirts and blouses, but mine always look too creased to cheat.

● *Freezer*

Really organised working mothers use their freezers to hoard a month or two's supply of home-made meals. Several years ago, I batch-cooked eight chickens and, when I have recovered my stamina, I will repeat the performance. Meanwhile I would not be without my freezer for its supply of bread (sliced for toast and sandwiches, rolls for a quick lunch or to accompany a salad at suppertime, croissants for a special breakfast when friends come to stay), frozen vegetables and shop-bought frozen dishes for emergencies. I even admit to a packet or two of fishfingers and some beefburgers. I do also try to make double quantities sometimes when I cook casseroles and stews, so that half can be eaten and half stashed away for another time.

● *Microwave*

I had a microwave oven thrust upon me, already built in to the kitchen of our new house. To begin with, I treated it rather like a nuclear reactor, rationing myself to a few quick bursts each day and taking great pains to stand well clear of the door for fear of escaping waves. Now, three years later, I cannot envisage life without it. I do not use it for roasting meat or cooking casseroles and I have not yet managed to defrost successfully – everything ends up partly cooked or, in the case of cold puddings and cakes, melted. But I do use it all the time for heating things up (anything from baked beans to a complete meal on a plate), to cook baked potatoes in 4 minutes flat, and for niggly little jobs such as melting cooking chocolate and making white sauce.

One word of warning though: before you switch on, think whether the food needs covering – a microwave may cut cooking time drastically and save washing up but you will not be any better off if you have to spend 10 minutes scraping exploded peas from the roof of the oven.

● *Dishwasher*

Those who do not have one say they are a waste of money; those who do, could not manage without. Emptying the dishwasher *is* a chore, but think of the advantages – no untidy piles of crockery and cutlery waiting for the next washing-up session, no heaps of streaky glasses and plates drip-drying on the draining board, everything squeaky clean and sparkling.

To get the most out of a dishwasher you need plenty of crockery and cutlery. In theory, most dishwashers hold up to twelve place settings, so you must have sufficient to keep going whilst the washing-up from several meals waits for the next wash cycle. Be careful that what you buy is dishwasher proof – some cutlery comes apart at the handle if put in a dishwater, and gold or silver decoration on crockery may gradually be washed away. You may even think it worth replacing existing items that cannot go in the dishwasher, as you are likely to become so spoilt that you will resent washing up even a few odds and ends.

Decide at the outset, whether you are going to put big things such as pans and mixing bowls in the dishwasher. I do, but my husband (who pays the electricity bills) considers this an extravagant use of the machine and removes them again if he finds them.

Do not monopolise the machine; invite the family to use it too. With persistence, even quite young children and staunchly anti-housework men can be trained to load up their eating utensils after use.

- *Vacuum cleaner that works*

  Does yours gobble up fluff at one end of the hall and then spit it out at the other? Does it reject bits of paper and cotton threads? Does it have brushes that drop off or a fan belt that is always snapping?

  Get it mended or buy a new one.

  You might also consider buying an extension flex for use with your vacuum cleaner – it should save a lot of plugging and unplugging as you move round the house.

- *Domestic help*

  If you can possibly afford it and if you can get hold of the right person, treat yourself to paid domestic help.

  Enquire locally what the going rate is, decide how much money you can spare, and work out how many hours of help this would buy you.

  Then decide upon your priorities. Do you want your ironing done for you each week? If you find it restful to stand in front of the television ironing shirts, perhaps not. But if your first job each morning is to iron enough clothes to get the family through the day, farming the ironing out may relieve you of a lot of pressure. Is it the cleaning that is a problem? Even if you cannot afford to pay someone to do it all, it may be worth having help for a few hours a week to take care of the jobs you hate most.

  Once you have decided what help you want and can afford, your next task is to track down the appropriate helper. As anyone who has ever tried to get domestic help knows, this is easier said than done.

  One tried and trusted method is to advertise in the local paper or in local shop windows. There is no point in paying to insert a long, flowery description of what you want. A bald statement of what is required (for example, 'Domestic help required 4 hours a week in the Clifton area – ring Bristol 000000') seems to attract just as many applicants. Weed out obvious no-hopers over the telephone, but be prepared to set aside some time to interview those who sound promising. Take up references for the ones on your shortlist. Ask about trustworthiness and ability to do the job and read between the lines of what you are told. 'She's fine if you make her a list of what to do every day' means 'she has no initiative and will sit about drinking coffee all day unless you supervise her'. 'She does the ironing beautifully' means 'she is hopeless at cleaning'.

  Consider offering the person you choose a week's trial and do not throw away the details of the others on your shortlist until you are sure she is satisfactory. Do not expect her to be able to do everything your way immediately. It is your responsibility to tell her, at first, what you want done and how you want it done. If you want her to tidy up for you or to put your clothes away when she has ironed them, you will have to explain this to her specifically or she may be reluctant to move your belongings around or to invade your privacy. If you have been lucky in your choice, time spent in training will be time well spent. On the other hand, if you decide you have made a mistake, be ruthless. There is absolutely no point spending your hard-earned money on a domestic help and your free time clearing up after her. Fire her and try again.

Another possibility is to approach a domestic cleaning service. They can be traced through the Yellow Pages and may be prepared to undertake anything from regular housework to spring cleaning and babysitting. You pay them an hourly rate (probably quite a lot more than the normal going rate for domestic help) and they send one of their employees to do whatever it is you require. Enquire whether you will be able to have the same person on a regular basis – you need to be able to rely on someone who you know is trustworthy and who knows where the vacuum cleaner is kept and what the household routine is.

## Other useful equipment

Into this category come all sorts of items that can make life run more smoothly. This is a selection from my own list. Your choice of gadgetry will depend very much upon your personal taste and lifestyle – the food processor that I consider an indispensable kitchen tool might be an insuperable kitchen storage problem for you.

- *Food processor*
  Not very good for making cakes or for any other cooking process that depends upon air being incorporated into a mixture, but marvellous for making pastry, bread and scones, grating large quantities of cheese, chopping and slicing vegetables, making breadcrumbs, liquidising soups and patés and so on. Choose one that is not too elaborate and is relatively easy to wash up.
- *Mixer or hand whisk*
  For the cakes, puddings, egg whites, etc. with which the food processor cannot cope. I do not do much baking so I am content with a small hand whisk. If you make a lot of cakes, you may like to consider investing in a large heavy-duty mixer such as the Kenwood Chef, providing you have somewhere to keep it when it is not in use.
- *Electric toaster*
  So that you do not burn the toast in the breakfast rush.
- *Electric kettle that switches off automatically*
  So that you do not boil it dry and burn out the element.
- *Duvets*
  Every bed in our house except our own has a duvet. There is no doubt that they speed up bed-making considerably and need not make a room look messy if covered with a heavy quilt or counterpane. We would have a duvet on our bed too if only we could learn the secret of peaceful coexistence under the covers – every time we try one out, we either spend the night fighting each other for sole possession of it or end up inextricably tangled up in it together in the middle of the bed.
- *Good steam iron*
  A good steam iron can cut ironing time dramatically. Mine will even make a reasonable job of bone-dry cotton. Keep the sole plate clean or the iron will stick and may make nasty brown marks on your clothes; you can buy iron sole plate cleaner for the purpose. It is also important to remember to empty out the steam tank at the end of each session or you may find rusty water dripping on to the ironing next time you get out the iron.

131

● *Pantry*

I have a large pantry with lots of shelves and cupboards and a cold keeping slab, and I would not be without it. I can buy items with a long shelf-life (such as tinned foods, kitchen paper, jams and marmalade, even cereals) in quantity, which simplifies the weekly shopping considerably and cuts down on the crises that occur when something unexpectedly runs out.

There is no reason why your storage space has to be in the kitchen. At one house, we built shelves for tins in the cupboard under the stairs and my mother stores boxes of cereals in the airing cupboard (where they never go soggy) and keeps cases of lavatory rolls in the attic.

● *Large fridge*

If you have room, a large fridge is a big help. You will need a lot of space for perishable goods if you are going to reduce the number of times you visit the shops each week (see Chapter 15) and, if you are organised, you will need somewhere to store meals that you have made in advance. If you have a separate freezer, you may be able to increase the usable space inside your fridge by buying a larder fridge which does not have a freezer compartment.

● *Noticeboard*

We have a large cork noticeboard in the playroom; it is invaluable for messages and all those other bits of paper that simply must not be lost, not to mention the efforts of infant artists.

● *Television and videorecorder*

I pondered long and hard before I added this one to my list, anticipating shouts of horrified disapproval. I have to confess, however, that I consider the current anti-telly lobby rather misguided. Some of the children's programmes screened nowadays are of an extremely high standard and a child can pick up a great deal of general knowledge in half an hour glued to the screen. If he also wants to watch cartoons or a third-rate quiz show every now and then, does it really matter? As children, my brother, sister and I regularly watched those frightful half-hour shows that followed the children's programmes – The Beverly Hillbillies, The Lucille Ball Show, and the like. They were mindless rubbish, but we enjoyed them, they kept us from under our mother's feet while she prepared supper and I doubt they did any lasting damage to our intellects.

I am sure it is important, though, to ensure that *you* remain in charge of television watching rather than your child and that the television is not left on constantly in the background, but switched on for a particular programme and then switched off so that he can get on with something else without distraction. Used in this way (especially in conjunction with a videorecorder, which you can use to manipulate the schedules to suit yourself), television can be a boon. Replace the bedtime story with half an hour of *Thomas the Tank Engine* on the video when you really cannot face reading about Milly Molly Mandy yet again. Issue an episode of *Black Beauty* as a treat when you want some time to get ahead with the cooking or just to read the Sunday papers. Watch the current children's serial companionably with your child when you are too exhausted to play games with him. He will enjoy a peaceful half-hour watching television far more than a torrid half-hour of snappy mummy supervising plasticine modelling because she feels she should.

## Routine

To survive as a working mother, you must be organised and this means having a routine.

Work out what simply has to be done to keep things ticking over. Try not to be unduly particular. If you set yourself the standards of a five-star hotel, you will be back to square one within the fortnight. The spirit may be very willing to black-lead the grate and dust the picture rails but, after a hard day at work, the flesh will almost certainly be too weak to cooperate. Stick to the basics without which life cannot go on: the food, the washing and ironing, a bit of tidying and a modicum of cleaning.

Allocate each job to a particular day and time. How you do this is very much a matter of personal preference. One working mother I know gets up early every morning so that she is always on top of the chores. In our house, we scrape by all week and have a monumental blitz at the weekend.

When you have drawn up your programme, inform the rest of the family how it is going to affect them. We went through a spell when my husband never had any pyjamas to wear – he put one pair in the wash each Friday through habit and I took the other pair away for washing each Saturday in accordance with my schedule.

Enlist whatever help you can, but guard against duplication of effort. If you cannot farm jobs out on a permanent basis, at least make sure that each member of the family remembers to mention to the other helpers when he has done a particular chore or if he intends to do a particular chore during the day. It will not improve tempers if you and your partner bump into each other in the super-market carpark, each with a trolley full of the weekly shopping.

Once you have your routine up and running, stick to it as far as you can but do not let it take you over. In the years to come it will not

be the pristine house, the up-to-date ironing or your delicately fla-
voured asparagus mousse that you and the children will remember,
but the wonderful picnic you all had at the seaside or that marvellous
trip to the railway museum when you stopped at MacDonalds for a
burger and chips on the way back. So, if the sun shines and you feel
like joining the kids in the garden or taking off for a day in the
country or a weekend break, grab the chance, whatever domestic
delights you originally had scheduled.

## Lists

Lists are an invaluable tool for the working mother. Not only does
a good list serve as a reliable reminder of anything and everything,
transferring jobs to be done from brain to paper also helps to eliminate the interminable nagging and memory jogging to which we
subject ourselves. How many times a day do you say to yourself, 'I
must remember to write to so and so/ do the nanny's tax return/
wash Johnny's football kit in time for school tomorrow'? Put it on the
list the first time you think of it and you can then put it out of your
mind until you have time to attend to it.

There are pitfalls that the would-be list maker must avoid. The
principal danger is the lost list. Although I come from a long line of
list makers and have inherited a talent for making good lists, nature
has not bestowed upon me a corresponding ability to keep track of
my lists once they are made. Somehow they always find their way
under the car seat or into the pocket of a little-used mackintosh only
to be re-discovered weeks later, dog-eared and out of date.

Here are some ideas that might help you to get the best out of
your lists:

&#9734; *Filofax or similar*
I have a friend who is a high priestess of lists and list management, and she swears by her Filofax. She subjected her
family to a diet of lentils and macaroni cheese for weeks
in order to buy herself the genuine article in leather. In it
she keeps her weekly menus, a list of standard household
items to jog her memory when making her shopping list,
her shopping list itself, addresses, birthdays, a list of jobs
to be done, notes of books/places to visit/shops etc. that
people recommend to her, and a lot more besides. It also
has a diary section in which to record the many comings
and goings of herself and her husband, their two children
and helpers.

I do not suggest that a new convert to list making should
dash out and buy a Filofax immediately. The purchase itself
will not solve your problems overnight and the expense is

only justifiable if you are sure you will actually use it. Ordinary handbag-sized ring binders and wads of file paper are available from good stationers at a much more reasonable price and can be used to set up your own system quite cheaply. If you get hooked, then is the time to reward yourself with the more swanky alternative if you feel you can square the cost with your conscience.

☆ *Post-it notes*

These are smallish pads of paper with a sticky strip on the back that will adhere to virtually any smooth surface and are available from most stationers in several sizes and a number of different colours. Use them for ordinary lists, which can be stuck firmly inside your diary or to the dashboard of the car, for urgent reminders in conspicuous positions such as the middle of the bathroom mirror, and for telephone messages – the kitchen cupboard by our phone is always covered with them.

☆ *Blackboard/noticeboard*

Keep a blackboard or wipeable noticeboard in a prominent place for lists and messages. Always keep a piece of chalk/felt tip/biro with your message pad or board, attached if possible or it is bound to have disappeared just when you need it.

☆ *Paper and pencil by the bed*

If you tend to be kept awake by the next day's jobs going round and round in your head, keep a piece of paper and a pencil by your bed and write things down as they occur to you – it will help you to relax.

☆ *Preserve lists that deal with situations that are likely to recur.* I make a new list of things to take on holiday every time we go away; the contents are virtually identical to the list I made the time before and the time before that, and I would conserve a lot of time and energy if I simply saved the list for future reference.

## How not to forget the ballet class or turn up for swimming on the wrong day

As children get older, one of the problems of the working mother is to keep track of their social life and to fit in her duties as chauffeur.

Your diary can be a great help if you use it properly. I do not always remember to enter engagements in mine and have been known to turn up for a dinner party the evening after it actually took place. My nanny is a lot more organised. She has an enormous desk diary which is always left open in the kitchen. Each page is in the form of a timetable, and her engagements, my work plans and the children's activities are recorded so that she knows precisely what is due to happen on a particular day and when.

My Filofax friend had some success with a forward planner chart of the type that is often used for office holidays. Each member of the family and the nanny became a blob of a particular colour and each one's engagements were recorded on the chart so that everyone knew where everyone else should be and whose obligation it was to get them there.

# Trouble-free mornings

I find that the tone of the whole day is set by what happens between getting up and going to work and I am sure that it pays to invest a certain amount of care and attention to ensure a trouble-free start each morning.

This is a time when it is particular important to have a routine and to stick to it. Work out what has to be done each morning and decide honestly how long it will all take – usually longer than you think. Add 5 or 10 minutes to allow for mishaps and plan your getting-up time accordingly.

## Getting yourself out of bed

This may not be a problem if you have young children who rise early. If you can train them to require your attention at just the right time in the morning, they will take their duties very seriously and are guaranteed to continue to pester you until you drag yourself out of bed to start the day with them. But young children do seem to be saddled with an imperfect sense of timing and there is always a risk that you will be awakened at 4 in the morning by the alarm call from the cot that you requested for 7. When you point out the error to your diligent toddler, he may settle down for a doze but he will almost certainly have switched into his repeater mode and will proceed to waken you half-hourly until it is time to get up.

Those without human alarms must rely on the mechanical sort. If you are prone to oversleeping, take action as follows:

☆ Replace your mild, unassuming alarm clock with something more offensive. A continuous, ear-splitting wail is less easy to ignore than a few namby-pamby peeps or a bit of Mozart on Radio Three. Go for a clock that is powered by mains electricity or long-life batteries. Although wind up alarms make a tremendous din, they only do so for a limited period before they run down, leaving you to slumber on in peace.

☆ Position your noisy, persistent alarm clock well out of reach of the bed so that, when it goes off, you have no choice but to get up and silence it. All you have to do then is to resist the temptation to dive straight back into bed.

## Organising the morning rush in advance

Leave as little as possible to be done in the morning once you are all up.

When I am really organised, I lay out my own and the children's clothes for the next day before I go to bed. This eliminates the last-minute scrabble for the lost sock and the tedious discovery that the only clean school shirt is screwed up at the bottom of the ironing bag.

I also try to collect together all that each member of the family will need for the following day in the way of swimming things, reading books, briefs, notebooks, and so on. These are plonked in an extremely inconvenient place by the front door where we are guaranteed to fall over them as we go out, together with sundry Post-it notes (stuck to the door itself) to remind me to 'collect lunchbox from fridge' and 'fill up with petrol'.

If he has the stamina, my husband's last job before going to bed is to set the breakfast table. A civilised breakfast requires organisation and takes time (at least a quarter of an hour in our already tight schedule) but is a priority for us. It is the one time of the day when the whole family sits down together and, though there may be nothing much to be said, the silence is relatively companionable. What is more, the children are not tempted to walk off round the house spilling half-finished pots of yoghurt and dropping pieces of buttery toast – it seems to me that parents who gobble their own breakfast standing in the kitchen are at rather a disadvantage when it comes to enforcing a rule that the children should sit up at the table to eat theirs.

## How to arrive at the office looking presentable

A serious problem for the working mother is how to arrive at work looking as smart and well-groomed as her childless and male colleagues. How many of them, I wonder, have had to wash up the breakfast pots, make the beds, help with the construction of a papier mache model, refit a child's bicycle chain, and mop up an overturned potty, all before they set off for the office?

One way to overcome the difficulty is to leave it until the very last minute before putting on your work clothes. Face and hair can be done in the normal way as they seem to survive the ravages of the morning rush relatively unscathed, but stay in your nightclothes and dressing gown or fling on an old tracksuit until just before you leave.

This tactic does not, in fact, work for me. The image of Mummy still in her nightclothes or wearing a comfortable tracksuit is far too leisurely. Each member of the family, including myself, interprets it in his or her own way to mean that I have all the time in the world and can be expected to read a story, help with a project, clear away all the breakfast pots, chase up the garden contractors, etc., etc. In self-defence therefore, I have to get dressed in my work clothes as soon as I get up. I protect myself from affectionate jammy fingers and runny noses by having an oversized dressing gown which I put on again on top of everything else, exposing just enough of my clothing to ensure that the family know I mean business and no more. The dressing gown does not come off again until the moment before I step out of the front door, and I must confess to a private nightmare that one day I will glance down at myself whilst sitting in a rush hour traffic jam on the outskirts of Leeds only to find that I am still wearing it. An enormous apron might work quite well as an alternative (and would certainly look less odd if I forgot to take it off) but I have yet to find an apron that has full-length sleeves and reaches to the floor, both features essential for complete protection.

If you have to take your child to a childminder or a nursery before going to work, neither getting dressed at the last minute nor the dressing gown tactic will protect you from hazards such as your child's grubby feet extended towards you as you lean over to strap him into his car seat or the wheels of his dusty pushchair as you fold it up and manhandle it on and off the bus. If you cannot afford to risk turning up at work with black marks all over your suit, consider investing in a spare washable mack to wear until you parted company with your offspring. This can work very well if you have a car – as soon as your child is safety out of the way in the morning, swop the old mack for your good coat which you have ready on the back seat and then reverse the process at picking up time. However, it will not be so straightforward if you travel on foot or use public transport. If you cannot prevail on a friendly childminder or nursery to act as cloakroom for you, your spare mack will have to be large, light and easily packed away so that you can wear it as an overall and then stuff it into your briefcase when you metamorphose from tramp to career woman.

## Where to live

You may have no choice about where you live. However, if you are about to move anyway or could move if you wanted to, it is worth giving some careful consideration to the area that would be most convenient for you and the sort of house that would suit you best. Just living in the right place can do a great deal to make life as a working mother manageable.

Different families have different priorities, but there are some questions that most people need to ask themselves. For example, do you want your home to be near to your own work, near to your partner's work or half way between the two? You might think it makes most sense to live near to your own workplace if you are the one who is primarily responsible for home and children. It certainly means you waste less time on routine travelling, you can get home in a hurry if there is a disaster, and you might even be able to see more of the children by popping in during the day. In fact we did the reverse and bought a house barely 2 miles from my husband's office and 25 miles from my own and it too has proved to be a very satisfactory arrangement. I find the journey to work is an excellent opportunity to put nappies and Marmite soldiers behind me and assume my working face ready for the day ahead. The distance involved is such as to rule out any possibility of nipping home for lunch, so I am under no pressure to cut corners and rush jobs in an attempt to do so. And in the evening, after half an hour in the car with Vivaldi at full volume and my brain in neutral, I have relaxed sufficiently to cope with two noisy and excited children in the run-up to bedtime. In contrast, my husband arrives home from the office with his mind still full of niggly problems of easements, defective titles and statutory declarations, ill prepared for an infant onslaught and, understandably, apt to snap. He therefore tends to leave the tea and bedtime routine to me, delaying his arrival until after the children are safely in bed with their stories read, but he is near at hand and ready, willing and able to step into the breach if there is an emergency or I get held up at court later than anticipated.

Another factor that you have to consider is schools and play-schools. If you buy that picturesque cottage miles from civilisation, who is going to do the school run? Perhaps it would be better to settle for the house in town so that the nanny will be able to walk round to the school gates?

Consider whether it would be possible to move to live near a willing relative. There is no doubt that grandparents, aunts and uncles and even close family friends can provide a first-class backup service for emergencies when your are stuck late at work or your child is ill and cannot go to nursery or nanny fails to appear at the appointed hour. They can also help in all sorts of other ways such as babysitting, shopping, being there to let in the gas man or the plumber, and collecting from school. But, however well intentioned they may be, it is straining the quality of mercy to expect them to make a round trip of 100 miles every time you need bailing out.

Think about the type of house you propose to buy. A big garden may seem wonderful in prospect but, as we have found from bitter experience, it can prove to be a millstone when both partners have very little free time. A derelict wreck may provide an outlet for your creative talents, but what opportunities do you have to choose door

139

handles, consider kitchen units and hassle recalcitrant plumbers? If you intend to have someone living in (or may do at a future date), make sure that you choose somewhere big enough to give her her own room. If you can afford a house with two bathrooms, not having to share a bathroom with the nanny is a boon. If you are going to work from home during the day while the children are around, see if you can find a house where you will be able to shut yourself away and achieve relative peace and quiet.

And a word of warning: if you are not sure whether you really want to work or not, do not stretch yourselves to the limit with your mortgage. The more you feel under pressure financially to work, the more desperate your longing to be at home with the children is likely to become.

# 15

# Chief cook and bottle washer

## 'What's for dinner, mum?'

Feeding the family must be one of the biggest nightmares of any working mother's life. There are two parts to the problem – the shopping and the cooking. The key to both is forward planning.

Before you begin to formulate your plan of campaign, take a long hard look at your present arrangements. Tot up how many times you have been shopping for food in the last week. How many different food shops have you visited? What did you buy in each shop? With hindsight, is there any reason why you could not have done all that food shopping by making one visit to one supermarket? If you are within reach of a good supermarket and have a freezer, or even a fridge with a small freezer compartment, once-a-week one-stop shopping is almost certainly feasible provided you are prepared to put your mind to it.

## The weekly shopping list

Set aside half an hour each week to draw up a comprehensive shopping list. Insist that you have some time to yourself to do this: if you break off every few minutes to wipe one child's nose or to get the other a drink, you will forget something and the whole object of the exercise will be defeated.

Start by planning at least a week's eating in advance. Remember to take into account that whatever you are going to eat at the end of the week will have to be capable of being stored until then, so do not plan fish for the following Friday unless you can freeze it. Record your menus somewhere where they will not get lost, or by the middle of the week you will be left with a pile of ingredients and no idea what you intended to do with them. If you have a Filofax, you could use that or, if not, you might use an ordinary notebook and tether it inside a kitchen cupboard. If you must use the back of an old envelope, pin it up on the noticeboard or put it away in your safe-keeping drawer.

Now take stock of other basic items such as butter, cereal, lavatory paper, cleaning equipment and deodorant, and add any that you need to your list. It may be helpful to have a master list of all the food and household items you ever buy and to skim through it to jog your memory. I find it is a mistake to allow too much individuality in matters such as cereals and personal toiletries; if you have to buy Signal for your husband, Crest for yourself and Sainsbury's own-brand toothpaste for the children, you have three items to check up on for your list, three items to remember at the supermarket and three to cart home. Bring home one fairly average tube of toothpaste and let anyone who wants anything different, and who is old enough to do so, buy their own if they do not like it.

Look over your list and consider whether any of the items cannot be obtained at the local supermarket. If so, decide whether it is worth making a detour to another shop for the offending articles or whether you would prefer to change your menus so that you can do without capers or vine leaves or whatever it might be.

## The big shop

Armed with your list, set off for the supermarket, but do choose your time carefully. There is not much point in going late on a Saturday when stocks have been depleted by the weekend rush, unless you particularly want to go then for the bargains that have been reduced for a quick sale because they will not survive until Monday. Nor is there any point in trying to do your big shop on Monday; the shelves will be virtually bare and what there is may well be left over from Saturday so will not keep very long when you get it home. Shopping on Friday evening or Saturday morning means fighting the crowds, but it does have the advantage that you can usually get exactly what you want and that you then have the rest of the weekend to put part 2 of your food campaign into action if you are so inclined.

## Part 2 of the food campaign

Part 2 of the food campaign involves preparing the majority of the week's meals in advance. It is, of course, optional. Once upon a time I used to adhere to it religiously. Nowadays I never have the energy or the inclination, though I know that by the middle of the working week I will wish that I *had* put it into operation.

There is no doubt that it is a wonderful feeling at the end of a working day to know that supper is all ready in the fridge or freezer and only requires heating through. What you have to decide is whether it is worth the half-day or so that it will probably take out of your weekend in preparation time. Perhaps the best course is to compromise by making one or two meals in advance (for instance, a casserole and a potato-topped pie of some sort) and planning for the other days either meals that require little preparation (such as chops or sausages, baked potatoes and a vegetable) or shop-bought ready-made meals. There is no need to feel guilty because you have not made the lasagne yourself – I am not at all sure that my family do not prefer something ready-cooked from Sainsbury's to the half-hearted efforts I sometimes knock up after a day's work. Ready-made meals can be bought frozen or unfrozen and there are some pretty classy dishes to be had – pasta dishes, curries, casseroles, fish pies, various potato concoctions, etc. If you read the labels carefully, you will find plenty that do not contain the dreaded additives and even vegetarians are not forgotten. From my own personal experience, I can recommend Sainsbury's, Tesco and Marks and Spencer as providing a good selection, and I am sure there must be many more shops that do the same. And for variety, what is wrong with the occasional take-away, be it fish and chips, Chinese, pizza or whatever you have nearby?

## Relieving the pressure

Even if you cannot exact from yourself the discipline required for the full two-part food campaign, you might consider adopting some of the following ideas to make feeding the family less of a strain:

☆ *No puddings*
They are time consuming to make and bad for you. If a second course is required, provide fruit or cheese and biscuits or a yoghourt.

☆ *Simple menus*
Keep your menus relatively simple, avoiding elaborate recipes unless you are sure that crêpes Suzette will still seem a good idea by the time you have to cook them on Wednesday evening after an awful meeting that has kept you late at work. There are lots of cookery books devoted to fast main dishes and many of the recipes taste just as good, if not better, than those that take twice as long to prepare and involve three times as many ingredients.

☆ *One-pot cooking*
Look out for recipes that can be cooked in one pot, vegetables and all. They make for particularly satisfying advance cooking and cut down enormously on washing up.

☆ *Pasta, rice and bread*
Remember pasta and rice as easy alternatives to potatoes; they may take much the same time to cook, but they do not need all that peeling and washing, eyeing and cutting up. Bread is even easier and, provided you avoid the tasteless plain white sliced variety, quite delicious as an accompaniment to many dishes. Serve garlic or herb bread as a special treat. You can

buy garlic butter in packets from the supermarket (at a price of course) or, if you are too idle even to butter your own French loaf, you can buy garlic bread from Tesco or Marks and Spencer all ready to bake in the oven.

☆ Even if you cannot face drawing up the week's menus in advance, at least perform sufficient mental gymnastics as you go round the supermarket to ensure that you accumulate enough ingredients (meat/fish/cheese/eggs/vegetables) to provide a meal on each day of the coming week. That way you should eliminate the mad dash to the shops during your lunch hour or on your way home.

☆ Include in your shopping some items with a 'best before' date a good while ahead. Root these out from the back of the shelf in preference to the packets at the front that are marked with a date only one or two days away. This cuts down on the need for freezing and so avoids panic defrosting under the hot tap when you have forgotten to take out the meat for the evening meal in advance. It will also ease your conscience when you succumb to an unplanned take-away if you know that the pork chops you did not have the energy to cook will last until the next day and will not be wasted.

☆ *Tins*

Have a store of useful tins. Nothing excites irritability (your own and the rest of the family's) quite like the realisation that you have forgotten to get anything for supper and there is nothing edible in the house. Personally I am not fond of the tinned meat often recommended as emergency rations, but I do find tins of tuna a versatile stand-by. Mixed with some tinned red kidney beans, chopped cucumber, onions, tomatoes and a little French dressing (bottled if you like), tuna makes a quick, easy and satisfying salad. My tin store also includes tinned tomatoes, baked beans, pineapple slices (a surprisingly frequent ingredient in all sorts of recipes) and some rather more exotic items such as Chinese water chestnuts (which add a delicious crunch to casseroles and stir-fry dishes and give the impression you have made a special effort to please).

☆ *UHT milk*

Keep a few cartons of UHT milk on the shelf for the times when you forget to set the milk dial or the milkman forgets you and you run out of milk.

☆ Decide what your priorities will be when you get home and let everyone know roughly what time they can expect to eat, so that they are not hovering around waiting to be fed from the moment you walk in. In our household, food has to wait until after I have had a chance to play with the children, bath them, read stories and get them off to bed. This works because the nanny has already given the children their tea by the time I come home and there are only the adults to feed, but it might be less satisfactory if you have unfed children who clamour for food as soon as they catch sight of you coming up the drive.

If you decide to make food your first priority, at least avoid plastering your best suit with flour by changing out of your work clothes before you start cooking or by wearing a large apron.

☆ See whether you can arrange that everyone will eat their main meal at lunchtime on at least one day (the same day!) each week. Quite apart from saving on cooking in the evening when boiled eggs or baked beans will do, this gives you a good excuse to enjoy meeting a friend for lunch instead of working through your lunch hour or racing round the shops stocking up on disposable nappies or children's underwear.

☆ Keep a list of your staple dishes and their ingredients in your handbag. Use it to inspire you whenever you cannot think what to give the family to eat and to jog your memory when you have to shop for the evening meal at the last minute.

## Washing, ironing and mending

The last thing any working woman wants to do when the evening meal is finally out of the way is to start washing and ironing clothes for the next day. Make sure, therefore, that each member of the family has sufficient clothing to survive from Monday to Friday without any laundry service. In doing your calculations, take into account that babies and young children can easily get through more than one outfit in a day so what seems like an extravagant quantity of clothing may, in fact, be only just enough to get by. If you cannot afford to bring everyone up to full quota straight away, do it gradually when you can find the money.

If possible, choose washable garments in preference to those that need dry cleaning. There will rarely be a day when you do not get someone else's breakfast or worse on your clothes, and you do not want to spend your entire time ferrying dry cleaning around and all your money paying for it. If you must buy clothes that need dry cleaning, go for dark colours and all-over patterns. Stunning cream-coloured dry clean only suits and dresses are strictly for childless women with a full complement of household staff and no need to work – for the working mother, they are absolutely out.

Try also to avoid the temptation to buy articles that really are hand wash only. In our household, clothes that cannot go in the washing

machine seem to spend more time at the bottom of the laundry basket waiting to be washed than they do being worn. However, I have
found that a hand wash only label does not necessarily mean that an
item cannot be washed successfully in the washing machine. On a
wool programme using cold water, I have had excellent results with
silk blouses, mohair and cotton jumpers and other delicate articles.
If I am at all worried about whether a particular item will survive,
I protect it by putting it inside a pillow case before putting it in the
machine (or you can buy a special zip bag made of fine net to use
instead of the pillow case).

If you have a baby still in nappies, use disposables if you possibly can. Have them delivered to your home in bulk – Boots and
Mothercare provide this service (see page 213 in the Facts Section).
Do not despair if you try disposables in the very early stages and find
that they leak; matters will almost certainly improve once the baby
starts to take more solid food and less milk and you will be able to try
again then. Leaking can, however, continue to be a problem at night
and you may have to take additional precautions if you want to avoid
having wet bedding to deal with in the morning. Try putting a pair of
plastic pants on top of the disposable nappy and/or putting a length
of disposable nappy roll (or a nappy pad) inside the disposable nappy
for extra absorbency. If these tricks fail, put a terry nappy on top
of the disposable and plastic pants on top of that. The terry nappy

should never be too unpleasant as the disposable will do most of the work and you should not need to have a nappy bucket, just add the terry to your normal wash.

Cut out any niggly little washing jobs that you can. For instance, I have replaced dishcloths, which needed frequent washing and bleaching, with J-cloths, which are thrown away instead – extravagant, but so much easier. Save yourself a battle with time-consuming items such as large cotton or linen sheets and tablecloths by sending them to the laundry if you have one that collects and delivers.

Avoid accidents when doing the washing. They take far more time to put right than they do to prevent. Separate dark clothes from light, think about colour-fastness and make sure that you choose a wash programme and temperature that will suit everything you have put in the machine. Remove all paper tissues and other items from pockets before washing. Your time will have been well spent if you save yourself the headache of pale-pink cricket whites and towels covered in a fur of disintegrated paper handkerchief.

Stop ironing towels, underpants, pyjamas, socks and the like forthwith.

Consider whether you could bear to iron other items selectively i.e. only where they show. I used to do this with sheets before I discovered the laundry, but I have never been able to bring myself to leave the backs and sleeves of shirts unironed.

Have a policy about what you do and what you do not mend. I once knew someone who darned her tights and the thought makes me rather ashamed that I do not even mend socks – they are worn until there is more hole than sock and then they are thrown away. Items that you do mend should be done straight away in order avoid a wholesale repair job at a later date. Loose buttons should be sewn on as soon as you notice them or they will come off in your hand just when you are in a tearing hurry to get ready for work and will be lost for ever.

## Cleaning

Doing the washing and feeding the family *demand* your attention. Cleaning and tidying the house fall into a different category – life will go on without them and it is entirely up to you how much or how little you do.

Do not let yourself be steam-rollered into hours and hours of dusting, polishing and vacuuming simply because you are worried about what Mrs Jones next door will think about the state of your house. If she does call, she is extremely unlikely to notice cobwebs on the ceiling and dust on the mantelpiece unless you draw them to her attention by apologising about them. And even if she does notice, far from condemning you, it may give her a comfortable feeling to know that you have as many shortcomings as a cleaner as she does – there is something very daunting about the woman who manages to keep her house in perfect condition, her children clean and tidy, and her freezer full of nourishing meals.

Decide for yourself what your own cleanliness/tidiness threshold is. Some people can live happily surrounded by complete chaos and, if you are one of them, thank your lucky stars as your load of housework will be considerably the lighter. At the other extreme are those poor unfortunates who cannot function without complete order and freedom from dirt. The rest of us occupy the middle ground – we tolerate a modest level of dirt and clutter, but we begin to become irritable once the state of the house deteriorates beyond that point.

Having evaluated your tolerance to domestic disorder, decide how to go about maintaining your minimum standards. Different methods suit different people.

If you are a blitz person, you will descend upon the house in a burst of feverish and productive energy on an ad hoc basic whenever the chaos penetrates your consciousness and you cannot stand the filth a moment longer.

More tidy-minded individuals may prefer to set aside a particular time each week/fortnight/month for cleaning. When we were first married, my husband and I used to spend Friday evenings cleaning our house from top to toe, followed by the reward of a visit to the pub. It was immensely satisfying to wake up to the spotless house every Saturday morning, but I am afraid that the routine did not last long.

Alternatively you may choose to keep the place reasonable tidy and clean all the time, setting aside perhaps half an hour each day to work systematically through your list of household chores.

Whatever your routine, the following tips might help:

- Do not allow anyone to accumulate junk. Be totally ruthless and get rid of anything you do not really want – from old newspapers and letters to broken toys and clothes that have been outgrown or have remained unworn for more than a year. As my tidy husband is always reminding me, a house is much easier to look after without piles of clutter all over the place.
- Insist on as much storage space (preferably cupboards, but shelves are better than nothing) as you have room for and can afford. Give everything a home and try to ensure that it is replaced there routinely after use so that it does not contribute to the general mess and you are able to find it next time you want it. Putting away should be a habit – my mother used to drive me mad telling me that it was just as easy to put things away immediately as it was to put them down, but she was right.

- Never go upstairs without taking something with you; most houses seem to have a heap of items at the bottom of the stairs waiting to go up and this is an excellent way of keeping it under control.
- Remember that giving a room a rigorous tidy often makes it look nearly as good as if you had cleaned it. Cleaning the basin and polishing the taps does wonders for the bathroom and, if you have a limited amount of time to make the house look nice for a special occasion, consider using part of it to arrange some flowers – flower arrangements are hard to beat when it comes to giving the less than perfect house a cared-for appearance.
- If your children still have bath toys, provide a suitable container for them or you will find it impossible to keep the bathroom tidy. You could use one of those synthetic mesh bags that hang from the bath taps but I find that an upended plastic booster step is better. Choose one with cut-out handles through which you can strain the bathwater that finds its way in with the toys.
- Try to prevent the oven and hob becoming a major cleaning problem by wiping them over after each use. Whenever possible wrap food that is to be cooked in the oven in foil or a roasting bag or cover it with a lid. You might even consider investing in an oven with self-clean linings, although I have yet to find one that does not require any cleaning at all.

# 16

# 'Why should I run round after you lot?'

E ver feel you are doing more than your fair share? Perhaps there is something you can do about it.

## Men

Some women have the supreme good fortune to be married to saints who see it as a natural part of a husband's role to do the shopping, share the cooking, hoover the stairs and take time off when the children are ill. Others – I suspect, the majority – do not.

Men who do not pull their weight about the house and with the children can be divided into two categories. There are the potentially usefuls (those who can be persuaded to do their bit amiably enough if approached in the right way) and the incurables (who most definitely cannot). When tackling the problem of the unhelpful partner, your first step must therefore be to decide into which category your partner falls.

If you have one of the incurables, I suggest you do not waste time and energy cajoling and bullying and feeling badly done to. Accept with the best possible grace that you are going to have to do everything yourself and devote your energies to planning a routine and getting on with it. I know it is neither right nor fair but it makes sense in terms of time – it takes longer to indulge in a full-scale argument over who should wash the kitchen floor than it does to do the job itself and, when you lose the argument, you still have the floor to do as well – and it makes sense in terms of domestic harmony. However righteous you feel, you will not persuade a man who has never yet lifted a finger and does not intend to start that it is his *duty* to help about the house. He knows as well as you do that they are his children too, that you have had a busy day at the office as well, that there is nothing biological that prevents men from cooking and that he could find out from the instruction booklet how to work the washing machine. What he does not agree with is your interpretation of these facts. Reminding him of them at the top of your voice is not going to persuade him to lay the table, do the shopping, peel the potatoes or wash his own shirts if he is convinced that these jobs are women's work. All you will succeed in doing is fuelling your own sense of righteous indignation and making him bad-tempered from resentment and vague feelings of guilt.

Let us suppose, though, that you decide that you have one of the potentially usefuls; how do you go about roping him in to help? Obviously it depends very much upon what type of person your partner is and what sort of relationship you have with him, but your chances of success will be increased if you plan your campaign with care. If he is to be of any real assistance, you need him to have the enthusiasm of the willing volunteer, so you must conceal from him the fact that he is, in fact, being conscripted. It is a delicate balance to strike. You cannot allow him to wriggle off the hook with a lot of vague promises. On the other hand, you must not make him feel that you are criticising him for his lack of help so far, or he will instantly be on the defensive.

Be prepared to take things slowly. You may be aiming for equality but do not risk frightening him off by demanding your pound of flesh immediately. If it suits you both to negotiate a comprehensive domestic demarcation agreement straight away, all well and good, but do not be surprised if your partner rebels at the prospect of a lifelong commitment to a particular job or jobs. Do not push him; content yourself with his offer to do the weekly shop (or whatever it might be) this week, and then next week, and then the week after. With any luck, by the time he has done the same job for four or five consecutive weeks, he will begin to feel proprietorial about it and it will become a habit.

When you plan your campaign consider *why* you are not getting as much help as you would like.

- Are you so efficient for instance, or is your partner so wrapped up in his work, that he simply has no idea of all the jobs with which you have to cope? If this is the problem, a direct request for help may be enough. Reinforce the request with a certain amount of industrial action if necessary, just to let him see exactly what you do do – he will soon realise that butter has to be bought from a shop when there is none for his toast for three breakfasts in a row.
- Are you churlish and ungrateful when help is offered? When he says 'Is there anything I can do?', do you snap back with a martyred 'No thank you' because you are irritated that he has to ask when he should be able to see for himself that there are a hundred and one ways in which he could help? Far be it from me to preach about adopting this sort of attitude; I have rejected well-meant offers of help more times than I care to remember. But I always wish I had not done it after

the event. Looking at the situation rationally, if you have a partner who is willing to be the manual labourer and let you be the brains, it is a lot better than nothing. Who knows, as he becomes more familiar with the job, he may even aspire to a senior management post.

- Do you make helping too difficult? Do you issue instructions so complex that even the simplest task seems daunting? When he offers to buy the packet of cornflakes that you have forgotten, do you insist that they must be Kelloggs', that the packet must be of a particular size so that it will fit in the pantry cupboard, that it must be one of the packets with tokens for a free kitchen roll holder, and that when he pays he must use the discount voucher that came through the letterbox yesterday? Do you stand over your partner to make sure he vacuums right up to the edges of the carpet? Do you rush out when he is hanging out the washing to tell him that he has pegged out all the socks upside down?

If this is you (and it is certainly me from time to time), stop issuing instructions and think whether you really want to be helped or whether it is more important to you to have things done your way. If help is the top priority, let people help you in their own way and interfere only when it is absolutely necessary to prevent a disaster. If you are not happy to let your standards slip, do not delegate – do it yourself. Above all, resist the temptation to demonstrate how a job should be done 'properly' by doing it again ostentatiously as soon as your partner has finished. This sort of insensitive behaviour is likely to result in a complete withdrawal of labour indefinitely – deservedly so. If you must make good his mistakes, for heaven's sake wait until he is out.

If you have planned your campaign for more help well, there is a good chance that it will begin to produce results. This is the point at which I am beset with feelings of guilt that my poor husband (who, I remind myself, does after all have a very demanding job) is having to do household chores that I have been brought up to think of as my responsibility. Having won the battle, not only do I fail to consolidate my position, I suddenly capitulate and scuttle off to beat him to all the tasks that he has just agreed to do. This is the most appalling waste of everyone's time and energy and it would be hard to imagine a more blatant way of looking a gift horse in the mouth. If only I could keep my conscience under control, I would be suitably grateful (but not effusively so, because after all he is only doing his fair share) and let him get on with it while I relished my victory.

Always be on your guard against counter-attack. There are certain household jobs that are traditionally seen as the man's province, for instance mowing the lawn, heavy digging in the garden, washing the cars, do-it-yourself and household repairs. If you once allow yourself to demonstrate that you are capable of doing this sort of thing, you may be landed with the whole lot permanently. I have never ever mowed a lawn. I am quite sure that I could not start or even push the motor mower and, in order to prove this beyond doubt, I have never tried. Either my husband mows the lawn or it goes on growing. I have recently, however, learned to change a plug and to wield an electric drill. I did not initiate myself in these mystic rites without a lot of heart searching, but in the end I decided it was easier to do minor DIY jobs myself than to do without the iron or the door safety chain for weeks whilst I nagged my husband to attend to them. To my surprise, I found drilling and brandishing a screwdriver immensely satisfying, much more so than washing up and ironing, but I have had to abandon thoughts of complete role reversal due to lack of cooperation from other quarters.

## Offspring

I do not for a moment suggest that children should be used as slave labour, but I think most people would agree that both the children and the family as a whole will benefit if they are expected to lend a hand now and then.

The secret is to start them young. Young children love to help and, if you are prepared to put up with their ham-fisted efforts in the early days, there is a good prospect that they will grow up to see helping as a perfectly normal part of their childhood. Even a 4 or 5-year-old can do (and enjoy doing) useful jobs and my 6-year-old daughter is a dab hand at getting herself washed and dressed and tidying her bedroom each morning and, assuming she has got out of bed the right side, likes nothing better than to go downstairs before us to start giving her brother his breakfast.

There is no doubt that, in the early stages of training a young child to help, it is often easier and a lot quicker to do the job yourself. This is counter-productive in the long run. What you want to do is to make the child take full responsibility for the task himself and he is not going to do this if he knows that, when he does not feel like it, he has only to indulge in a bit of whingeing and dawdling and you will take over. So stick to your guns and be patient but firm, encouraging but unrelenting. Providing you have chosen a job that is within the capabilities of your child, you will win in the end.

Older children may need more subtle persuasion. There may be children who do their bit simply because they are inherently good-natured or because they always do as their parents ask, but my researches suggest that such children do not exist outside the minds of childcare experts and the pages of their learned books. So if something more is required for your offspring, you might try:

☆ *A rota system*
My parents used to introduce rotas sporadically during my childhood, but they were always short-lived for one reason or another. I suspect they are rather like diets – they seem to be a miraculous solution at the outset but are doomed to fail once the initial enthusiasm wears off.

☆ *A bit of bribery*
I am not against bolstering up normal parental control with a bit of good honest bribery now and again. After all, the whole world works on an 'if you scratch my back, I'll scratch yours' basis and, providing the child is not allowed to become an infant blackmailer, I can see no harm in introducing him to the system young. In some households, children are even required to earn their pocket money by doing jobs, which carry a prearranged rate of pay.

☆ *The threat approach*
This is the other side of the bribery coin and sometimes very effective. What you do is to point out to the child that unless he helps you get on with the chores (be it by entertaining himself and keeping out of your way for an hour or by tidying his own bedroom or whatever), you will not have time to take him to the park/read his bedtime story/transport him to

the disco. If you adopt this approach however, you must be prepared to obey three simple rules: you must use it only when the task you want to impose upon the child is one that it is right and fair to ask him to do; you must make your terms and conditions plain to the child in advance; and you must be prepared to enforce your threat if he does not comply, so that next time it happens he will know that you mean business.

# 17

# 'But what about me?'

It may come as no surprise to you that this is the last chapter in the book and nearly the shortest one! Finding time for oneself is vitally important, but for most of us virtually impossible.

## Other people's bright ideas

Those who are not working mothers have all sorts of suggestions as to how working mothers might make time for themselves. Have you considered the following bright ideas, for example?

> ☆ *Retiring to your bedroom upon arriving home from work* and taking 10 minutes to unwind, refusing to be disturbed for anything other than dire emergencies.
>
> According to a magazine I read recently, you should undress and have a warm shower, put on loose clothes, sit or lie down comfortably and do a few exercises – no doubt wonderfully relaxing but who is going to breastfeed that screaming baby and prevent the toddler from investigating the kitchen cupboards or falling down the stairs whilst you are incommunicado?
>
> ☆ *Going to bed later*
> What, even later? I do not know about you, but I cannot work up much enthusiasm for embroidery or learning a foreign language after midnight.
>
> ☆ *Getting up early*
> I do have some limited success with this tactic, particularly in the summer when the mornings are light, and I do like the comfortable glow of virtue and superiority which I get from beating the rest of the world to it. But my early morning peace and quiet tends to be short-lived and I am usually joined by one or the other child within 15 minutes or so. I cannot get up any earlier to overcome this problem – I

have barely fallen asleep before it is time to get up as it is.

☆ *Arranging to have a regular evening out alone each week*, for example at an evening class. It is very refreshing to do something completely different for a couple of hours once a week and I wholeheartedly recommend it to those with sufficient stamina, but I do not have the energy after a day in court, an hour playing with the children, baths and stories, grown ups' supper and the washing up to turn out again to learn French polishing or African mask-making.

☆ *Arranging for Granny to have the children for part of each weekend*
This really is a good idea if you happen to have a granny near at hand, but it ignores the fact that many of us have such a guilty conscience about being away from our children during the week that we feel the need to make it up to them by spending every available moment with them at weekends.

## Harsh reality

As a working mother, you are probably making full use of all the available hours in the day as it is, and other people's bright ideas are unlikely suddenly to conjure up the extra time you need to indulge yourself.

Review your priorities by all means. You may be able to cut down on the cleaning, buy ready-made meals from the supermarket more often, change over to duvets, and stop entertaining so frequently in order to make time for yourself. But minor adjustments apart, I have come to the conclusion that the best I can do is to resign myself gracefully to the fact that life as a working mother does not allow much leeway for self-indulgence.

This is a pity. It has meant giving up hobbies that I enjoy such as dress-making and making soft furnishings. But the point is that, having given up my hobbies entirely, I no longer resent the fact that I cannot find time for them. So, while I do not now have the fun of a project well done, equally I am no longer reproached by the sight of half-finished dresses bristling with pins and bolts of furnishing fabric waiting to be turned into curtains. I have also ceased to measure the success of a day in terms of what has been achieved – a room wallpapered, a piece of embroidery complete, the desk turned out and all outstanding paperwork attended to. By these standards, most of my days are failures. With my expectations at rock bottom, I can enjoy whatever happens to be fun during the day, be it half an hour in a hot bath with my book or a walk with the children or an evening slumped in front of the television.

If I still find myself hankering for time for me, I have only to look at those of my friends who are full-time mothers with young children to know that it is not really the work that is the obstacle but the young children. Non-working mothers may be at home all day, but their time is no more their own than mine is. The household chores spin out over much of the day and the children take up the rest. In fact, they envy me because of all the time I have to myself during working hours!

## Making time for your partner

Resigning yourself to having no time for yourself does not mean resigning yourself to having no time with your husband. It is all too easy for each partner to become so bound up in the business of simply getting through each day that neither gives a thought to how the other is managing. Things tend to be arranged so that one looks after the children while the other catches up on housework/paper-work/office work and vice versa, with the result that husband and wife are never on the same shift. When they do meet, they are both so exhausted that they can manage no more than a grunted greeting before switching off in front of the television or falling fast asleep in bed. Before long, they have started to grow apart.

Halting (or better still preventing) the process requires effort. Try consciously to make time for your partner, however busy you are and even if it means you will not get all the chores done. Watch out for the occasions when your normally taciturn partner wants to talk and try not to brush him off because you have work to do. If you can, arrange to go out together as a couple on a regular basis. I know this is easier said than done – something always crops up at work at the last minute and babysitters are thin on the ground – but it is well worth doing, even if you only go for a walk or to the local pizza place or the cinema. Consider going away for the occasional weekend together without the children if you are fortunate enough to have someone to look after them. You may feel awful about leaving them but it will not hurt them once in a while. It may even do them good to stand on their own two feet without you, and it will certainly do you good to be without them. Be prepared for excuses from your partner as to why he cannot possibly get away, but do not take no for an answer. In our household, I have to choose and book a holiday before my husband will accept that he is going to have to take one. Even then, we have to go abroad because it is only the fact that the plane leaves at a scheduled time and will not wait for us that prevents him from continuing to work right up to the last minute and beyond.

Do things together as a family too. It may take longer to get the shopping done if you all go, but it can be fun and might include a leisurely morning coffee somewhere or a visit to the toy shop.

# THE FACTS SECTION

# 1

# Maternity rights and benefits

## How to use this section

All pregnant women are automatically entitled to:

- Free dental treatment
- Free prescriptions.

All mothers are entitled to:

- Child benefit.

Find out more about these rights in Part 1 of this section.

By law, pregnant *employees* generally have the following additional rights:

- The right to paid time off for ante-natal care
- The right not to be unfairly dismissed because of pregnancy
- The right to statutory maternity pay
- The right to return to work after the baby is born.

Turn to Part 2 for details.

If you are *self-employed*, Part 2 does not concern you. Turn to Part 3 instead to find out whether you might be entitled to:

- Maternity allowance, or
- Sickness benefit.

Part 4 contains calendars, a sample letter and a checklist for use in conjunction with Parts 2 and 3.

Part 5 suggests where you might obtain further information and advice.

**Note**
*The Department of Health and Social Security (DHSS) is now known as the Department of Social Security (DSS).*

# Part 1: Benefits to which everyone is entitled

## 1. Free prescriptions

1.1 Whilst you are pregnant and for a year after your baby is born, you are entitled to free prescriptions.

1.2 *How to claim*
Ask your doctor, midwife or health visitor for form FW8 (which confirms you are pregnant). Fill it in and send it to your local Family Practitioner Committee (Health Board in Scotland). They will send you an exemption certificate.

## 2. Free dental treatment

2.1 Whilst you are pregnant and for a year after your baby is born, you are entitled to free dental treatment.

2.2 *How to claim*
Simply tell your dentist that you are pregnant and you will not have to pay for your NHS treatment.

## 3. Child benefit

3.1 Once your baby is born, you can claim child benefit. The present rate is £7.25 per week per child.

If you are a single parent, you can also claim one parent benefit. This is a supplement which you get on top of your eldest child's child benefit (at the moment, an extra £4.90 a week). So, for example, a mother bringing up three young children on her own would be entitled to £12.15 a week for her first child and £7.25 a week for each of the others.

Both child benefit and one parent benefit are tax free.

3.2 *How to claim*
Your local social security office will supply you with the application form(s) (see the Address Book for how to contact them). You cannot apply until after your baby is born because you will need to send your baby's birth certificate with your application.

When your application has been processed, you will be sent a payment book which you will use to draw your benefit at a named Post Office.

# Part 2: Maternity rights for employees

If your baby is born very prematurely, you should seek further information on your rights, particularily with regard to SMP and statutory maternity leave. Certain of the general rules set out in this book may be modified in your case.

## 1. Paid time off for ante-natal care

1.1 Pregnant employees are entitled not to be unreasonably refused paid time off for ante-natal care. Unlike the other maternity rights, there is no minimum period of service required – you are covered even if you have just started the job. Nor is there any distinction made between part-timers and full-timers – the law applies to both. *However*, you must realise that what you get is the right not to be unreasonably refused time off for your ante-natal care, not the right to swan off to the ante-natal clinic as and when you feel like it. So, for example, a part-timer would not be entitled to insist on attending the clinic during her working hours if she could arrange to attend during her time off.

1.2 *How to claim your time off*
If it is your first appointment for which you want time off, simply ask your employer.
    When you request time off for subsequent appointments, if your employer asks you to, you must:

> ☆ produce a certificate from a doctor, midwife or health visitor confirming that you are pregnant;
> ☆ produce your appointment card or some other written confirmation of your appointment for inspection.

1.3 *If you do not get the time off/pay to which you are entitled*
If you think your employer has unreasonably refused to let you have time off or refused to pay you properly for the time when you were away from work, you may be entitled to financial compensation. You can claim this by making a complaint to an industrial tribunal (see Part 2, paragraph 6).

## 2. The right not to be unfairly dismissed because of pregnancy

2.1 Obviously you do not want to find yourself out of a job just because you are pregnant. The law gives you special protection against dismissal because of your pregnancy, providing you satisfy certain conditions with regard to the length of your service with your employer and the number of hours you do each week.

2.2 *Minimum period of service/hours of work – do I qualify?*
If you are a full-timer (i.e. you work 16 or more hours a week), you

qualify for protection if you have done at least *two years* continuous service with your employer.

If you are a part-timer working between 8 and 16 hours a week, the minimum period of service is *five years*.

If you do fewer than 8 hours a week, you have no protection, however long you have worked for your employer.

### 2.3 *What are my rights?*

As a general rule, if you qualify for protection, your employer cannot dismiss you because you are pregnant or for any reason to do with your pregnancy. If he does so, the dismissal is automatically classed as unfair and you can make a complaint to an industrial tribunal (see Part 2, paragraph 6). The tribunal can order your employer to give you your job back or to pay you financial compensation.

There is an exception to the general rule if:

* your pregnancy makes you incapable of doing your work adequately (for example, where you have to do a lot of heavy lifting as part of your job and the bump makes this impossible), or
* it would be against the law for you to carry on with your particular job whilst pregnant (for instance if you work with X-rays or certain chemicals).

In these circumstances, your employer is likely to be entitled to dismiss you. However, he must first offer you any suitable alternative job that is available. If he does not do so, your dismissal is unfair and you can complain to an industrial tribunal.

### 2.4 *If you do not qualify for special protection*

If your employer sacks you because of your pregnancy and you have not worked for him for long enough/for enough hours each week for this to be classed as unfair dismissal, you may be able to claim that you have been the victim of sex discrimination. Contact the Equal Opportunities Commission (address and phone number in the Address Book) for advice and help.

## 3. Statutory maternity pay (SMP)

3.1 SMP is a weekly payment made over a period of a maximum of 18 weeks from the time when you stop work to have your baby. Although SMP is actually a social security benefit, you will receive your payments through your employer just as you do your salary. Your employer is then reimbursed by the DHSS.

### 3.2 *Identifying your 'EWC' and your 'qualifying week'*

In order to work out your SMP rights, you need to do some mental gymnastics with dates. On page 177 you will find a calendar to help you work out your position. Take a pencil and mark the calendar according to the following instructions. Do not worry that you do not understand what you are doing at this stage. Refer back to your annotated calendar as you read the rest of the section and all should become clear.

☆ SMP calculations work backwards from the date your baby is due, so start by putting a ring round the date you have been given as your expected date of confinement and labelling it 'Baby due'.

☆ Mark off the week (Sunday to Saturday inclusive) in which your expected date of confinement falls. This is your expected week of confinement – label it 'EWC'.

☆ Treating the week before your EWC as week 1, count back 15 weeks from your EWC. Put a ring round the 15th week (Sunday to Saturday inclusive) before your EWC. This is your qualifying week. Label it 'QW – don't give up work before the beginning of this week'.

☆ Treating the week before your EWC as week 1, count back 7 weeks from your EWC. Put a line after the Saturday of the 7th week. Label it 'Stop work by now to secure full SMP'.

☆ Treating the week before your EWC as week 1, count back 11 weeks from your EWC. Put a ring round the 11th week. Label it 'Earliest SMP can start'.

☆ Treating your qualifying week as week 1, count back 26 weeks. Put a ring round the Sunday of the week you arrive at and label it '26 weeks continuous employment starts now'.

If you get stuck, look at the example on page 179.

### 3.3 Do I qualify?

The SMP scheme does not apply to members of the armed forces. Nor does it apply, apparently, to some lady mariners or to prisoners! The rest of you can claim SMP providing you satisfy the following conditions:

● You must continue to be employed by your employer into your QW.

● By the end of your QW, your employment must have lasted for at least 26 weeks without a break (you can count the whole of your QW towards this 26-week period even if you give up work part way through it).

● Your average weekly earnings for the 8 weeks ending with your QW must not have been below the national insurance contribution threshold (currently £43.00 per week).

Clearly you will not be able to satisfy these conditions if you were dismissed before your QW because your pregnancy made it unlawful for you to do your job or meant that you could not do it properly (see Part 2, paragraph 2.3). In these circumstances, you can still claim SMP providing:

- you *would have* completed at least 26 weeks continuous employment by the end of your QW had you not been dismissed, and
- your average weekly earnings for your last 8 weeks of work were not below the national insurance contribution threshold.

### 3.4 *How much?*
There are two rates of SMP:

○ *The higher rate*
The higher rate is equivalent to 9/10ths of your average weekly earnings and is payable for the first 6 weeks of your SMP entitlement providing you have put in sufficient continuous service with your employer. The required periods are as follows:

Full-timers (i.e. at least 16 hours a week): at least two years' continuous service ending with the QW.

Part-timers (i.e. between 8 and 16 hours a week): at least five years' continuous service ending with the QW.

Note that if you do fewer than 8 hours a week, you will not qualify for the higher rate, whatever the period of your employment.

○ *The lower rate*
The lower rate is a fixed rate which is prescribed by regulations. At the time of writing, it is £36.25 a week, but you should ask your employer what the current rate is as it does change from time to time.
If you are *not* eligible for the higher rate, all your SMP will be at the lower rate. If you *are* entitled to the higher rate, you will go on to the lower rate after your first 6 weeks on SMP.

### 3.5 *When do SMP payments start?*
SMP cannot start until:

☆ you have reached the 11th week before your EWC, and
☆ you have stopped work.

The earliest you can get SMP is therefore the 11th week before your EWC. If you have not given up work by then, payment of SMP will be delayed until you do give up. Read the following paragraph when deciding your timing – you may lose some of your SMP if you continue working for too long.

### 3.6 *For how long do I get SMP?*
The maximum SMP period is 18 weeks. This divides up into:

* ☆ a core period of 13 weeks, which starts with the 6th week before your EWC;
* ☆ 5 floating weeks, which you can take before or after the core period or partly before and partly after, depending on when you want to finish work.

This means that, if you want to claim your full 18 weeks' SMP, you must stop work by the beginning of the 6th week before your EWC. For every extra week or part week you work after that point, you will lose a week's SMP.

### 3.7 *How do I get my money?*
SMP is paid by your employer in the same way as your normal salary with the usual deductions for tax, national insurance, etc. You do not have to put in a formal claim but there are important steps that you must take to safeguard your entitlement:

* ● *Notice that you are going to be absent*
  At least 21 days before you are due to stop work (or if that is not reasonably practicable, as soon as it *is* reasonably practicable), you must give your employer notice that you are going to be absent because of your pregnancy or confinement. Your employer can ask you to put your notice in writing if he wishes.

  Note that you need not give notice where you have been dismissed because your pregnancy made it unlawful for you to do your job or meant that you could not do it properly (see Part 2, paragraph 2.3). Your employer knows you are going to be away to have a baby – he has just sacked you himself.

* ● *Medical evidence of the date your baby is due*
  No SMP is payable until you have provided your employer with medical evidence of your expected date of confinement. This medical evidence should be in the form of a maternity certificate, which you can get from your doctor or midwife once you have reached the start of the 14th week before your EWC and must normally be produced to your employer no later than 3 weeks after the date on which your SMP was due to start.

3.8 *How does SMP tie in with contractual maternity pay?*
You may find that your contract of employment provides for you to receive some sort of maternity pay. Unfortunately this does not mean that you are entitled to both your contractual pay *and* SMP. You simply receive whichever payment is the larger.

3.9 *Problems with your SMP*
If your employer refuses to pay you SMP or you think he is paying you too little, ask for an explanation. If you are not happy with what your employer tells you, ask him for a written statement setting out his position. If you are not happy with that either, you can ask for an adjudication officer to decide on your entitlement. Contact your local social security office to find out how to do this.

If it turns out that you are not entitled to SMP, you may be able to get maternity allowance instead. Turn to Part 3 to investigate.

## 4. Statutory maternity leave

4.1 *What are my rights?*
If you satisfy the conditions set out in paragraph 4.2, you can take maternity leave without prejudicing your job. The maximum period of leave is approximately 40 weeks (slightly more if your baby is late, slightly less if your baby is early), starting with the beginning of the 11th week before the week in which your baby is due. You must return to work before the end of 29 weeks beginning with (and including) the week in which you had your baby. Upon your return to work, you are entitled to step back into your old shoes as far as seniority, pension rights, etc. are concerned.

4.2 *Do I qualify?*
To qualify for maternity leave, you must normally satisfy the following conditions:

- You must continue to be employed by your employer at least until immediately before the beginning of the 11th week before your EWC.
- You must have completed the requisite period of continuous service with your employer:

    Full-timers (16 hours or more a week): at least two years' continuous service by the beginning of the 11th week before your EWC.

    Part-timers (between 8 and 16 hours a week): at least five years' continuous service by the beginning of the 11th week before your EWC.

Note that those working fewer than 8 hours a week do not qualify, however long their service.

If you have been dismissed before the 11th week because your pregnancy made it unlawful for you to do your job or meant that you could not do it adequately, you will not be able to satisfy these conditions. However, you will still be entitled to return to work after your baby is born if you would have been employed for two years (full-timers) or five years (part-timers) had you been allowed to go on working up to the beginning of the 11th week.

4.3 *Steps you must take to protect your right to return to work*
In order to protect your right to return to work, you must negotiate a legal obstacle course. This involves giving your employer several notices. In each case, a simple letter will do very nicely providing it covers the relevant points.

- *Advance notice*
  At least 21 days before you stop work (or if that is not reasonably practicable, as soon as it is reasonably practicable), you must give your employer *written* notice stating:

  - that you are leaving to have a baby
  - when your expected week of confinement is
  - that you intend to return to work after the baby is born.

  Simply copy out the example on page 180 inserting your own details.
      If your baby arrives unexpectedly early, you may find yourself giving notice after it has been born. In this case, your notice should state:

  - that you are absent from work because you have had a baby
  - the date on which the baby was born
  - that you intend to return to work.

  If you have been dismissed because your pregnancy made it unlawful for you to do your job or meant that you could not do it adequately, you may not be able to give advance notice that you are leaving. What you must do, though, is to notify your employer (in writing if he so requests) before your dismissal takes effect or as soon thereafter as reasonably practicable that you intend to return to work.

- *Proof of your expected week of confinement*
  If your employer asks, you must produce for his inspection a maternity certificate from a doctor or midwife showing your expected week of confinement. You can get this certificate at any time after the beginning of the 14th week before your EWC.
- *Confirmation that you intend to return*
  Some mothers change their minds about returning to work after their baby is born. Your employer must give you 49 days after the beginning of your EWC to sample motherhood. He can then write to you requesting you to give him written confirmation of your intention to return. You must give confirmation within 14 days of receiving his request (or, if this is not reasonably practicable, as soon afterwards as is reasonably practicable). At this stage it is only necessary to say that you will be coming back; you do not have to stipulate when they should expect you. Do not let the dirty nappies take precedence over this bit of paperwork – if you do not do as you are told, you will lose your right to return to work.
- *Notice* as *to when you intend to return*
  At least 21 days before the day on which you intend to return to work, you must notify your employer in writing of the proposed date. Remember that, as your letter must actually reach your employer at least 21 days before your proposed starting date, you will need to post it a few days beforehand. The date you choose for your return is entirely up to you, providing it is before the end of the period of 29 weeks beginning with the week in which your baby was born.

### 4.4 *Your return*

Normally you will return to work on the day you have notified to your employer. However, there are one or two situations in which your return may be delayed by you or your employer. Notably:

- If you are ill at the end of the 29-week period, you can postpone your return for a further period of up to 4 weeks. To do this, you must produce a medical certificate to your employer before the date on which you are due back at work.
- Your employer can postpone your return for up to 4 weeks from the date on which you have said you are coming back, providing he gives you his reasons and tells you when he *will* allow you to return.

### 4.5 *How does my statutory maternity leave tie in with my rights under my contract of employment?*

You may find that you have a right to time off on maternity leave by virtue of your contract of employment, possibly with pay.

- If you qualify for statutory maternity leave as well as contractual maternity leave, you can pick and choose your rights according to whether you will do better under your contract or under the statutory scheme.
- If you do not qualify for statutory maternity leave for some reason, you will have no choice but to rely on your contractual rights. This was the position I was in when I had my first child. I was not entitled to any statutory maternity leave as I had been working for my employer for less than two years. However, my contract provided for a short period of maternity leave as long as I had completed at least one year of service, and I was therefore able to have about 4 months off and still return to my old job.

4.6 *What if my employer refuses to let me return to work?*
If the reason why your employer is refusing to take you back is because you have become redundant during your maternity leave and he cannot offer you suitable alternative work, you may be able to seek a redundancy payment. It is not possible to cover redundancy in this book; further information can be obtained from the Department of Employment's free booklet entitled *Redundancy Payments*. This should be available from Jobcentres and Unemployment Benefit Offices.

If, for some reason other than redundancy, your employer wrongly refuses to let you return to your old job (or, if that is not reasonably practicable, to a suitable alternative job), you can complain to an industrial tribunal that you have been unfairly dismissed and seek an order obliging your employer to take you on again or to pay you financial compensation (see Part 2, paragraph 6).

4.7 *Special Cases*

☆ *Small employers*
If, immediately before your maternity leave, your employer employed five or less employees (including you) and it is not reasonably practicable for him to permit you to return to work in your old job or a comparable one, you have no statutory right to return to work.

☆ *Excluded employments*
Certain employees are excluded from the right to return to work because of the nature of their employment, notably policewomen.

4.8 *If you are not sure whether you want to go back to work*
Many women are not sure whether they will want to go back to work
or not. This is perfectly understandable. If you feel like this, protect
your right to return by following the procedure set out in paragraph
4.3. This may seem unfair to your employer, but it is the only way in
which you can keep your options open. Make up your mind finally
when it is time to notify your employer of the date on which you
intend to return.

4.9 *Two babies in quick succession*
Gluttons for punishment who decide to have another baby soon after
returning from maternity leave will be pleased to know that the time
spent on maternity leave can be counted as part of a period of continuous employment. In other words, you do not have to put in a
completely fresh period of two years (full-timers) or five years (part-
timers) with your employer to qualify for protection from dismissal
because of your new pregnancy or indeed for further maternity
leave. Similarly, your time on maternity leave can be counted when
reckoning your entitlement to SMP.

## 5. What if I am off sick during my pregnancy?

If you have to have time off work because you are ill during your
pregnancy (for example, if you have to rest because you are threat-
ening to miscarry or you have high blood pressure), your normal
arrangements for sick pay will apply. You may therefore be entitled
to sick pay either under the statutory scheme or by virtue of your
contract of employment.

Your absence through sickness will not affect your maternity
rights providing it is clear that you have not actually resigned your
post. Your contract of employment normally continues even if you
are not able to be there to fulfil your duties under it.

## 6. Complaining to an industrial tribunal

6.1 *Time limits*
Normally you must make your complaint within three months.
When the three months start to run depends upon the nature of
the complaint:

- If you are complaining that you have been unreasonably
  refused time off for ante-natal care or that your employer
  has not paid you properly for your time off, the three-month
  period begins with the day of the appointment concerned.
- If you are complaining that you have been unfairly dismissed
  because of your pregnancy or a reason associated with it, the
  three months begins with the effective date of termination of

your employment (which generally means the date on which your notice expires).

- If you are complaining that you have been unfairly dismissed because your employer has refused to let you return to work at the end of your maternity leave, the three months begin with the day on which you intended to return.

The three-month time limit can be extended by the tribunal if it is satisfied that it was not reasonably practicable for you to present your complaint within the normal period.

### 6.2 How to complain

You can obtain the relevant form from a Jobcentre or Unemployment Benefit Office. They will also supply you with an explanatory leaflet telling you what to do.

Think carefully before you launch into a complaint. In particular, ask yourself the following questions:

☆ Have I done all I can to sort the matter out with my employer by agreement?

☆ Am I absolutely sure of my ground? If not, seek expert advice and help (for example from a Citizens' Advice Bureau, law centre or solicitor) before going any further. This is perhaps particularly important if you are claiming that you have been denied your right to return to work after your baby is born. The legal provisions on maternity leave are extremely complex and this book provides an outline only.

☆ Can I be bothered with the hassle? Is it worth it? It may well be if you want your job back, but perhaps not if it is just a couple of hours' pay that is at stake.

### 6.3 What can the tribunal do for me?

The orders that the tribunal can make depend upon the nature of your complaint:

- If you have been unreasonably refused time off for ante-natal care, your employer will be ordered to pay you compensation. The tribunal will establish your average hourly rate of pay, assess how long you should have been allowed off for your appointment and multiply one by the other to arrive at the amount you should receive as compensation. Your employer will have to pay this on top of any wages that you have already been paid under your contract.

- If you have been allowed time off for ante-natal care but not been paid properly, your employer will be ordered to pay you the money due.

- If you have been unfairly dismissed, your employer will be ordered to reinstate you in your old job or re-engage you in a comparable one, providing that this is what you want and that it is practicable for your employer to take you back. If neither re-engagement nor reinstatement is practicable, you will receive cash compensation.

# Part 3: Maternity allowance and sickness benefit

## 1. Maternity allowance

### 1.1 *What is it?*
Maternity allowance is a weekly benefit paid by social security.

### 1.2 *Identifying important dates*
To understand maternity allowance, you need to identify certain important dates. Turn to the calendar on page 177 and follow these instructions:

    ☆ Put a ring round the date you have been given as your expected date of confinement and label it 'Baby due'.

    ☆ Mark off the week (Sunday to Saturday inclusive) in which your expected week date of confinement falls. This is your expected week of confinement. Label it 'EWC'.

    ☆ Treating the week before your EWC as week 1, count back 14 weeks from your EWC. Put a ring round the 14th week (Sunday to Saturday inclusive) and label it '14th week before EWC'.

    ☆ Treating the week before your EWC as week 1, count back 11 weeks. Put a ring round the 11th week. Label it 'Earliest maternity allowance can start'.

    ☆ Treating the week before your EWC as week 1, count back 7 weeks. Put a line after the Saturday of the 7th week and label it 'Stop work by now to secure full maternity allowance'.

### 1.3 *Do I qualify?*
You cannot qualify for maternity allowance if you are entitled to SMP (see Part 2, paragraph 3).

In all other cases, whether or not you qualify will depend upon your work record and the national insurance contributions you have made. Broadly speaking, you need to have worked and paid class 1 or class 2 contributions for at least six months of the year preceding the 14th week before your EWC.

Do not waste too much time trying to work out whether you are eligible – if you think you might be, simply contact your local social security office and let them check for you. I was not expecting to get maternity allowance when I stopped work to have Andrew but I put in a claim anyway and was pleasantly surprised to find that I qualified.

## 1.4 *How do I claim?*

- *Form MA 1*
  A claim for maternity allowance must be made by sending form MA1 (which you can get from your local social security office or possibly from the ante-natal clinic) to your social security office.
- *Maternity certificate*
  If possible, you will need to send a maternity certificate with your claim. You can get one from your doctor or midwife once you have reached the 14th week before your EWC. If you have not yet got a maternity certificate, send in your claim anyway and forward the certificate separately later.
- *Form SMP1*
  If you are employed, check with your employer that you are not entitled to SMP before making your maternity allowance claim. If your employer says SMP is not payable, he will give you form SMP1 setting out his reasons. Send this to the DHSS with your form MA 1.
- *Birth certificate*
  If you make your claim after your baby is born, you will need to send his birth certificate with your claim unless your maternity certificate shows both your expected week of confinement and the actual day on which your baby was born.
- *Your national insurance contribution card*
  If you are self-employed and stamp your own card, this will need to be sent with your application.

## 1.5 *When to make your claim*

Claim as soon as possible after the beginning of the 14th week before your EWC. Do not delay even if you are still working – if you claim later than the end of the 4th week after your allowance should have started, you may lose part of your entitlement unless you can show that you had good cause for making a late claim.

## 1.6 *How much do I get?*

If you are entitled to maternity allowance, you will get a payment book which you can cash each week at a named post office. Most people get the standard weekly rate (currently £33.20 per week), though you can claim extra money if you have an adult dependant.

You do not have to pay tax on maternity allowance.

## 1.7 *When do maternity allowance payments start?*

Your maternity allowance cannot start until:

☆ you have stopped work, and
☆ you have reached at least the 11th week before your EWC.

So, if you have stopped work by the 11th week before your EWC, your maternity allowance will start from that week. But if you decide to work later into your pregnancy, all you will get from your Social Security Office in response to your maternity allowance claim will be a form confirming that you are entitled to an allowance and asking you to notify them when you stop work so that payments can start at that point.

Read paragraph 1.8 before deciding when to give up work – you may lose out if you continue working for too long.

### 1.8 *The payment period*

Maternity allowance is paid for a maximum of 18 weeks. This divides up into:

> ☆ a core period of 13 weeks, which starts with the 6th week before your EWC;
> ☆ 5 floating weeks, which you can take before or after the core period or partly before and partly after, depending on when you finish work.

This means that, if you want to claim your full 18 weeks' maternity allowance, you must stop work by the beginning of the 6th week before your EWC. For every week or part week you work after that point, you will lose a week's allowance.

## 2. Sickness benefit

If you do not qualify for SMP or maternity allowance, you may be entitled to sickness benefit towards the end of your pregnancy and for a short time after your baby is born. Like maternity allowance, sickness benefit is a weekly benefit paid by social security. The present rate is £33.20 a week. Entitlement depends upon your national insurance contributions.

If your claim for maternity allowance is unsuccessful, you should be considered automatically for sickness benefit. However, you might like to ask about this specifically to be on the safe side.

# Part 4: Calendars, sample letter and checklist

## 1989

**Jan**

| S | M | T | W | T | F | S |
|---|---|---|---|---|---|---|
| 1 | 2 | 3 | 4 | 5 | 6 | 7 |
| 8 | 9 | 10 | 11 | 12 | 13 | 14 |
| 15 | 16 | 17 | 18 | 19 | 20 | 21 |
| 22 | 23 | 24 | 25 | 26 | 27 | 28 |
| 29 | 30 | 31 | | | | |

**Feb**

| S | M | T | W | T | F | S |
|---|---|---|---|---|---|---|
| | | | 1 | 2 | 3 | 4 |
| 5 | 6 | 7 | 8 | 9 | 10 | 11 |
| 12 | 13 | 14 | 15 | 16 | 17 | 18 |
| 19 | 20 | 21 | 22 | 23 | 24 | 25 |
| 26 | 27 | 28 | | | | |

**Mar**

| S | M | T | W | T | F | S |
|---|---|---|---|---|---|---|
| | | | 1 | 2 | 3 | 4 |
| 5 | 6 | 7 | 8 | 9 | 10 | 11 |
| 12 | 13 | 14 | 15 | 16 | 17 | 18 |
| 19 | 20 | 21 | 22 | 23 | 24 | 25 |
| 26 | 27 | 28 | 29 | 30 | 31 | |

**Apr**

| S | M | T | W | T | F | S |
|---|---|---|---|---|---|---|
| | | | | | | 1 |
| 2 | 3 | 4 | 5 | 6 | 7 | 8 |
| 9 | 10 | 11 | 12 | 13 | 14 | 15 |
| 16 | 17 | 18 | 19 | 20 | 21 | 22 |
| 23 | 24 | 25 | 26 | 27 | 28 | 29 |
| 30 | | | | | | |

**May**

| S | M | T | W | T | F | S |
|---|---|---|---|---|---|---|
| | 1 | 2 | 3 | 4 | 5 | 6 |
| 7 | 8 | 9 | 10 | 11 | 12 | 13 |
| 14 | 15 | 16 | 17 | 18 | 19 | 20 |
| 21 | 22 | 23 | 24 | 25 | 26 | 27 |
| 28 | 29 | 30 | 31 | | | |

**June**

| S | M | T | W | T | F | S |
|---|---|---|---|---|---|---|
| | | | | 1 | 2 | 3 |
| 4 | 5 | 6 | 7 | 8 | 9 | 10 |
| 11 | 12 | 13 | 14 | 15 | 16 | 17 |
| 18 | 19 | 20 | 21 | 22 | 23 | 24 |
| 25 | 26 | 27 | 28 | 29 | 30 | |

**July**

| S | M | T | W | T | F | S |
|---|---|---|---|---|---|---|
| | | | | | | 1 |
| 2 | 3 | 4 | 5 | 6 | 7 | 8 |
| 9 | 10 | 11 | 12 | 13 | 14 | 15 |
| 16 | 17 | 18 | 19 | 20 | 21 | 22 |
| 23 | 24 | 25 | 26 | 27 | 28 | 29 |
| 30 | 31 | | | | | |

**Aug**

| S | M | T | W | T | F | S |
|---|---|---|---|---|---|---|
| | | 1 | 2 | 3 | 4 | 5 |
| 6 | 7 | 8 | 9 | 10 | 11 | 12 |
| 13 | 14 | 15 | 16 | 17 | 18 | 19 |
| 20 | 21 | 22 | 23 | 24 | 25 | 26 |
| 27 | 28 | 29 | 30 | 31 | | |

**Sept**

| S | M | T | W | T | F | S |
|---|---|---|---|---|---|---|
| | | | | | 1 | 2 |
| 3 | 4 | 5 | 6 | 7 | 8 | 9 |
| 10 | 11 | 12 | 13 | 14 | 15 | 16 |
| 17 | 18 | 19 | 20 | 21 | 22 | 23 |
| 24 | 25 | 26 | 27 | 28 | 29 | 30 |

**Oct**

| S | M | T | W | T | F | S |
|---|---|---|---|---|---|---|
| 1 | 2 | 3 | 4 | 5 | 6 | 7 |
| 8 | 9 | 10 | 11 | 12 | 13 | 14 |
| 15 | 16 | 17 | 18 | 19 | 20 | 21 |
| 22 | 23 | 24 | 25 | 26 | 27 | 28 |
| 29 | 30 | 31 | | | | |

**Nov**

| S | M | T | W | T | F | S |
|---|---|---|---|---|---|---|
| | | | 1 | 2 | 3 | 4 |
| 5 | 6 | 7 | 8 | 9 | 10 | 11 |
| 12 | 13 | 14 | 15 | 16 | 17 | 18 |
| 19 | 20 | 21 | 22 | 23 | 24 | 25 |
| 26 | 27 | 28 | 29 | 30 | | |

**Dec**

| S | M | T | W | T | F | S |
|---|---|---|---|---|---|---|
| | | | | | 1 | 2 |
| 3 | 4 | 5 | 6 | 7 | 8 | 9 |
| 10 | 11 | 12 | 13 | 14 | 15 | 16 |
| 17 | 18 | 19 | 20 | 21 | 22 | 23 |
| 24 | 25 | 26 | 27 | 28 | 29 | 30 |
| 31 | | | | | | |

# 1990

## Jan
| S | M | T | W | T | F | S |
|---|---|---|---|---|---|---|
|   | 1 | 2 | 3 | 4 | 5 | 6 |
| 7 | 8 | 9 | 10 | 11 | 12 | 13 |
| 14 | 15 | 16 | 17 | 18 | 19 | 20 |
| 21 | 22 | 23 | 24 | 25 | 26 | 27 |
| 28 | 29 | 30 | 31 |   |   |   |

## Feb
| S | M | T | W | T | F | S |
|---|---|---|---|---|---|---|
|   |   |   |   | 1 | 2 | 3 |
| 4 | 5 | 6 | 7 | 8 | 9 | 10 |
| 11 | 12 | 13 | 14 | 15 | 16 | 17 |
| 18 | 19 | 20 | 21 | 22 | 23 | 24 |
| 25 | 26 | 27 | 28 |   |   |   |

## Mar
| S | M | T | W | T | F | S |
|---|---|---|---|---|---|---|
|   |   |   |   | 1 | 2 | 3 |
| 4 | 5 | 6 | 7 | 8 | 9 | 10 |
| 11 | 12 | 13 | 14 | 15 | 16 | 17 |
| 18 | 19 | 20 | 21 | 22 | 23 | 24 |
| 25 | 26 | 27 | 28 | 29 | 30 | 31 |

## Apr
| S | M | T | W | T | F | S |
|---|---|---|---|---|---|---|
| 1 | 2 | 3 | 4 | 5 | 6 | 7 |
| 8 | 9 | 10 | 11 | 12 | 13 | 14 |
| 15 | 16 | 17 | 18 | 19 | 20 | 21 |
| 22 | 23 | 24 | 25 | 26 | 27 | 28 |
| 29 | 30 |   |   |   |   |   |

## May
| S | M | T | W | T | F | S |
|---|---|---|---|---|---|---|
|   |   | 1 | 2 | 3 | 4 | 5 |
| 6 | 7 | 8 | 9 | 10 | 11 | 12 |
| 13 | 14 | 15 | 16 | 17 | 18 | 19 |
| 20 | 21 | 22 | 23 | 24 | 25 | 26 |
| 27 | 28 | 29 | 30 | 31 |   |   |

## June
| S | M | T | W | T | F | S |
|---|---|---|---|---|---|---|
|   |   |   |   |   | 1 | 2 |
| 3 | 4 | 5 | 6 | 7 | 8 | 9 |
| 10 | 11 | 12 | 13 | 14 | 15 | 16 |
| 17 | 18 | 19 | 20 | 21 | 22 | 23 |
| 24 | 25 | 26 | 27 | 28 | 29 | 30 |

## July
| S | M | T | W | T | F | S |
|---|---|---|---|---|---|---|
| 1 | 2 | 3 | 4 | 5 | 6 | 7 |
| 8 | 9 | 10 | 11 | 12 | 13 | 14 |
| 15 | 16 | 17 | 18 | 19 | 20 | 21 |
| 22 | 23 | 24 | 25 | 26 | 27 | 28 |
| 29 | 30 | 31 |   |   |   |   |

## Aug
| S | M | T | W | T | F | S |
|---|---|---|---|---|---|---|
|   |   |   | 1 | 2 | 3 | 4 |
| 5 | 6 | 7 | 8 | 9 | 10 | 11 |
| 12 | 13 | 14 | 15 | 16 | 17 | 18 |
| 19 | 20 | 21 | 22 | 23 | 24 | 25 |
| 26 | 27 | 28 | 29 | 30 | 31 |   |

## Sept
| S | M | T | W | T | F | S |
|---|---|---|---|---|---|---|
|   |   |   |   |   |   | 1 |
| 2 | 3 | 4 | 5 | 6 | 7 | 8 |
| 9 | 10 | 11 | 12 | 13 | 14 | 15 |
| 16 | 17 | 18 | 19 | 20 | 21 | 22 |
| 23 | 24 | 25 | 26 | 27 | 28 | 29 |
| 30 |   |   |   |   |   |   |

## Oct
| S | M | T | W | T | F | S |
|---|---|---|---|---|---|---|
|   | 1 | 2 | 3 | 4 | 5 | 6 |
| 7 | 8 | 9 | 10 | 11 | 12 | 13 |
| 14 | 15 | 16 | 17 | 18 | 19 | 20 |
| 21 | 22 | 23 | 24 | 25 | 26 | 27 |
| 28 | 29 | 30 | 31 |   |   |   |

## Nov
| S | M | T | W | T | F | S |
|---|---|---|---|---|---|---|
|   |   |   |   | 1 | 2 | 3 |
| 4 | 5 | 6 | 7 | 8 | 9 | 10 |
| 11 | 12 | 13 | 14 | 15 | 16 | 17 |
| 18 | 19 | 20 | 21 | 22 | 23 | 24 |
| 25 | 26 | 27 | 28 | 29 | 30 |   |

## Dec
| S | M | T | W | T | F | S |
|---|---|---|---|---|---|---|
|   |   |   |   |   |   | 1 |
| 2 | 3 | 4 | 5 | 6 | 7 | 8 |
| 9 | 10 | 11 | 12 | 13 | 14 | 15 |
| 16 | 17 | 18 | 19 | 20 | 21 | 22 |
| 23 | 24 | 25 | 26 | 27 | 28 | 29 |
| 30 | 31 |   |   |   |   |   |

## Sample annotated calendar

*26 weeks continuous employment starts now*

### 1989

**Jan**

| S | M | T | W | T | F | S |
|---|---|---|---|---|---|---|
| 1 | 2 | 3 | 4 | 5 | 6 | 7 |
| 8 | 9 | 10 | 11 | 12 | 13 | 14 |
| 15 | 16 | 17 | 18 | 19 | 20 | 21 |
| 22 | 23 | 24 | 25 | 26 | 27 | 28 |
| 29 | 30 | 31 | | | | |

**Feb**

| S | M | T | W | T | F | S |
|---|---|---|---|---|---|---|
| | | | 1 | 2 | 3 | 4 |
| 5 | 6 | 7 | 8 | 9 | 10 | 11 |
| 12 | 13 | 14 | 15 | 16 | 17 | 18 |
| 19 | 20 | 21 | 22 | 23 | 24 | 25 |
| 26 | 27 | 28 | | | | |

**Mar**

| S | M | T | W | T | F | S |
|---|---|---|---|---|---|---|
| | | | 1 | 2 | 3 | 4 |
| 5 | 6 | 7 | 8 | 9 | 10 | 11 |
| 12 | 13 | 14 | 15 | 16 | 17 | 18 |
| 19 | 20 | 21 | 22 | 23 | 24 | 25 |
| 26 | 27 | 28 | 29 | 30 | 31 | |

**Apr**

| S | M | T | W | T | F | S |
|---|---|---|---|---|---|---|
| | | | | | | 1 |
| 2 | 3 | 4 | 5 | 6 | 7 | 8 |
| 9 | 10 | 11 | 12 | 13 | 14 | 15 |
| 16 | 17 | 18 | 19 | 20 | 21 | 22 |
| 23 | 24 | 25 | 26 | 27 | 28 | 29 |
| 30 | | | | | | |

**May**

| S | M | T | W | T | F | S |
|---|---|---|---|---|---|---|
| | 1 | 2 | 3 | 4 | 5 | 6 |
| 7 | 8 | 9 | 10 | 11 | 12 | 13 |
| 14 | 15 | 16 | 17 | 18 | 19 | 20 |
| 21 | 22 | 23 | 24 | 25 | 26 | 27 |
| 28 | 29 | 30 | 31 | | | |

**June**

| S | M | T | W | T | F | S |
|---|---|---|---|---|---|---|
| | | | | 1 | 2 | 3 |
| 4 | 5 | 6 | 7 | 8 | 9 | 10 |
| 11 | 12 | 13 | 14 | 15 | 16 | 17 |
| 18 | 19 | 20 | 21 | 22 | 23 | 24 |
| 25 | 26 | 27 | 28 | 29 | 30 | |

**July**

| S | M | T | W | T | F | S |
|---|---|---|---|---|---|---|
| | | | | | | 1 |
| 2 | 3 | 4 | 5 | 6 | 7 | 8 |
| 9 | 10 | 11 | 12 | 13 | 14 | 15 |
| 16 | 17 | 18 | 19 | 20 | 21 | 22 |
| 23 | 24 | 25 · 26 | 27 | 28 | 29 | |
| 30 | 31 | | | | | |

**Aug**

| S | M | T | W | T | F | S |
|---|---|---|---|---|---|---|
| | | 1 | 2 | 3 | 4 | 5 |
| 6 | 7 | 8 | 9 | 10 | 11 | 12 |
| 13 | 14 | 15 | 16 | 17 | 18 | 19 |
| 20 | 21 | 22 | 23 | 24 | 25 | 26 |
| 27 | 28 | 29 | 30 | 31 | | |

**Sept**

| S | M | T | W | T | F | S |
|---|---|---|---|---|---|---|
| | | | | | 1 | 2 |
| 3 | 4 | 5 | 6 | 7 | 8 | 9 |
| 10 | 11 | 12 | 13 | 14 | 15 | 16 |
| 17 | 18 | 19 | 20 | 21 | 22 | 23 |
| 24 | 25 | 26 | 27 | 28 | 29 | 30 |

*QW – don't give up work before the begining of this week*

*earliest SMP can start*

**Oct**

| S | M | T | W | T | F | S |
|---|---|---|---|---|---|---|
| 1 | 2 | 3 | 4 | 5 | 6 | 7 |
| 8 | 9 | 10 | 11 | 12 | 13 | 14 |
| 15 | 16 | 17 | 18 | 19 | 20 | 21 |
| 22 | 23 | 24 | 25 | 26 | 27 | 28 |
| 29 | 30 | 31 | | | | |

**Nov**

| S | M | T | W | T | F | S |
|---|---|---|---|---|---|---|
| | | | 1 | 2 | 3 | 4 |
| 5 | 6 | 7 | 8 | 9 | 10 | 11 |
| 12 | 13 | 14 | 15 | 16 | 17 | 18 |
| 19 | 20 | 21 | 22 | 23 | 24 | 25 |
| 26 | 27 | 28 | 29 | 30 | | |

**Dec**

| S | M | T | W | T | F | S |
|---|---|---|---|---|---|---|
| | | | | | 1 | 2 |
| 3 | 4 | 5 | 6 | 7 | 8 | 9 |
| 10 | 11 | 12 | 13 | 14 | 15 | 16 |
| 17 | 18 | 19 | 20 | 21 | 22 | 23 |
| 24 | 25 | 26 | 27 | 28 | 29 | 30 |
| 31 | | | | | | |

*EWC*

*stop work by now to secure full SMP*

*Baby due*

## Letter to employer for maternity leave purposes

> 10 Acacia Avenue,
> Scunthorpe
>
> 10 Oct 1989
>
> I. Fairboss
> ABC Ltd
> Fieldview Industrial Estate
> Scunthorpe
>
>
> Dear Mr Fairboss,
>
> I am writing to inform you that I shall be absent from work because I am having a baby. My expected week of confinement is the week beginning        . I intend to return to work with ABC Ltd after the baby is born.
>
>
> Your sincerely,
>
>
> Mrs A. N. Mother

# Checklist of important dates for your diary

This checklist should help you to make sure that you do not miss any important deadlines. Insert your own dates in the left-hand column. Your EWC is the week (Sunday to Saturday inclusive) during which your are due to have your baby. All ante-natal dates are reckoned backwards from your EWC, but be careful when reckoning post-natal dates to identify the correct starting point as this varies.

| *Wk beginning* | | |
|---|---|---|
| | Conception onwards | Free prescriptions and dental treatment. Obtain Form FW8 from your GP or midwife. Right not to be unreasonably refused time off for ante-natal care. Obtain certificate confirming pregnancy and be prepared to show appointment card for appointments after the first. |
| | At least 3 weeks before stopping work | Give written notice to your employer of your EWC and that you will be stopping work but intend to return (for SMP and maternity leave purposes). |
| | 15th wk before EWC | Qualifying week for SMP – do not give up work before the beginning of this week if you wish to claim. Also work this week if you want to claim maternity allowance. |
| | 14th wk before EWC | Obtain maternity certificate from doctor or midwife and produce it to your employer (for SMP and maternity leave purposes). If you cannot get SMP, claim maternity allowance. |
| | 13th wk before EWC | |
| | 12th wk before EWC | Work up to the end of this week to secure maternity leave. |

| | |
|---|---|
| 11th wk before EWC | Earliest SMP/maternity allowance can start. |
| 10th wk before EWC | |
| 9th wk before EWC | |
| 8th wk before EWC | |
| 7th wk before EWC | Must stop work at the end of this week to secure full SMP/maternity allowance. |
| 6th wk before EWC | Latest start date for full SMP/maternity allowance. |
| 5th wk before EWC | |
| 4th wk before EWC | |
| 3rd wk before EWC | |
| 2nd wk before EWC | |

Expected week of confinement (EWC)

| | |
|---|---|
| Actual birth date | Register birth within 6 weeks (3 in Scotland). Claim child benefit (and one parent benefit) once you have the birth certificate. |
| 7th week after EWC | Your employer can write asking you to confirm your intention to return to work. Reply within 14 days if he does so. |
| At least 21 days before the day on which you intend to return to work | Notify your employer in writing of your proposed return date. |

| 29 wks from the beginning of the week in which your baby was born | Must return to work before the end of the 29th week unless you contract allows you longer or you are ill or your employer postpones your return. |

# Part 5: Further Information and Advice

## 1. Free leaflets

1.1 *What is available?*
The three principal official guides are:

- *Babies and benefits*
  This DHSS leaflet provides lots of useful information for the expectant or new mother about social security benefits, etc. It also incudes a checklist setting out clearly what you must do to make sure that you get all the benefits to which you are entitled and that you protect your right to return to work after the baby is born.
- *Maternity benefits*
  Another DHSS guide giving more comprehensive details about SMP and other maternity benefits.
- *Employment rights for the expectant mother*
  This booklet, produced by the Department of Employment, explains your right to paid time off for ante-natal care, your right to return to work, etc.

The DHSS also produce detailed leaflets on particular benefits, for example child benefit, NHS prescriptions, etc.

Other organisations also produce free literature, for example *Pregnant at Work* and *Money for Mothers and Babies* from the Maternity Alliance. Those on their own might be interested in buying *Single and Pregnant, a guide to benefits for single mothers* from the National Council for One-Parent Families. For contact details, see the Address Book.

### 1.2 *How to get hold of the official guides*

DHSS leaflets can be obtained from social security offices and some post offices or by post from the DHSS Leaflets Unit (address in the Address Book).

The Department of Employment booklet can be obtained from some Jobcentres and Unemployment Benefit offices.

## 2. More personal information and advice

If you want to talk to someone about your rights, there are the following possibilities:

- *Freeline Social Security*
  This is the DHSS free telephone enquiry service dealing with general queries about social security benefits – ring 0800 666555.
- *Your local social security office*
  Specific queries about benefits should be directed to your local social security office. Try to avoid visiting the office in person – you might waste hours waiting in an interminable queue. Ring up or write with your query instead.
- *Regional offices of the Advisory, Conciliation and Arbitration Service (ACAS)*
  ACAS will advise you on all your employment rights except with regard to SMP (see the Address Book for how to contact ACAS or get the address and phone number of your ACAS regional office from the leaflet *Employment rights for the expectant mother*).
- *Your trade union, a Citizens' Advice Bureau, local law centres, the Maternity Alliance* (address and phone number in the Address Book), *The National Council for Civil Liberties Women's Rights Unit* (address and phone number in the Address Book) *or a solicitor.*

## 3. Books

There are lots of books on employment law, DHSS benefits, etc. Some are rather technical but the *Rights guide to non-means-tested social security benefits* gives an excellent straightforward résumé of SMP, maternity allowance, child benefit and one parent benefit. It is updated every year and can be obtained from bookshops or direct from the Child Poverty Action Group (address and phone number in the Address Book). You might also find *Maternity Rights at Work* by Jean Coussins, Lyn Durward and Ruth Evans useful. This is available from the National Council for Civil Liberties (address and phone number in the Address Book).

# 2

# Childcare – What is on offer?

| Option | Description | Cost | Further information |
|--------|-------------|------|---------------------|
| **Relative(s)** | Basically self-explanatory. Sometimes mum and dad manage between them without any outside help. Sometimes members of the wider family such as grandparents, uncles and aunts are roped in. Some relatives provide a comprehensive backup service including shopping, cooking, cleaning, etc., as well as looking after the children. | Entirely up to you and the relative concerned. Some would not dream of accepting payment, others expect to be paid the going rate for the job. | Chapter 5 |
| **Au pair** | A foreign girl, aged between 17 and 27, who comes to live in as part of the family and, in return for pocket money, should help out around the house and lend a hand with the children. Usefulness limited by requirement of very generous time off. Not a sensible option for a full-time working mother with young children but may suit part-timers or mothers with school-age children. | Will expect upwards of £25 per week plus board and lodging | Chapter 6 |
| **Child-minder** | Looks after your child in her own home. Though there is no formal training for the job, most childminders are mothers | Charges set by minder herself. As a guide, the minimum charge for one child for a full week of up | Chapters 7 and 9<br><br>*continued* |

themselves and well used to all aspects of child care. Some also have experience of working with children in other capacities, e.g. as nursery nurses, nannies or teachers. Most minders work conventional hours (say 8 a.m. to 6 p.m.) but with luck you may be able to find one who is flexible enough to fit in with the most outlandish timetable, and it is not unknown for a minder to look after her charges overnight occasionally.

Service not restricted to under-5s – some minders will take older children before and after school and during school holidays.

to 40 hours is likely to be £35, and some minders charge over £50 per week. If you pay by the hour, expect to pay at least 90p per hour or part hour.

**Day Nursery/ creche**

Not to be confused with pre-school playgroups and nursery schools. Day nurseries provide a full-time childcare service. They normally open sufficiently early for parents to drop their children off on the way to work and then look after the children – providing meals, rest facilities and entertainment – until the end of the working day. Some are open all the year round apart from bank holidays, some close down for a few weeks' annual holiday.

Age limits vary. Some nurseries take tiny babies; some accept school-age children during the school holidays.

Fees range widely from nothing at all (where a needy family gets a place in a local authority nursery) to quite a sizeable chunk of your earnings, particularly if you have more than one child there. Expect regional variations. As a rough guide, here in Yorkshire, the rate for a full-time place ranges from approximately £30 to £55 per week.

Chapters 8 and 9

*continued*

| | | | |
|---|---|---|---|
| **Mother's help** | Provides general household assistance, in theory, including most things from light cleaning and cooking to child care. Some mother's helps will take sole charge of the children for you (as opposed to just helping you with them), others are unwilling or cannot be trusted with the responsibility.<br><br>Can live in (possibly going home for weekends) or come in daily. | Difficult to say as wages vary widely. Agencies quote figures starting at about £55 per week gross, though you may find a girl who will settle for less. | Chapter 10 |
| **Nanny** | Experienced child care in your own home plus child-related housework such as the children's laundry, looking after their bedrooms, cooking their meals. Should be competent to take sole charge of the children right from the word go, probably even overnight if you need it. Normally will not touch ordinary housework.<br><br>Can live in (possibly going home at weekends) or come in daily. | Varies enormously according to area, experience, hours, duties, perks, etc. Agencies quote figures starting at about £90 p/wk gross. | Chapter 10 |
| **Shared nanny/ mother's help** | Sharing a nanny/ mother's help with another working mother cuts the cost dramatically. You can tailor the arrangement to your particular requirements. Two full-timers could club together to employ a girl to look after both sets of children en masse; two | Might expect slightly more than a nanny/ mother's help working solely for one family, but you only have to contribute part of her wage. Exact contributions will depend on what you each get in terms of service, convenience, etc. | Chapter 10 |

*continued*

187

part-timers could
take it in turns
to have exclusive
use of the nanny/
mother's help, and
so on.

**A bit of everything**

Many mothers put
together a
package – dad
drops off at
nursery school,
granny collects
and provides
lunch, a friend
copes with the
afternoon, etc.
etc.

Great cost in
nervous energy
(so many things
to organise and
so many things
that can go wrong),
but can be
economical in
money terms.

# 3

# National Childminding Association: Contract/agreement between Parents and Registered Childminder

NAME OF CHILDMINDER: _____    NAME OF CHILD: _____

ADDRESS: _____    ADDRESS: _____

_____    _____

TELEPHONE: _____    TELEPHONE: _____

REGISTERED BY: _____
    Social Services Department

NAME OF PARENT RESPONSIBLE FOR PAYMENT: _____

DATE THE CHILDMINDING ARRANGEMENT IS TO START: _____

HOURS: From _____ am/pm To _____ am/pm

DAYS: _____

MEALS TO BE PROVIDED: _____

| FEES: | | | |
|---|---|---|---|
| | Weekly | £ _____ | per week |
| | Hourly | £ _____ | per hour |
| | Daily (maximum 8 hours) | £ _____ | per day |
| | Overtime (after ____ pm) | £ _____ | per hour |
| | Unsocial hours (before 8am or after 6pm) | £ _____ | per hour |
| | Occasional minding | £ _____ | per hour |
| | Weekends or Statutory Public Holidays | £ _____ | per hour |

CHARGES FOR ABSENCE:

| | | |
|---|---|---|
| Due to child's or parent's sickness | £ _____ | |
| Due to childminder's sickness | £ _____ | |
| Parent(s)' occasional days off | £ _____ | |
| Parent(s)' annual holidays ( ____ wks/yr) | £ _____ | |
| Childminder's annual holiday ( ____ wks/yr) | £ _____ | |
| On Statutory Public Holidays | £ _____ | |

PAY DAY: _____ in advance

NOTICE REQUIRED OF HOLIDAYS (on both sides) _____

NOTICE REQUIRED OF TERMINATION OF THIS CONTRACT _____ WEEKS OR FULL FEE IN LIEU OF NOTICE (this applies to both minder and parent).

PARENTS TO PROVIDE: _____

PLAYGROUP FEES TO BE PAID BY: _____

CHILDMINDER CAN TAKE CHILD ON OUTINGS: _____

ANY SPECIAL ARRANGEMENTS: _____

This agreement is subject to review every ____ months. Date of next review _____

SIGNED: _____ (parent) Date: _____

SIGNED: _____ (childminder) Date: _____

please note that childminders cannot normally undertake the care of sick children

# 4

---

# National Childminding Association: Record Of Information About A Minded Child

### RECORD OF INFORMATION ABOUT A MINDED CHILD

**To be completed by the parent(s) and handed to the childminder**

CHILD'S NAME_____

DATE OF BIRTH_____

HOME ADDRESS_____

_____ TEL. NO._____

MOTHER'S NAME_____

MOTHER'S PLACE OF WORK_____

_____ TEL. NO._____

FATHER'S NAME_____

FATHER'S PLACE OF WORK_____

_____ TEL. NO._____

WHO TO CONTACT IN AN EMERGENCY_____

NAME OF PERSON WHO WILL COLLECT CHILD_____

CHILD'S DOCTOR_____

ADDRESS_____

_____ TEL. NO._____

IMMUNISATIONS/VACCINATIONS_____

_____

INFECTIOUS ILLNESSES_____

HEALTH CLINIC_____

_____ TEL. NO._____

HEALTH VISITOR_____

IS CHILDMINDER TO TAKE CHILD TO CLINIC?_____

ANY SPECIAL DIET, ALLERGIES, HEALTH PROBLEMS ETC._____

_____

ANYTHING ELSE THE CHILDMINDER SHOULD KNOW ABOUT YOUR CHILD_____

_____

_____

Details of any serious accidents which occur while the child is in the care of the childminder can be recorded on the back of this form.

**NATIONAL CHILDMINDING ASSOCIATION**
**8 Masons Hill, Bromley, Kent, BR2 9EY. Telephone: 01-464 6164**

# 5

# Nanny or mother's help: *Job profile*

**Degree of responsibility for children**
Extra pair of hands, mother always present          .....
Extra pair of hands, mother occasionally          .....
absent for short periods
In charge whilst mother works at home          .....
Sole charge: for a few hours at a stretch          .....
              whole days          .....
              overnight          .....
              several nights          .....
Early mornings and breakfasts          .....
Bathtime          .....
Getting up in the night          .....
Other ...................................................................................
......................................................................................

**Child-related housework**
Required as follows:
children's washing          .....
children's ironing          .....
tidying children's bedrooms          .....
cleaning children's bedrooms          .....
tidying playroom          .....
cleaning playroom          .....
children's food shopping          .....
cooking children's meals          .....
   and washing up
chauffeuring to school,
   clinic, etc.          .....
shopping for
   children's clothes          .....
other – specify...............................................................
......................................................................................
......................................................................................
None required          .....

**Other housework**
Required as follows:
bedmaking          .....
tidying          .....
cleaning including the rotten          .....

jobs e.g. oven, loos, kitchen
floor
light cleaning                             .....

washing                                   .....

ironing            .....

shopping           .....

cooking           .....

responsibility for room if living in    .....

other – specify.................................................................

............................................................................................

None required           .....

## Household organisation

e.g. chivvying other help (cleaner, gardener, etc.), sorting out freezer, posting letters, contacting plumbers, etc. – specify ...........................

............................................................................................

............................................................................................

## Other

e.g. typing business correspondence or mucking out the horse – specify ...............................................................................

............................................................................................

............................................................................................

## Live in/live out

Live in all week           .....

Live in weekdays, go home weekends    .....

Come in daily           .....

Other – specify...............................................................................

............................................................................................

## Hours

............................................................................................

## Babysitting requirements

............................................................................................

............................................................................................

............................................................................................

## Minimum qualifications/experience

............................................................................................

............................................................................................

## Target price           £   per wk gross/net

## Proposed perks

e.g. use of car, free use of chalet abroad for own holidays, own self-contained flat – specify .................................................................

............................................................................................

# 6

# Nanny or mother's help: Contract of Employment

NAME OF EMPLOYER ...............................................................
ADDRESS...............................................................................
..........................................................................................
..........................................................................................
TELEPHONE NUMBER ..............................................................
NAME OF NANNY/MOTHER'S HELP............................................
ADDRESS...............................................................................
..........................................................................................
..........................................................................................
TELEPHONE NUMBER ..............................................................

POSITION IN WHICH EMPLOYED (i.e. 'nanny', 'mother's help,'
etc.).....................................................................................
ARRANGEMENTS WITH REGARD TO TRIAL PERIOD..............
..........................................................................................
OFFICIAL STARTING DATE .......................................................
PERIOD OF EMPLOYMENT (specifying the date on which the con-
tract expires if it is for a fixed term) .........................................
..........................................................................................
NOTICE TO BE GIVEN BY EMPLOYER.......................................
NOTICE TO BE GIVEN BY NANNY/MOTHER'S HELP ..............
DUTIES ................................................................................
..........................................................................................
..........................................................................................
..........................................................................................
..........................................................................................

HOURS OF WORK ...................................................................
BABYSITTING REQUIRED AS PART OF STANDARD
CONTRACT............................................................................
..........................................................................................
PLACE OF WORK (if you have more than one base or travel a lot,
or in cases of nanny sharing) ....................................................
..........................................................................................
SITUATIONS IN WHICH OVERTIME PAY WILL BE PAID........
..........................................................................................
..........................................................................................
STANDARD RATE OF PAY (specifying arrangements for
deduction of tax and NIC) .......................................................

OVERTIME RATE.............................................................................

WHEN PAYMENT WILL BE MADE (weekly/monthly/in
arrears, etc.) ..................................................................................

................................................................................................

OTHER BENEFITS (accommodation/meals at work/use of car/petrol
money, etc.)....................................................................................

................................................................................................

HOLIDAYS (specifying how many days/weeks holiday and
arrangements as to when this may be taken, which public holidays
will be allowed, holiday pay entitlement).............................................

................................................................................................

................................................................................................

SICKNESS (specifying arrangements for sick pay and sick leave or,
if there are no contractual arrangements, stating that fact)....................

................................................................................................

................................................................................................

MATERNITY AND OTHER SPECIAL LEAVE .............................

................................................................................................

SPECIAL ARRANGEMENTS...........................................................

................................................................................................

................................................................................................

................................................................................................

Note: there are no terms as to pensions or pension schemes

SIGNED ...................................................................(EMPLOYER)
SIGNED ...........................................(NANNY/MOTHER'S HELP)
DATED...........................................................................................

Notes for guidance:
- *Arrangements for trial period*
  More about this on pages 89–90.
- *Period of employment*
  You can leave this open-ended if you want, or you can engage
  the nanny for a fixed period, say one or two years. The only
  real effect of a fixed-term contract is psychological. It does
  not, in fact, prevent you dismissing an unsuitable nanny during the stipulated period, nor does it help if the nanny herself simply ups and offs during the contract term. Mentally
  though, both parties are geared up to a certain commitment
  to each other and this may lead to a greater stability over the
  period of the fixed term. The disadvantage is that the nanny
  may look upon the end of the stipulated period as a natural
  opportunity to move on and have a change, which is fine if

you have both had enough of each other, but not so good if she has turned out to be a treasure and you desperately want to keep her.

● *Notice*

Unless your nanny has been guilty of gross misconduct, she is entitled to notice from you as follows:

| *Period of employment with you* | *Notice required* |
|---|---|
| 1st month | No minimum period |
| 1 month or more but less than 2 years | Not less than 1 week |
| 2 years or more but less than 12 years | 1 week for every year of employment |
| 12 years or more | Not less than 12 weeks |

After she has been employed with you for a month, you are entitled by law to 1 week's notice from the nanny.

These are the minimum notice periods. You can agree more generous provisions if you wish – you will probably want at least 1 month's formal notice either way. Ask the nanny to let you have even more informal warning of her plans to leave if she can.

● *Duties*

Put them *all* down – refer to your job profile (section 5).

● *Hours of work*

Allow yourself plenty of time for a leisurely handover from mum to nanny in the morning and back again in the evening and for getting to and from work. Be realistic about the prospect that you will have to stay late at work occasionally. If it happens a lot, it may be best to fix a routine finishing time for the nanny that will cover you even when you are detained. That way she knows where she stands and you can gain Brownie points by letting her off early whenever you do manage to get home in good time. If your work schedule is particularly erratic, perhaps it would be wise simply to fix a total number of hours that the nanny is expected to work per week, agreeing to inform her of each week's exact schedule, say, one week in advance?

● *Babysitting*

Most live-in girls expect to do one or two night's babysitting each week. If you want to be sure of your full quota, stipulate in the contract which nights are babysitting nights so that the nanny knows she must keep those particular evenings free.

Some daily nannies babysit as well, sometimes for extra money, sometimes included in the basic salary. Expect to chauffeur as you would any other babysitter if the nanny does not have her own transport.

● *Pay (standard)*

Nannies tend, understandably, to be more interested in what they will have in their hand than in the gross wage you are offering. There is no harm in negotiating your nanny's salary by reference to the net sum she is to receive after deductions but, when you have arrived at a figure, work out what gross sum this requires you to pay and use the gross figure in the contract. If you guarantee the nanny the net sum and agree to pay whatever tax and NIC are due from your own pocket, you may find that you have entered into a 'free of tax' agreement. This is a fiscal nightmare which necessitates all sorts of complicated paperwork, guaranteed to send you round the bend in next to no time. For some help on working out gross figures, turn to page 202.

● *Pay (overtime)*

It is up to you whether you agree in advance to pay overtime in certain situations. For instance, some employers fix an overtime rate that comes into operation if the nanny has to stay later than her contractual finishing time, and this may be one way for the perpetual late-comer to keep the nanny sweet. I do not pay overtime though I *am* occasionally late. Instead I let my nanny finish early every now and then and occasionally I give her an extra whole or half-day off to compensate.

● *Other benefits*

These come in all shapes and sizes. I pay my nanny's phone rental because I require her to have a phone so that we can contact each other in case of illness or emergency – she would not otherwise have had one. We provide a newish VW Polo motor car for her own use and we pay insurance, road tax, servicing, etc. and reimburse the cost of petrol used chauffeuring the children around. She get meals at work and, if she invites other nannies and their charges round for a meal during the day, catering is on us. We also pay for her as well as the children when they go on an outing, for example to the teashop or on a visit to the fair or to a museum.

● *Holidays*

3 or 4 weeks (i.e. 15 or 20 working days) a year in addition to public holidays is reasonable, but there are nannies who get more or less. Our nanny has 4 weeks, of which 3 must be taken when we are on holiday and 1 can be taken whenever she chooses, provided she gives us reasonable advance notice of when it will be. In fact, she also normally gets the whole of the Christmas/New Year period off and the Tuesday of most bank holiday weekends as well as the Monday. We do not count periods when she accompanies us on holiday as part of her holiday entitlement.

- *Sickness*

  *If your nanny earns more than the national insurance lower earnings level* (see page 200), you will have to pay statutory sick pay (SSP) whenever she is off at least 4 days. How the scheme works is described on pages 205-208. It will not cost you anything as you will be reimbursed by the DHSS.

  You can agree more generous sick pay arrangements with your nanny if you wish. You might, for example, agree to top up her SSP to the level of her normal wage for a specified period or to pay sick pay for the first few days of her illness when she would not be entitled to SSP. Be careful to think things through, though, before committing yourself. What if your nanny slips a disc and has to spend three months flat on her back – can you afford to keep her *and* her temporary replacement on full salary?

  *If your nanny earns less than the national insurance lower earnings level*, she will not be eligible for SSP. You can agree to pay her some sick pay yourself if you can afford it. Otherwise, she will have to get in touch with the DHSS to find out whether they can help with state benefits.

- *Maternity and other special leave*

  For most mothers, maternity leave for the nanny is out of the question. You have no obligation to make any provision for it in the contract and you are most unlikely to have any duty to take the nanny back under the statutory maternity scheme if she leaves to have a baby.

- *Pension*

  Nobody expects you to provide your nanny with a pension. This note is only included because the law says it has to be.

# 7

# Information sheet for nanny or mother's help

*TELEPHONE NUMBERS*
Mother at work.................................................................

Father at work ...............................................................
Doctor ..........................................................................
Health visitor.................................................................
Helpful neighbour/friend.................................................
Useful grandparent .........................................................
Playschool/nursery school/school .....................................
Hospital casualty department............................................
Local police ...................................................................
Gas board......................................................................
Electricity board ............................................................
Plumber.........................................................................

*SOCIAL AND OTHER ACTIVITIES AND CONTACTS*

Details (times, venues, etc.):

Mother and toddler groups ...............................................
......................................................................................
Tumbletots or similar......................................................
......................................................................................
NCT post-natal support group ..........................................
......................................................................................
Playschool/nursery school/school .....................................
......................................................................................
Library ..........................................................................
......................................................................................
Swimming pools.............................................................
......................................................................................
Parks ............................................................................
......................................................................................
Baby clinic....................................................................
......................................................................................
Other nannies ................................................................
......................................................................................

## DAILY ROUTINE

...............................................................................................................

...............................................................................................................

...............................................................................................................

...............................................................................................................

## OPERATING INSTRUCTIONS FOR IDIOSYNCRATIC HOUSE-HOLD APPLIANCES

e.g. 'Clout starter motor with mole wrench before attempting to start car'

...............................................................................................................

...............................................................................................................

...............................................................................................................

## OPERATING INSTRUCTIONS FOR IDIOSYNCRATIC CHILDREN

...............................................................................................................

...............................................................................................................

...............................................................................................................

...............................................................................................................

## MEDICAL INFORMATION

Medication (including vitamin drops, fluoride, etc.)

...............................................................................................................

...............................................................................................................

...............................................................................................................

...............................................................................................................

Allergies ...........................................................................................

...............................................................................................................

Immunisations given so far (tetanus, etc.) .........................................

...............................................................................................................

Childhood ailments already endured (mumps, etc.) ............................

...............................................................................................................

Directions to doctor's surgery and casualty department .....................

...............................................................................................................

# 8

# Nanny or mother's help: Tax, national insurance and statutory sick pay

## Part 1: Tax and national insurance

As your nanny's employer, you will almost certainly have to deal with her tax and national insurance contributions (NIC). This is a nightmare for the uninitiated and a bore even when you know how.

### 1. Nannies who earn less than the lower earnings limit for NIC

Not only do low-paid nannies cost you less, they do not involve you in tax and NIC problems either!

At the time of writing, the lower earnings limit for NIC is £43.00 a week, but it does change regularly. Up-to-date figures can be obtained over the phone from the Social Security Advice Line for Employers (see Part 3) or from your local social security office. Alternatively you can refer to leaflet NI.208 *National Insurance contribution rates, Statutory Sick Pay and Statutory Maternity Pay rates.*

If your nanny earns less than the lower earnings limit for NIC, there is no tax or NIC to pay. You do not need to contact the DHSS or the Inland Revenue to tell them that you have taken her on, nor are there any official records to keep or returns to make. You should, however, keep a clear record of what you pay each week.

### 2. What to do when you take on a nanny who is going to earn more than the lower earnings limit for NIC

2.1 *If you are employing a nanny for the first time ever*
- Contact your tax office straight away
  Each tax office deals with a particular geographical area. If you are not sure which office covers your area, look up 'Inland Revenue' in the telephone book, ring one of the numbers listed under Inspector of Taxes and ask them to point you in the right direction.
- Tell your tax office that you have become an employer
  Stress that you have employed one solitary nanny not a factory full of mill workers and ask to be put on the *simplified domestic PAYE scheme.* I spent a couple of years wrestling unnecessarily with the normal PAYE scheme before discovering that there was an alternative; I do not recommend the experience.

Have the following details ready for your tax office:

- the new nanny's surname and first two forenames
- her national insurance number if you know it
- the date you took her on
- what you have agreed to pay her gross and whether it is to be a weekly or monthly payment
- her home address if you know it
- the name and address of her last employer if you know it.

They will also want to know a bit about the job in order to check that the simplified scheme is appropriate.

It is probably best to send all the information in a letter or, if you give the details over the phone, to confirm them in writing. Keep copies of all correspondence with the tax office.

- If the new nanny gives you a form P45 (Employee Leaving – Copy of Employer's Certificate) from her previous employer, send it to the tax office too. Ignore the 'Instructions to New Employer' at the bottom of the form – they do not apply to you.
- Await the arrival of a bewildering assortment of incomprehensible papers, guides, forms and leaflets from the tax office. Keep all these together in a safe place along with your reference number which will also be sent to you. The items you will need regularly are:

- the simplified deduction card (P12)
- 'How to fill in the simplified deduction card P12' with simplified tax tables attached (P16)
- the national insurance contribution tables (CF391)
- the yellow payslip booklet (P30BC(Z)).

### 2.2 *If you are replacing an existing nanny*

- Write to tell your tax office
  Provide them with the new nanny's name, national insurance number if you know it, the date you took her on, pay details, and her home address and that of her last employer if known to you.
- If the new nanny gives you a form P45 (Employee Leaving – Copy of Employer's Certificate) from her previous employer, send it to the tax office too. Ignore the 'Instructions to New Employer' at the bottom of the form – they do not apply to you.
- Follow the instructions on your old nanny's simplified deduction card and send it back to your tax office.

## GROSS AND NET PAY FOR THE TAX YEAR 1989/90

(Valid for nannies with the standard single person's tax code who pay Table A NIC)

| Net weekly pay | Nanny's NIC | Tax | Gross weekly pay | Employer's NIC | Total cost to you |
|---|---|---|---|---|---|
| £40 | NIL | NIL | £40.00 | NIL | £40.00 |
| £50 | £2.62 | NIL | £52.62 | £2.62 | £55.24 |
| £60 | £3.32 | £3.26 | £66.58 | £3.32 | £69.90 |
| £70 | £5.84 | £7.43 | £83.27 | £5.84 | £89.11 |
| £80 | £6.89 | £11.11 | £98.00 | £6.89 | £104.89 |
| £90 | £10.48 | £15.64 | £116.12 | £10.48 | £126.60 |
| £100 | £11.83 | £19.42 | £131.25 | £11.83 | £143.08 |
| £110 | £13.18 | £23.21 | £146.39 | £13.18 | £159.57 |

*Note that NIC changes are in the pipeline. This table will therefore remain valid only until October 1989. Thereafter it will serve as a rough guide only.*

## 3. Fixing your nanny's salary – an important note

Do not make the mistake of fixing your nanny's salary by reference to the amount she is to have in her hand each week/month and agreeing to meet her NIC and tax for her on top. Although this sort of arrangement is likely to be very popular with your nanny, you will be in for trouble from the tax man who will class it as a 'free of tax' arrangement and will not allow you to operate the simplified domestic scheme.

If you want to ensure that your nanny has a particular sum clear each week/month, what you must do is to work out the gross equivalent of the figure you have in mind. It is this gross figure that should appear in your nanny's contract and on her simplified deduction card (see paragraph 4) as her pay. There are no tables to help you calculate gross earnings from net and, if your tax office is like mine, you will not get much assistance from that quarter either. So, unless the table above helps, settle down for an hour or so of trial and error with the national insurance contribution tables and the simplified tax tables.

## 4. Filling in your nanny's simplified deduction card

*4.1 Your tax office will send you a simplified deduction card (P12) for your nanny*

The details on the top of the card will have been filled in for you and you will find a Free Pay figure in the box on the left-hand side.

This is the amount your nanny is allowed to earn each week without paying tax.

### 4.2 *Before using the card for the first time*
Before you can use the card, you must work out which NIC table applies to your nanny. The answer is in the 'National insurance contribution tables' (CF391).

Most nannies pay Table A (Standard rate) contributions but some older married women and widows pay Table B (Reduced rate) contributions and women of 60 and over are on Table C (Employer's contributions only).

Write the NIC table letter in the box on the left-hand side of the card.

### 4.3 *What to do each week/month*
On pay day each week (or month if you pay monthly), write up the deduction card. Straightforward instructions as to how to do this can be found attached to the simplified tax tables (P16).

When you have written up the card, take the week's (or month's) total pay figure from column 5 and subtract from it the figures that appear in column 1c (employee's contribution to NIC) and column 8 (tax deducted). The balance is the sum you should actually hand over to your nanny as her net pay for that week/month. She is entitled to an itemised payslip from you showing her gross wage, the deductions you have made, the amount of her net wage and, if different parts of her wage are paid in different ways, the amount and method of each part payment. You can buy pads of printed slips from stationery shops for the purpose.

### 4.4 *New deductions cards during the tax year*
If there is a general change that affects your nanny's tax code (for instance, if personal allowances are increased following the Budget), the tax office will automatically send you a new deduction card that takes account of the amended code.

If your nanny thinks that her code should be changed for personal reasons, she should write to the tax office about it herself. If the tax man agrees with her, you will be sent a new deduction card.

If you get a new card during the course of the tax year:

    ☆ total up the columns on the old card
    ☆ send the amount due on the old card to the accounts office as you would at the end of a quarter (see paragraph 5)
    ☆ send back the old card to the tax office.

Apart from the NIC table letter, no information needs to be carried forward from the old card to the new one, as the tax office will already have set up the new card for you ready for action.

## 5. Paying the accounts office each quarter

Each quarter, you must pay your dues to the accounts office. To do this, you will need the yellow payslip booklet (P30BC(Z)) and the simplified deduction card.

Take the following steps:

- Total up the columns on the deduction card.
- Turn to the beginning of the payslip booklet where you will find a chart headed 'Record of deductions from gross National Insurance' and one headed 'Record of Payments'. The 'Record of deductions' you can ignore unless you have paid SSP or SMP (turn to Part 2 to find out how to proceed if you *have* paid SSP). The 'Record of Payments' you must complete. Make your entries against the date that corresponds with the end of your quarter. Ignore the extra lines, which are there for those making monthly payments under the ordinary PAYE scheme.
- From your deduction card, copy:
  - the column 8 total into column 1 of the Record of Payments
  - the column 1b total into columns 2 *and* 4 of the Record of Payments.
- Write 'NIL' in column 3.
- Add your entry in column 1 of the Record of Payments to your entry in column 4 and put the answer into column 5. This is the amount you have to pay to the accounts office.
- Fill in the payslip for the relevant period according to the instructions at the front of the payslip booklet. Whatever you do, do not use a payslip for the wrong period. I once did and completely wrecked the system.
- Pay the total amount due by cheque, bank giro, etc. as outlined at the front of the payslip booklet. This can be quite a hefty sum, so, if money is tight, try to put aside enough to cover your nanny's tax and NIC and your employer's NIC each time you pay her.

If you do not pay the accounts office promptly at the end of the quarter, you will get a standard blue reminder. This will be followed by a red second reminder. Persistent dereliction of duty will elicit sterner warnings and threats of action. Do not ignore these – they mean what they say.

## 6. Year-end returns

The tax year ends on the 5th April. Shortly before this, you will receive instructions from the tax office as to what to do at the year end. This will include returning the current simplified deduction card and you will be sent a replacement for the new tax year. If new tables and leaflets have been issued, you will also receive copies of these in due course. Scrap your old copies if they have been superseded.

## 7. Self-employed nannies

Self-employed people are paid gross and handle their own tax and national insurance – no tax and NIC headaches for the employer.

If you have an independent nanny who wants to do her own administration, it is just possible that she may class as self-employed. However, it is vital that you check with your tax office before throwing your tax forms out of the window. You do not want a nasty bill for unpaid tax and NIC if it subsequently turns out that she is, in fact, your employee and you should have been making returns to the accounts office every quarter.

# Part 2: Statutory sick pay

The SSP rules are detailed and complex. This is just a broad outline. For more information, see the *Employer's Guide to Statutory Sick Pay* (leaflet NI.227), phone the Social Security Advice Line for Employers (SSALE – see Part 3) or contact your local social security office.

## 1. Who qualifies?

If your nanny is off sick for at least 4 days, you will normally be obliged to pay her SSP, providing:

> ☆ her average weekly earnings are not less than the NIC lower earnings limit (currently £43.00 per week)
> ☆ she is not on a short-term contract for 3 months or less
> ☆ she is not over 60
> ☆ she is not self-employed.

## 2. PIWs and waiting days

As no SSP is payable for short periods off work, the following conditions must be satisfied before payment is made:

> ● There must be a PIW (period of incapacity for work). A spell of sickness will qualify as a PIW only if it lasts for 4

consecutive days or more. All days of sickness are counted including Saturdays, Sundays and holidays, irrespective of whether or not your nanny's contract requires her to work weekends, bank holidays, etc.

- There must have been 3 'waiting days'. Not every day of illness is a waiting day. Only 'qualifying days' count. This usually means that you count your nanny's normal working days but not the days she would normally have off.

*Example:*

Your nanny wakes up with 'flu on Friday morning and cannot come to work. She continues to be ill over the weekend (which is not a problem as she does not normally work weekends) and is not fit to return to work until Thursday of the following week.

There is a PIW as there are at least 4 days of sickness in a row (Friday, Saturday, Sunday, Monday, etc.).

The first 3 qualifying days in the PIW are Friday, Monday and Tuesday. These are waiting days. You pay SSP for the Wednesday.

Note that where your nanny has two spells of sickness each lasting 4 days or more and separated by 8 weeks or less, the two periods are 'linked' (i.e. treated as one PIW). This means that waiting days put in during the first spell of sickness also count for the second spell of sickness, with the result that SSP may turn out to be payable from the very start of the second bout. More detail is available in the *Employer's Guide to Statutory Sick Pay* and tables are provided in DHSS booklet SSP/SMP55 to help you work out what links with what.

## 3. Proof of illness

You decide whether your nanny really is incapable of work because of her illness (in which case she is eligible for SSP) or whether she is malingering (in which case she is not). You are not entitled to ask for a doctor's sick note for the first 7 days of a spell of illness, but you can do so for longer spells if you see fit.

## 4. How much?

There are two rates of SSP depending on your nanny's earnings. The rates change on the 6th April each year. You will find the current figures in the DHSS booklet SSP/SMP55 or in leaflet NI.208 *National Insurance contribution rates, Statutory Sick Pay and Statutory Maternity Pay rates.*

You may find that you have to pay SSP for a part week. In the example in paragraph 2, for instance, SSP is due for one day only.

In this sort of situation, you will have to work out a daily rate. To do this, divide the appropriate weekly rate by the number of days your nanny normally works in a week.

## 5. The mechanics of payment

### 5.1 *Paying your nanny*
*You* calculate how much SSP your nanny is due and pay this to her (initially from your own pocket). You should deduct tax and NIC from the SSP in the usual way and it will probably be convenient to pay SSP when you would normally pay your nanny her wages. Remember to record the payments you make on your nanny's simplified deduction card (column 1d) and in your SSP records (see paragraph 6 below).

There is no reason why your nanny's pay packet should not include both some SSP and some of her normal wage. This would be so in the example given in paragraph 2 – the nanny would receive no pay for Monday and Tuesday of the week in which she returned to work (unless you had agreed to continue to pay her salary during short periods off sick), SSP for the Wednesday and normal pay for the Thursday and Friday.

### 5.2 *Reimbursement*
You are entitled to be reimbursed the full amount of the SSP you pay to your nanny. You are also entitled to compensation for your employer's NIC relating to that SSP. So, though you may be tearing your hair out by the time you have finished adding and subtracting and filling in forms, you should not be any the worse off financially.

Normally you get your money back by paying less NIC when you make your next quarterly payment to the accounts office. You should deduct the following amounts from the NIC and income tax that would otherwise be due:

* ☆ *The gross amount of the SSP you have paid*
  i.e. the amount of SSP before deduction of your nanny's tax and NIC
* ☆ *NIC compensation on SSP*
  Work out your NIC compensation by multiplying the gross amount of the SSP you have paid by the appropriate percentage. Leaflet NI.208 (*National Insurance contribution rates, Statutory Sick Pay and Statutory Maternity Pay rates*) tells you what that percentage is for the current tax year; so does CF391 (the national insurance contribution tables). Alternatively, consult your local social security office or SSALE.

Remember to record everything at the front of your payslip booklet. Deductions should be itemised in the 'Record of deductions from gross National Insurance' and your mathematics made clear in the 'Record of Payments'. You will find an example in the booklet NP.15 *Employer's guide to National Insurance contributions* if you get stuck.

Should the deductions work out at more than the amount of NIC and tax you are due to pay to the accounts office:

- Record the position at the front of your payslip booklet but do not send a payslip to the accounts office. Dispose of the payslip you would otherwise have used for that quarter so that you do not use it for the following quarter by mistake. In due course, you will receive a reminder from the accounts office. Complete the declaration on the back of the slip and return it without delay. This tells the accounts office that you owe nothing that quarter.
- Carry the unrelieved balance forward and deduct it from your next quarterly payment. Mark on your payslip for that quarter the total figures for both that quarter and the preceding one when you did not send a payslip to the accounts office.
- Alternatively, if you need to get your money back quickly, apply to the accounts office in writing for payment.

## 6. SSP records

You are required by law to keep the following SSP records:

- whenever there is a PIW (i.e. whenever your nanny is ill for at least 4 consecutive days), a record of the dates of your nanny's illness;
- a record of any days within the PIW for which you did not pay SSP, together with the reasons why you did not make payment;
- a record of the qualifying days in each PIW.

You may find it convenient to use an SSP record sheet (form SSP2), which you can obtain free from your local social security office.

The DHSS can inspect your records. They must be kept for at least three years after the end of the tax year to which they relate. Failure to keep records is an offence for which you can be fined.

# Part 3: Further information and advice

Copies of all the leaflets/booklets mentioned in Parts 1 and 2 can be obtained from your local social security office or from the DHSS Leaflets Section (see the Address Book for the address).

Further information and advice about the simplified domestic PAYE scheme can be obtained from your tax office.

Queries about NIC and SSP should be addressed to your local social security office; I have found mine very helpful. Alternatively, if you want to make a general enquiry, phone the Social Security Advice Line for Employers (SSALE) on 0800 393539. The call will cost you nothing.

# 9

## Shopping by mail order

I have listed below some of the companies offering a mail order service for children's clothes, maternity wear, etc.

Mail order has tremendous advantages for the working mother. Sitting down with a catalogue and a cup of coffee can be quite fun and it certainly beats shepherding a turbulent toddler round town or dashing to Marks and Sparks in your lunch hour. I look forward to the arrival of the new catalogues at the beginning of each season.

Buying something you have not actually seen can be disconcerting to begin with, but do not worry too much about it as most items can be returned if they do not come up to expectations. Simply check in the catalogue for the particular company's terms and conditions.

Mail order parcels that are too big to fit through the letter box can be more of a problem. Nothing is more irritating than finding that the postman/carrier has called to deliver your parcel but taken it away again because you were out. Rest assured, though, that you will get your parcel in the end. The Post Office drop a card through the letter box inviting you to collect from their depot or to let them know when it would be convenient for them to redeliver, and other carriers do likewise or, if they do not need your signature on the delivery documents, may find a safe place to leave the parcel for you.

If you do decide to order by post, beware the inertia factor. I used to think that I was the only one who ended up keeping goods that I did not really want simply because I never got round to sending them back. On making enquiries, I find that there are, in fact, many others who have drawers full of assorted items in lurid colours and outlandish sizes which have universally failed to please. Some people who suffer from the inertia factor protect themselves by never ordering by post. A more constructive approach might be to force yourself to parcel up and despatch unwanted items *immediately* before you have time to get used to them sitting on the hall table waiting for attention.

Obviously I cannot include a comprehensive list of mail order companies. This chapter includes a selection only – if you want more variety, look through the ads in magazines such as *Parents, Mother, Under Five, Mother & Baby*.

# Clothes

## Children

BLOOMING MARVELLOUS LTD
Dept MBK4
PO Box 12F
Chessington
Surrey KT9 2LS
Tel. 01–391 4822 (catalogues) /0338 (orders)

Ages 0 – 6

A few of everything from rompers, dungarees and pinafore dresses to tracksuits, T-shirts and cardigans. Not cheap but fun and, so far as I can tell from the items I have ordered, well made.

CLOTHKITS
Lewes Design Workshops Ltd
24 High Street
Lewes
East Sussex BN7 2LB
Tel. 0273 477111

Ages 0 – adult

Well-known company that started off specialising in children's wear but now also supplies a range of good-quality women's clothing. A few designs come in kit form but the majority of items are ready made (socks, T-shirts, jumpers, tracksuits, dresses, shirts, etc.).

In the past, many of the clothes have been made from fabric specially printed for Clothkits and have consequently had a very distinctive Clothkits stamp about them. Apparently the company has now been taken over and some changes seem to be in the pipeline.

There are Clothkits shops in Lewes, Oxford, Covent Garden, Guildford, Winchester, Bath and Cambridge, and more are due to open soon.

COTTON ON
29 North Clifton Street
Lytham FY8 5HW
Tel. 0253 736611

Ages 0 – adult

Most items made from 100% cotton. Nice range including tights, polo neck jumpers, school clothes, knitting yarn, nightwear, dresses, shorts and tracksuits. Particularly useful if you have a child who suffers from eczema or other skin problems.

## KIDS' STUFF
10 Hensman's Hill
Bristol
BS8 4PE
Tel. 0272 734980

Ages 6 months – 10 years

Wonderful selection of plain, hard-wearing dungarees, trousers, skirts and pinafores, which are strong enough to stand up to wear by two or more children in succession and get passed round our family from sister to brother and cousin to cousin. Not expensive for the wear that they give and certainly a lot cheaper than the more swanky Osh Kosh equivalent. Also available are jumpers, hats, socks, tights, tracksuits, nightwear, etc.

There is a shop under the factory at 10 Hensman's Hill and also at 50 Park Row, Bristol.

## MOTHERCARE
Mothercare-by-Post
PO Box 145
Watford
WD2 5SH
Tel. 0923 31616 (queries) /240365 (orders)

Age 0 – adult (maternity wear only)

Goods from the Mothercare range can be ordered by post. You may get a wider choice this way than when shopping in your local store. The order form is in the Mothercare catalogue, which you can get from any Mothercare store.

## NIPPERS
Gloucester House
45 Gloucester Street
Brighton
Sussex
BN1 4EW
Tel. 0273 693785

Ages 0 – 9

Upmarket catalogue offering an interesting selection of quite expensive jeans, dungarees, shirts, dresses, tracksuits, etc. Charlotte's sweatshirt has worn wonderfully and, though I have not tried anything else myself, I have heard that other items are just as good. As well as mail order, there is a shop at 19 Kensington Gardens in Brighton (0273 690176).

## Maternity wear

BLOOMING MARVELLOUS

Address as above

Catalogue tends to excel at informal clothes, with good lines in tracksuits (a very comfortable way of wearing trousers when you are pregnant), dungarees, T-shirts and sweatshirts (with or without slogans), but there are also dresses, blouses, pinafores, etc. Very reasonable prices.

NCT MATERNITY SALES

Dept MB389

Alexandra House

Oldham Terrace

Acton

London W3 6HN

Tel. 01–992 6762

Maternity swimming costumes and tracksuits, nightdresses for breastfeeding, an excellent range of nursing bras and a number of other useful items including breast pumps. Also available are various leaflets and books on many aspects of pregnancy, birth, breastfeeding and early parenthood.

# Disposable nappies

## Boots nappies

Boots will supply disposable nappies by mail order. They come in huge quantities – mostly upwards of 200 nappies at a time (about a month's supply). There is no charge for delivery and the enormous cardboard cartons in which the nappies arrive can be turned into playhouses, cars, boats, etc. and represent even more unbeatable value than the nappies.

You can order by telephone using Visa or Access – ring Linkline 0800 622525 (no charge for the call). Alternatively you can place your order at any branch of Boots or pick up an order form from your local store and order by post.

## Mothercare nappies

The free Home Delivery Service can deliver Smarty Pants or Smarty Pants Ultra-Dry nappies in packs of 168. You can order by phone (0923 240365) if you have a Storecard, Access card or Visa card or you can send in your order by post to Mothercare-by-Post (order form available in the Mothercare catalogue) or place your order at one of the shops. For Mothercare's address, see page 212

## Toys and books

EARLY LEARNING CENTRE
South Marston
Swindon
SN3 4TJ
Tel. 0793 831300

Comprehensive range of toys, games, etc. Early Learning Centre shops all over the country too, but it is nice to browse through the catalogue anyway.

TRIDIAS
The Ice House
124 Walcot Street
Bath BA1 5BG
Tel. 0225 469455

Large and varied selection of toys, party presents, games, jigsaws and so on. Shops in Bath, Richmond and Dartington as well.

WATERSTONE & CO
Mail order division
4 Milsom Street
Bath BA1 1DA
Tel. 0225 448595

Will supply any British book in print. A charge is made for postage and packing. Waterstone's *Guide to Books* (price £9.95) does not list every book available but carries details of 60,000 titles and is useful for reference.

# 10

# Address Book

ADDITIONS
52 Chiltern Street
London W1M 1PP
Tel. 01–486 3065

Smart shop selling everything in the maternity wear line from swim-suits to evening dresses. Middle price range – as a rough guide, a dress might cost you about £70.

ADVISORY, CONCILIATION AND ARBITRATION SERVICE (ACAS)
Various regional offices – look in your phone book under 'Advisory, Conciliation & Arbitration Service' or contact your local Jobcentre or Unemployment Benefit Office and ask for the address and phone number of your nearest ACAS office.

ACAS will advise you on all your employment rights as a pregnant employee except with regard to statutory maternity pay.

ASSOCIATION OF BREASTFEEDING MOTHERS
10 Herschell Road
London SE23 1EN
Tel. 01–778 4769 (a recorded list of breastfeeding counsellors throughout the country)

The ABM offers information, encouragement and practical mother-to-mother support for those who are breastfeeding. They will put you in touch with a breastfeeding counsellor and can also supply by post leaflets, books, breast pumps, breast shells and special teats designed to simulate the human nipple. Send an SAE for an order form listing what is available. The Association may also be able to put you in touch with an ABM group that meets in your area.

For an annual subscription, you can be a member of the Association and receive a newsletter about birth, babies and breastfeeding (10 issues a year).

BALLOON
77 Walton Street
London SW3 2HT
Tel. 01–589 3121

Maternity wear shop selling dresses, pinafores, skirts, jumpers, casual wear, etc. Price guide: £80 upwards for a dress.

## BRITISH ACTIVITY HOLIDAY ASSOCIATION
Rock Park
Llandrindod Wells
Powys
LD1 6AE
Tel. 0597 3902

Formed in 1986 in view of concern about children's activity holidays. The Association has drawn up a Code of Practice for operators of activity holidays. It encourages operators to take out membership of the Association and tries to ensure that all members come up to scratch. Any complaints from parents about particular holidays are investigated. The Association can provide parents with details of registered members who may be able to provide the sort of holiday for which they are looking.

## BUMPSADAISY
43 The Market
Covent Garden
London WC2E 8HA
Tel. 01–836 1105

Over 75 branches nationwide hiring out maternity clothes for special occasions or everyday wear. Ring or write for details of your nearest branch.

Also three retail shops (Covent Garden, Bristol and Tunbridge Wells) selling casual and working outfits. Interesting selection – no broderie anglaise collars and no tents. Price guide: £45 to £100 for a dress (to buy).

## CATHOLIC ADVISORY GROUP FOR AU PAIRS
24 Great Chapel Street
London W1V 3AF
Tel. 01–439 0116

Multinational association looking after the welfare of au pair girls (Catholics and non-Catholics alike) in this country.

## CENTRAL BUREAU FOR EDUCATIONAL VISITS
## AND EXCHANGES
Seymour Mews
London W1H 9PE
Tel. 01–486 5101

A government-funded organisation which produces a free fact sheet on au pairing. Contact the information section for a copy. The Bureau also publishes a book called *Working Holidays*, which comes out yearly and is available by mail order. Although this was originally written for young people looking for short-term employment during university holidays and the like, those considering employing an au pair may also find it helpful as it includes details about hours of work, pay, immigration requirements, reputable au pair agencies, etc., plus information on how to advertise abroad.

Au pairs might like to read *Young Visitors to Britain*, also available from the Bureau by mail order (in English, French, German, Italian and Spanish language editions). This guide advises on passports, permits, travel arrangements, language tuition, special interest courses, money, health and welfare, etc.

## CHILD POVERTY ACTION GROUP (CPAG)
4th Floor
1–5 Bath Street
London EC1V 9PY

The CPAG is an organisation pressing for improvements in the position of poor families. It publishes the *Rights guide to non-means-tested social security benefits*, which includes much useful information on statutory maternity pay, etc. The guide is updated annually and is available by mail order from the CPAG or in bookshops.

## CHILTERN NURSERY TRAINING COLLEGE
20 Peppard Road
Caversham
Reading RG4 8LA
Tel. 0734 471847

One of the top three nanny-training establishments. More detail in Chapter 10.

## THE DAYCARE TRUST
(See below under NATIONAL CHILDCARE CAMPAIGN)

## DEPARTMENT OF EMPLOYMENT

Source of a series of useful free booklets on employment rights, for example *Employment rights for the expectant mother*. Contact a Jobcentre or Unemployment Benefit Office for copies. However do beware when using the booklets – the law is always changing and certain information may be out of date. In the current edition of *Employment rights for the expectant mother* (1986) for example, there is a section on maternity pay; this should be ignored – the old maternity pay system has been replaced by SMP.

## DHSS LEAFLETS UNIT
PO Box 21
Stanmore
Middlesex HA7 1AY

A useful source of leaflets on maternity rights and benefits. You can also get free general advice by phone on Freeline Social Security – dial 0800 666555 (for advice on social security benefits including statutory maternity pay) or 0800 393539 (for advice in your capacity as your nanny's employer with regard to her national insurance contributions, statutory sick pay, etc.).

## ELEGANCE MATERNELLE
35 Chiltern Street
London W1
Tel. 01–487 5520

Small shop stuffed full of fashionable maternity wear (dresses, tops, trousers, clothes for special occasions, etc.). Price guide: £100 upwards for a dress.

## EQUAL OPPORTUNITIES COMMISSION
Overseas House
Quay Street
Manchester
M3 3HN
Tel. 061 833 9244

The EOC is a public body set up by Parliament in 1975 to prevent people being unfairly treated because of their sex. Amongst other things, it liaises with trade unions and employers, etc. to help them introduce and improve equal opportunity policies and programmes, and works with employers to help women combine their work and family responsibilities; it can also advise and help individuals.

If you are returning to work after a break, you may like to read *Signposts: a guide for women returning to work or learning* (available from the EOC by post). There is also a full publications catalogue.

## THE FEDERATION OF RECRUITMENT AND EMPLOYMENT SERVICES LTD
10 Belgrave Square
London SW1X 8PH
Tel. 01–235 6616

The Federation is a trade association for recruitment firms. It has a specialist section for agencies placing au pairs and nannies and can supply their addresses. The activities of members are regulated by means of the Federation's codes of practice.

## GINGERBREAD
35 Wellington Street
London WC2E 7BN
Tel. 01–240 0953

Gingerbread is an association of one-parent families set up in 1970. As well as a national headquarters, it has a network of self-help groups throughout Britain and Eire. Local groups provide a regular meeting place for parents and children, family activities and outings, emotional and practical support, and advice and information. Gingerbread also operates a number of community day nurseries and some after-school and holiday centres. Gingerbread's publications list includes *Maternity Rights* (a guide to rights and benefits for pregnant women on their own, price 20 pence plus postage) and *Who looks after the children?* (a guide to child care for lone parents, price 30 pence plus postage).

## GREAT EXPECTATIONS
78 Fulham Road
London SW3 6HH
Tel. 01–584 2451

Upstairs at 'Night Owls', Great Expectations sells a good range of quite reasonably priced maternity clothes (day dresses, evening wear, skirts, casual, etc). Price guide: £40 to £120 for a dress.

## HACKNEY JOB SHARE PROJECT
380 Old Street
London EC1V 9LT
Tel. 01–739 0741

Hackney Job Share Project has a number of years' experience of devising and implementing job share programmes. It offers general information on job sharing, specific advice to individuals and to employers on organising job shares, and training for those managing job shares or involved in recruitment. It can supply various publications about job sharing – how to organise it, preparing applications, etc.

## HOME OFFICE IMMIGRATION AND NATIONALITY DEPARTMENT
Lunar House
40 Wellesley Road
Croydon
Surrey
CR9 2BY
Tel. 01–686 0688

The Home Office produces a free leaflet entitled *Information about au pairs*. Staff at Lunar House will also answer individual queries about au pairs. Hang on patiently if you ring them – the line is very busy and calls are answered in turn.

## INTERNATIONAL YOUTH WELFARE
29 Bramley Road
London N14 4HE
Tel. 01–449 6648

Pressure group working to improve the status of au pairs. If you live in the North London area, may be able to put you in touch with prospective au pairs.

## THE LADY
39–40 Bedford Street
London WC2E 9ER

A weekly newspaper/magazine – the traditional place to advertise for a nanny or mother's help.

## LA LECHE LEAGUE
BM 3424
London WC1V 6XX
Tel. 01–242 1278

The La Leche League provides information and support for breast-feeders. There are LLL leaders all round the country who hold local meetings and also offer advice and support on an individual basis. The League produces over 100 different leaflets on breastfeeding (including *Practical Hints for Working and Breastfeeding*) and will supply these and a large selection of books on babies, breastfeeding, family life, etc. by post. Send a large SAE for a full list.

For an annual subscription, you can join the League and receive their newsletter (six issues a year), which deals with breastfeeding and all sorts of other topics as well. For instance, one issue that I have includes a short piece on combining motherhood with a part-time job as an accountant, a 'Toddler Column' and an article about schools giving sweets as a reward for good work.

## LA MAMA
| | |
|---|---|
| 228 High Street | or |
| Bromley | 38 High Street |
| Kent BR1 1PQ | Kingston-upon-Thames |
| Tel. 01–290 5725 | KP1 1HL |
| | Tel. 01–541 4635 |

La Mama's aim is to provide the sort of clothes that you would choose for the non-pregnant you but with room for the bump as well. Some items are very reasonable, others may seem relatively pricey compared to mass-market maternity wear but may turn out to be worth every penny in terms of quality, style and general usefulness. It is now quite a while since I was pregnant and I am still happily wearing my La Mama sweatshirts.

## LYALL EASON & DUDLEY DIVISION
Robert Barrow Ltd
24–26 Minories
London EC3N 1BY
Tel. 01–709 9611

Insurance brokers who will advise on insurance for nannies and mother's helps.

## THE MATERNITY ALLIANCE
15 Britannia Street
London WC1X 9JP
Tel. 01–837 1265

A national organisation that campaigns for improvements in rights and services for mothers, fathers and babies. Two of the leaflets that the Alliance produces (*Money for Mothers and Babies* and *Pregnant at Work*) are particularly useful for working mothers as they contain a run-down of your rights to SMP, maternity leave, time off for ante-natal care, maternity allowance, etc.

## NATIONAL CHILDBIRTH TRUST (NCT)
Alexandra House
Oldham Terrace
Acton
London W3 6NH
Tel. 01–992 8637

The NCT is a well-established national organisation concerned with all aspects of childbirth, breastfeeding, post-natal support, etc. It runs ante-natal classes and has a network of breastfeeding counsellors who offer individual help and advice on all aspects of breastfeeding. My area has a thriving post-natal support group, which holds regular daytime meetings for mothers and children in members' houses (my nanny belongs to this as my proxy), plus a separate working mothers' group, which organises evening meetings and keeps a register of childcare facilities available in the area.

There are numerous NCT leaflets on pregnancy, birth, breast-feeding and early parenthood (e.g. *Breastfeeding – Returning to Work*) and you can order these and various recommended books by post. Other items (such as nightdresses, nursing bras, breast pumps, etc.) are available by mail order from NCT Maternity Sales (see section 9). You may also be able to hire an electric breast pump through your local breastfeeding counsellor.

If you wish to support the NCT, you can become a national member or simply join your local branch (look in your local phone book under National Childbirth Trust).

## NATIONAL CHILDCARE CAMPAIGN
Wesley House
4 Wild Court
London WC2B 5AU
Tel. 01–405 5617/8

A voluntary organisation that campaigns for better daycare facilities for children. Its sister organisation, the Daycare Trust, provides free information and advice to parents, educationalists, employers, childcare workers, etc. about where child care is to be found, how to improve it and how to go about setting up a project. Its publications list includes *Daycare for Kids: A parents' survival guide* (£4.95 plus postage and packing).

## NATIONAL CHILDMINDING ASSOCIATION (NCMA)
8 Masons Hill
Bromley
Kent BR2 9EY
Tel. 01–464 6164

Set up in 1977 by childminders, parents and childcare workers, the NCMA works to improve the status, conditions and standards of childminding. It produces a number of leaflets and handbooks on childminding and will supply these (and various books, T-shirts, car stickers, etc.) by mail order.

The NCMA will answer queries from the general public but parents are welcome to join the Association if they want and, as members, can ask the NCMA to take up childminding problems on their behalf and will automatically receive the newsletter several times a year.

## NATIONAL COUNCIL FOR CIVIL LIBERTIES (NCCL)
21 Tabard Street
London SE1 4LA
Tel. 01–403 3888

Amongst other things, the NCCL (through its Women's Rights Unit) campaigns for equality for women in the workplace. It is concerned that women workers are undervalued, earn much less than men and are hampered by the lack of childcare facilities. It aims to change the climate of opinion by publicising women's issues and through work in trade unions and in parliament, lobbying MPs and policy-makers, preparing legislative proposals and pressing for amendments to government Bills.

NCCL publications (which include the useful *'Maternity Rights at Work'* by Ruth Evans, Lyn Durward and Jean Coussins, price £1.50 + postage and packing) can be obtained from the NCCL by post. A full publications list is available free of charge.

For an annual subscription, you can join the Women's Rights Fund, which entitles you to a variety of benefits such as access to expert advice, workshops and seminars at national and local level and a quarterly newsletter dealing with women's issues.

## NATIONAL COUNCIL FOR ONE-PARENT FAMILIES
255 Kentish Town Road
London NW5 2LX
Tel. 01-267 1361/2/3

One-Parent Families works to improve the position of lone parents and their children. As well as campaigning for the policies and services that one-parent families need, it provides free help, advice and counselling to individuals (on legal matters, housing problems, social security, etc.), and produces up-to-date leaflets and information sheets on a variety of subjects including social security, housing, tax, legal aid and health. You might find *Single and Pregnant* (price £1.30 including postage and packing) particularly helpful. It deals with SMP, rights at work, etc.

## NATIONAL OUT OF SCHOOL ALLIANCE (NOOSA)
Oxford House
Derbyshire Street
Bethnal Green Road
London E2 6HG
Tel. 01-739 4787

The Alliance seeks to promote good quality after-school and school holiday care facilities. It produces a directory of the schemes available in London (*Out of School in London*) and will also advise on what schemes are available outside London. If you cannot find an existing scheme, it will advise you on how to go about pressuring your local authority into making provision and can also tell you how to go about setting up a scheme yourself. *Starting from scratch* (available by mail order) is a practical guide to setting up and running a locally based scheme.

## NATIONAL PLAYING FIELDS ASSOCIATION
25 Ovington Square
London SW3 1LQ
Tel. 01-584 6445

The Association aims to ensure that there is safe play and recreation space for all children and young people. It may be able to help parents interested in setting up a holiday playscheme either by advising or by supplying, by mail order, various books on playschemes. *How to organise a holiday playscheme* (price £4.00) may be of particular interest.

## NEW WAYS TO WORK
309 Upper Street
London N1 2TY
Tel. 01–226 4026

New Ways to Work is a small educational charity that promotes job sharing and other flexible ways of working. It provides advice and information, runs seminars and training sessions and carries out research on job sharing in the UK. It produces a free leaflet entitled *Introduction to Job Sharing*, which answers some basic questions about job sharing. It also produces a series of booklets and factsheets (all at modest prices) on various aspects of job sharing and other flexible working arrangements.

For Londoners, the New Ways to Work London Job Share Register might be useful – it seeks to help people find job share partners.

## NNEB
8 Chequers Street
St Albans
Herts AL1 3XY
Tel. 0727 67333

NNEB stands for Nursery Nurse Examination Board. The NNEB certificate is the traditional nannying qualification in this country (more details in Chapter 10). The Board can supply a list of colleges that run approved courses in preparation for the certificate examination – you can then contact your local college with a view to snapping up their most prized graduate the moment she receives her certificate.

## NORLAND NURSERY TRAINING COLLEGE LTD
Denford Park
Hungerford
Berkshire RG17 OPQ
Tel. 0488 82252

One of the top three nanny-training establishments – see Chapter 10 for more details.

## NURSERY WORLD
Schoolhouse Workshop
51 Calthorpe Street
London WC1X OHH
Tel. 01–837 7224   Fax. 01–278 3896

A fortnightly magazine read by nannies and others working with children and a possible place for an advert for a new nanny or mother's help. See Chapter 10 for more details.

## PRINCESS CHRISTIAN COLLEGE
26 Wilbraham Road
Fallowfield
Manchester M14 6JX
Tel. 061–224 4560

One of the top three nanny-training establishments – see Chapter 10 for more details.

## PROFESSIONAL ASSOCIATION OF NURSERY NURSES (PANN)
99 Friar Gate
Derby DE1 1EZ
Tel. 0332 43029

An independent registered trade union for all qualified nursery nurses including nannies. Members of PANN have access to information and advice on employment and training and membership automatically includes insurance which covers any damages that are awarded against the nanny as a result of negligent care.

## PUBLICITAS LTD
525/527 Fulham Road
London SW6 1HF
Tel. 01–385 7723

Advertising representatives for a variety of newspapers and magazines throughout Europe, the Americas and the Far East.

I have not used them but they say that they will suggest appropriate publications and make arrangements for the placement of adverts.

## ST PATRICK'S INTERNATIONAL YOUTH CENTRE
24 Great Chapel Street
London W1V 3AF
Tel. 01–439 0116

Welfare organisation looking after the interests of au pair girls and other young foreigners in this country. Although the Centre is not an employment agency, staff may have details of girls looking for au pair posts or, at the very least, will be able to put you in touch with some au pair agencies.

## SOCIAL SERVICES DEPARTMENT
Address and telephone number in the phone book, normally under the name of your local authority, e.g. 'North Yorkshire County Council'.

A good starting point when looking for nurseries, childminders, out-of-school schemes, etc.

## UNIVERSAL AUNTS LTD
250 Kings Road
Chelsea
London SW3 5UE
Tel. 01–351 5767

A long-established agency that is very used to providing emergency cover nationwide at the drop of a hat, e.g. when the nanny breaks her leg and cannot work for three weeks just when you are about to depart for a business trip to the States. Note that I have not actually used the agency myself and cannot therefore give it a personal recommendation.

## VACATION WORK
9 Park End Street
Oxford OX1 1HJ
Tel. 0865 241978

Publishers of *Adventure Holidays*, a directory of activity holidays in Britain and further afield. Copies available direct from the publishers or from bookshops.

## VOLUNTARY ORGANISATIONS LIAISON COUNCIL FOR UNDER FIVES (VOLCUF)
77 Holloway Road
London N7 8JZ
Tel. 01–607 9573

VOLCUF is a charity that provides information and support for voluntary groups working to promote and develop improvements in services for children under 5. It produces a free leaflet entitled *Finding and choosing day care for your under-fives*.

## WOMEN RETURNERS' NETWORK
c/o Ruth Michaels
Senior Tutor for Continuing Education
Hatfield Polytechnic
PO Box 109
College Lane
Hatfield
Hertfordshire AL10 9AB
Tel. 07072 79490/1

The Network aims to facilitate the re-entry of women into the labour force after a career break by promoting education, training and employment opportunities. It organises conferences and produces publications including *Returning to Work: Education and Training for Women* (published by Longman, price £9.75), which is a directory containing details of 1,400 courses in England and Wales, local contacts for detailed advice, childcare/creche facilities, etc.

## WORKING MOTHERS' ASSOCIATION
77 Holloway Road
London N7 8JZ
Tel. 01-700 5771

The Working Mother's Association was formed in 1985 to promote the interests of working women with children. The Association provides information, advice and moral support. There are quite a number of local groups meeting throughout the country. The Association will put you in touch with your nearest group and you can also obtain from them their inexpensive *Working Mother's Handbook*, a practical guide to the alternatives in the child care. For a modest yearly sum, you can be a member of the Association and receive the quarterly newsletter.

## WORKPLACE NURSERIES CAMPAIGN
Southbank House
Black Prince Road
London SE1 7SJ
Tel. 01-582 7199

The Campaign was launched in 1984 to fight the Inland Revenue's decision to tax higher-paid employees on subsidised nursery provision. It aims to promote the development of work-related child care, particularly workplace nurseries, and to provide advice, information and encouragement to employers, trade unions, etc.

## WORKPLACE NURSERIES LTD
Southbank House
Black Prince Road
London SE1 7SJ
Tel. 01-582 7199

Started in 1986, the organisation (sister of the Workplace Nurseries Campaign, see above) specialises in providing information and advice on employer-subsidised childcare provision. It has compiled an information pack called the *Employer's Guide to Workplace Nurseries* (which outlines the arguments in favour of employer-subsidised child care and provides practical information for employers on how to set up a workplace nursery) and a trade union pack (which provides advice for those involved in negotiating for child care at work). Both packs are available by mail order. The organisation also offers a consultancy service providing specialist advice to individual employers, trade unions, etc.

# INDEX